# VALUATION OF FIXED INCOME SECURITIES

# VALUATION OF FIXED INCOME SECURITIES

## Frank J. Fabozzi, CFA
School of Organization & Management
Yale

Published by Frank J. Fabozzi Associates

Editorial & Production Consultant: Stephen Arbour
Editor: Stacia Mellbourne

© 1994 BY FRANK J. FABOZZI ASSOCIATES
SUMMIT, NEW JERSEY 07901

ALL RIGHTS RESERVED. No part of this publication may be reproduced, stored in a retrieval system, or transmitted, in any form or by any means, electronic, mechanical, photocopying, recording, or otherwise, without the prior written permission of the publisher and the copyright holder.

This publication is designed to provide accurate and authoritative information in regard to the subject matter covered. It is sold with the understanding that the publisher is not engaged in rendering legal, accounting, or other professional services.

ISBN 1-883249-02-3

Printed in the United States of America
1 2 3 4 5 6 7 8 9 0

*To the memory
of my mother,
Josephine*

Other books by
Frank J. Fabozzi Associates

*Collateralized Mortgage Obligations:
Structures and Analysis*
(Second Edition)
by
Frank J. Fabozzi,
Charles Ramsey,
and Frank R. Ramirez

*CMO Portfolio Management*
Edited by
Frank J. Fabozzi

# PREFACE AND ACKNOWLEDGMENTS

Today's fixed income market includes securities with complex structures resulting in a wide-range of risk/return relationships. The traditional valuation method fails to properly value complex fixed income securities for two reasons. First, it values each cash flow that is expected to be received from a security using a single discount rate. Thus, no recognition is given to the term structure of interest rates. Second, it fails to properly value any option embedded in a security.

The purpose of *Valuation of Fixed Income Securities* is to provide a framework for properly valuing any fixed income product. The valuation framework takes into account the term structure of interest rates and the value of any embedded options. The framework relies on state-of-the-art technology for valuing interest rate options. The two valuation methodologies described in this book are the binomial lattice method and the Monte Carlo simulation method. Applications of these methodologies to valuing callable and putable bonds, mortgage-backed securities (particularly, collateralized mortgage obligations), inverse floating-rate securities, and convertible bonds are provided.

### *Acknowledgements*

I am grateful to several individuals who have assisted me in various stages of this project.

Andrew Kalotay and George Williams (Andrew Kalotay Associates) provided helpful comments on Chapter 6 and furnished the software used to generate the illustrations in that chapter. Yu Zhu and Mihir Bhattacharya (Merrill Lynch) commented on Chapter 9 and provided the information for one of the illustrations. Several of the illustrations in Chapter 7 are drawn from my work with Scott Richard (Miller, Anderson & Sherrerd). I am grateful to Harsh Kumar (Goldman Sachs) for furnishing the information on the credit term structure of interest rates reported in Chapter 2.

Special thanks to John Carlson (Lehman Brothers), Dwight Churchill (Fidelity Investments), Dessa Fabozzi (Merrill Lynch), and Jan Mayle (TIPS) for their review of the entire book.

I have benefitted from discussions with: Cliff Asness (Goldman Sachs Asset Management), Worth Bruntjen (Piper Capital Management), Steve Coma (Merrill Lynch), Ike Epley (Alex. Brown & Sons), Gifford Fong (Gifford Fong Associates), Robert Gerber (Sanford Bernstein), Andrew Greenberg (CMB Investment Counselors), Joseph Guagliardo, Jr. (Gifford Fong Associates), Deepak Gulrajani (BARRA), David Jacob (Nomura Securities), Frank Jamison (Alex. Brown & Sons), M. Song Jo (Alex. Brown & Sons), Frank Jones (The Guardian Life), David Kotok (Cumberland Advisors), William Leach (The Boston Company), Martin Leibowitz (Salomon Brothers), Brent Lockwood (Alex. Brown & Sons), Franco Modigliani (MIT), Edward Murphy (Merchants Mutual Insurance Company), Scott Pinkus (Goldman Sachs), Bill Powers (PIMCO), Sharmin Mossavar-Rahmani (Goldman Sachs Asset Management), Frank Ramirez (Alex. Brown & Sons), Chuck Ramsey (Alex. Brown & Sons), Ben Rinkey (Piper Capital Management), Charles Smither (Alex. Brown & Sons), Ron Staff (Compass Bank), William Stewart (Alex. Brown & Sons), C.T. Urban (Norwest Investment Management), Nicholas Wentworth (Investment Advisors, Inc.), and David Yuen (Alex. Brown & Sons).

Finally, I am grateful to Stacia Mellbourne who edited the manuscript and Stephen Arbour who was responsible for all phases of production.

*Frank J. Fabozzi*

# TABLE OF CONTENTS

| | |
|---|---:|
| Preface | *ix* |
| Table of Contents | *xi* |
| List of Advertisers | *xiii* |
| 1. Fundamental Valuation Principles | *1* |
| 2. Spot Rates and Their Role in Valuation | *17* |
| 3. Forward Rates and Term Structure Theories | *45* |
| 4. Measuring Price Sensitivity to Interest Rate Changes | *75* |
| 5. Overview of the Valuation of Bonds with Embedded Options | *93* |
| 6. Binomial Method | *109* |
| 7. Monte Carlo Method | *145* |
| 8. Valuation of Inverse Floaters | *175* |
| 9. Valuation of Convertible Securities | *195* |
| Index | *213* |
| Advertisements | *225* |

# LIST OF ADVERTISERS

Alex. Brown & Sons
Andrew Kalotay Associates
BARRA
BondCalc Corporation
Ernst & Young
Integrated Decision Systems, Inc.
Intex Solutions, Inc.
Muller Data
Myers-Kohl Corporation
Reuters
Securities Software & Consulting
Thomson Financial Services
TIPS
Trepp & Company, Inc.

# 1
# FUNDAMENTAL VALUATION PRINCIPLES

Valuation is the process of determining the fair value of a financial asset. The fundamental principle of valuation is that the value of any financial asset is the present value of the expected cash flow. This principle applies regardless of the financial asset. Consequently, it applies equally to common stock, preferred stock, a bond, a mortgage loan, and real estate.

> **The objectives of this chapter are to:**
>
> 1. explain what is meant by the cash flow of a financial asset;
>
> 2. discuss the process involved in valuing a fixed income security;
>
> 3. explain the situations in which determination of the cash flow of a fixed income security is complex;
>
> 4. review the provisions that allow the cash flow to be altered by either the issuer or the investor;
>
> 5. explain why a fixed income security should be viewed as a package of zero-coupon securities;
>
> 6. review risk measures associated with investing in fixed income securities; and,
>
> 7. explain the role of valuation in deriving risk measures.

## ESTIMATING CASH FLOW

The first problem encountered in valuing a financial asset is interpreting what is meant by "cash flow." Accountants have a set answer: it is the net income after taxes plus noncash outlays such as depreciation. Nice definition, but useless for our purposes. Cash flow is simply the cash that is expected to be received each period from an investment. In the case of a fixed income security, it does not make any difference whether the cash flow is interest income or repayment of principal.

The cash flow for only a few types of fixed income securities are simple to project. Noncallable Treasury securities have a known cash flow. For a Treasury coupon security, the cash flow is the coupon interest payments every six months up to the maturity date and the principal payment at the maturity date. So, for example, the cash flow per $100 of par value for a 7%, 10-year Treasury security is the following: $3.5 (7%/2 × $100) every six months for the next 20 six-month periods and $100 20 six-month periods from now. Or, equivalently, the cash flow is $3.5 every six months for the next 19 six-month periods and $103.50 20 six-month periods from now.

In fact, for any fixed income security in which neither the issuer nor the investor can alter the repayment of the principal before its contractual due date, the cash flow can easily be determined assuming that the issuer does not default.

The difficulty in determining the cash flow is for securities under the following circumstances:

1. either the issuer or the investor has the option to change the contractual due date of the repayment of the principal;
2. the coupon payment is reset periodically based on some reference rate and there are restrictions on the new coupon rate (that is, there is a cap or a floor); or,
3. the investor has an option to convert the fixed income security to an equity issue.

### Provisions for Altering Principal Repayment

Most non-Treasury securities include a provision in the indenture that grants the issuer or the security holder the right to change the scheduled date or dates when the principal repayment is due. Assuming that the issuer does not default, the investor knows that the principal amount will be repaid, but does not know when that principal will be received. Because of this, the cash flow — which includes principal repayment and coupon interest payments — is not known with certainty.

The four most common provisions in fixed income securities that allow for the altering of the principal repayment are described below.

***Call and Refunding Provisions in Bond Indentures:*** An important question in negotiating the terms of a new bond issue is whether the issuer shall have the right to redeem the *entire amount* of bonds outstanding before the maturity date. Issuers generally want this right because they recognize that at some time in the future the general level of interest rates may fall sufficiently below the issue's coupon rate, so redeeming the issue and replacing it with another issue with a lower coupon rate would be attractive. This right is a disadvantage to the bondholder.

Thus, a call provision is an "embedded option" granted to the issuer. By an embedded option we mean an option that is part of the structure of a bond, as opposed to bare options, which trade separately from an underlying security.

The usual practice is a provision that denies the issuer the right to redeem bonds during the first 5 to 10 years following the date of issue with proceeds received from issuing lower-cost debt obligations ranking equal to or superior to the debt to be redeemed. This type of redemption is called *refunding*. While most long-term issues have these refunding restrictions, they may be immediately callable, in whole or in part, if the source of funds comes from other than lower interest cost money. Cash flow from operations, proceeds from a common stock sale, or funds from the sale of property are examples of such sources.

Investors often confuse refunding protection with call protection. Call protection is much more absolute in that the issue can not be redeemed *for any reason*. Refunding restrictions only provide protection against the one type of redemption mentioned above.

As a rule, bonds are callable at a premium above par. Generally, the amount of the premium declines as the bond approaches maturity and often reaches par after a number of years have passed since issuance.

***Accelerated Sinking Fund Provisions in Bond Indentures:*** A bond indenture may require the issuer to retire a specified portion of an issue each year. This is referred to as a *sinking fund requirement*. This kind of provision for repayment of debt may be designed to liquidate all of a bond issue by the maturity date, or it may be arranged to pay only a part of the total by the end of the term. If only a part is paid, the remainder is called a *balloon maturity*. The purpose of the sinking fund provision is to reduce credit risk.

Generally, the issuer may satisfy the sinking fund requirement by either (1) making a cash payment of the face amount of the bonds to be retired to the corporate trustee who then calls the bonds for redemption using a lottery, or (2) delivering bonds purchased in the open market with a total face value equal to the amount that must be retired to the trustee. Usually, the sinking fund call price is the par value if the bonds were originally sold at par.

Many corporate bond indentures include a provision that grants the issuer the right (i.e., option) to accelerate the repayment of the principal. This is an another embedded option granted to the issuer since the issuer can take advantage of this provision if interest rates decline below the coupon rate. While the acceleration provision is supposedly included in an indenture to reduce the credit risk, by allowing the issuer to retire more of the principal prior to the maturity date, it effectively is a call option granted to the issuer.

***Put Provision in Bond Indentures:*** A put provision grants the bondholder the right to sell the issue back to the issuer at par value on designated dates. The advantage to the bondholder is that if interest rates rise after the issue date, thereby reducing the value of the bond, the bondholder can put the bond to the issuer for par. This will insure that the bond will stay close to par, somewhat like instruments earning a short-term floating rate, except unlike floating-rate instruments, putable bonds also provide protection against deterioration in credit rating.

***Prepayment Provision in Mortgage Loans:*** A mortgage loan is a loan in which the funds borrowed are used to purchase real estate. In the United States, residential mortgage loans grant the borrower the right to prepay the loan, in whole or in part, without penalty at any time. Thus, the borrower has the right to pay off a loan without penalty if mortgage interest rates in the market fall below the contracted rate on the loan.

Note that in all but the put provision, the option to alter the principal repayment schedule rests with the issuer/borrower. The put provision allows the investor to alter the scheduled principal repayment date. Also it should be noted that the exercise of an option to change the cash flow will depend on the prevailing market interest rate relative to the interest rate paid by the borrower. Consequently, the valuation of securities with any of the embedded options described above must take into account future interest rates.

## Floating-Rate Securities

A floating-rate security is one in which the coupon rate is reset periodically. The new coupon rate for the period is contractually determined to be some *reference rate* adjusted for a spread. The spread can either be added to or subtracted from the value of the reference rate. Two examples of the coupon reset formula for a floating-rate security are:

>   Reference rate + 100 basis points
>   Reference rate − 50 basis points

The coupon rate need not increase with the reference rate as in the two examples. Today, there are floating-rate securities whose coupon interest rate decreases when the reference rate increases. Such floating-rate securities are called *inverse floating-rate securities*, or simply, *inverse floaters*. These securities are described in Chapter 8. An example of the coupon reset formula for an inverse floater is:

>   18% − Reference rate

The reference rate for any floating-rate instrument could be a market interest rate (such as the London Interbank Offered Rate (LIBOR) or a Treasury rate), or a calculated interest rate (such as the 11th District Cost of Funds), or the rate on some non-interest rate financial benchmark (such as the Standard & Poor's 500 stock market index).

Regardless of the reference rate, because of the uncertainty about its future value, future coupon interest is not known with certainty. This means that the cash flow is not known with certainty.

In addition, there are provisions in some floating-rate securities that can restrict the coupon rate. There can be a provision that sets a maximum coupon rate for the security. This provision is referred to as a *cap* or *ceiling*. There can be a provision that sets a minimum coupon rate for the security. This provision is referred to as a *floor*. Effectively, caps and floors are options. In the case of a cap, the security holder effectively sold an option to the issuer specifying that if the coupon reset rate based on the formula is above a specified rate, the security holder has to compensate the issuer by accepting the maximum coupon rate. For a floor, the issuer effectively sold an option to the security holder specifying that if the coupon reset rate based on the formula is below a specified rate, the issuer has to compensate the security holder by paying the minimum coupon rate. Thus, just as the provisions described earlier for altering the principal repayment can be viewed as embedded options, cap and floor provisions are also embedded options.

## Conversion or Exchange Provision

The conversion provision grants the security holder the right to convert the security into some financial asset or commodity either at any time during the life of the security or only at the maturity date. For example, a bond may be exchangeable into two ounces of gold at the maturity date. The more common type of conversion provision is one in which the investor has the right to convert the security into a predetermined number of shares of common stock of the issuer. A convertible security is therefore a security with an embedded call option to buy the common stock of the issuer. An *exchangeable security* grants the security holder the right to exchange the security for the common stock of a firm *other* than the issuer of the security.

Because there is uncertainty about the future value of the underlying stock into which the investor may convert, the cash flow of a convertible security is not known with certainty. Also, these securities are typically callable and some are putable which makes the valuation of a convertible security even more complicated.

## Cash Flow and Interest Rate Uncertainty

In our description of embedded options, a key factor that determines whether either the issuer of the security or the investor would exercise an option is the level of interest rates in the future relative to the security's coupon rate. Specifically, for a callable bond, if the prevailing market rate at which the issuer can refund an issue is sufficiently below the issue's coupon rate to justify the costs associated with refunding the issue, the issuer is likely to call the issue. Similarly, for a mortgage loan, if the prevailing refinancing rate available in the mortgage market is sufficiently below the loan's mortgage rate so that there will be savings by refinancing after considering the associated refinancing costs, then the homeowner has an incentive to refinance. For a putable bond, if the rate on comparable securities rises such that the value of the putable bond falls below the value at which it must be repurchased by the issuer, then the investor will put the issue.

What this means is that to properly estimate the cash flow of a fixed income security it is necessary to incorporate into the analysis how interest rates can change in the future and how such changes affect the cash flow. As we will see in later chapters, this is done in valuation models by introducing a parameter that reflects the volatility of interest rates.

## DISCOUNTING THE CASH FLOW

Once the cash flow for a fixed income security is estimated, the next step is to determine the appropriate interest rate. To determine the appropriate rate, the investor must address the following three questions:

1. What is the minimum interest rate the investor should require?
2. How much more than the minimum interest rate should the investor require?
3. Should the investor use the same interest rate for each estimated cash flow or a unique interest rate for the estimated cash flow of each period?

The minimum interest rate that an investor should require is the yield available in the marketplace on a default-free cash flow. In the U.S., this is the yield on a U.S. Treasury security. The premium over the yield on a Treasury security that the investor should require should reflect the risks associated with realizing the estimated cash flow. Below we address the third question.

### Exhibit 1: Cash Flow for Three 10-Year Hypothetical Treasury Securities Per $100 of Par Value
(Each period is six months)

| Period | 12% coupon | 8% coupon | 0% coupon |
|---|---|---|---|
| 1 | $60 | $40 | $0 |
| 2 | 60 | 40 | 0 |
| 3 | 60 | 40 | 0 |
| 4 | 60 | 40 | 0 |
| 5 | 60 | 40 | 0 |
| 6 | 60 | 40 | 0 |
| 7 | 60 | 40 | 0 |
| 8 | 60 | 40 | 0 |
| 9 | 60 | 40 | 0 |
| 10 | 60 | 40 | 0 |
| 11 | 60 | 40 | 0 |
| 12 | 60 | 40 | 0 |
| 13 | 60 | 40 | 0 |
| 14 | 60 | 40 | 0 |
| 15 | 60 | 40 | 0 |
| 16 | 60 | 40 | 0 |
| 17 | 60 | 40 | 0 |
| 18 | 60 | 40 | 0 |
| 19 | 60 | 40 | 0 |
| 20 | 1,060 | 1,040 | 1,000 |

## Traditional Valuation Approach

The traditional practice in valuation has been to discount every cash flow of a fixed income security by the same interest rate (or discount rate). For example, consider the three hypothetical 10-year Treasury securities shown in Exhibit 1: a 12% coupon bond, a 8% coupon bond, and a zero-coupon bond. The cash flow for each security is shown in the exhibit. Since the cash flow of all three securities is viewed as default free, the traditional practice is to use the same discount rate to calculate the present value of all three securities and the same discount rate for the cash flow for each period.

## Contemporary Approach

The fundamental flaw of the traditional approach is that it views each security as the same package of cash flows. For example, consider a 10-year U.S. Treasury bond with an 8% coupon rate. The cash flow per $100 of par value would be 19 payments of $5 every six months and $105 20 six-month periods from now. The traditional practice would discount the cash flow for all 20 periods using the same interest rate.

The proper way to view the 10-year 8% coupon bond is as a package of zero-coupon instruments. Each period's cash flow should be considered a zero-coupon instrument whose maturity value is the amount of the cash flow and whose maturity date is the date of the cash flow. Thus, the 10-year 8% coupon bond should be viewed as 20 zero-coupon instruments. The reason that this is the proper way is because it does not allow a market participant to realize an arbitrage profit. This will be made clearer in the next chapter.

By viewing any financial asset in this way, a consistent valuation framework can be developed. For example, under the traditional approach to the valuation of fixed income securities, a 10-year zero-coupon bond would be viewed as the same financial asset as a 10-year 8% coupon bond. Viewing a financial asset as a package of zero-coupon instruments means that these two bonds would be viewed as different packages of zero-coupon instruments and valued accordingly.

The difference between the traditional valuation approach and the contemporary approach is depicted in Exhibit 2 which shows how the three bonds whose cash flow is depicted in Exhibit 1 should be valued. With the traditional approach, the minimum interest rate for all three securities is the yield on a 10-year U.S. Treasury security. With the contemporary approach the minimum yield for a cash flow is the theoretical rate that the U.S. Treasury would have to pay if it issued a zero-coupon bond with a maturity date equal to the maturity date of the estimated cash flow.

Therefore, to implement the contemporary approach it is necessary to determine the theoretical rate that the U.S. Treasury would have to pay to issue a zero-coupon instrument for each maturity. Another name used for the zero-coupon rate is the *spot rate*. As explained in the next chapter, the spot rate can be estimated from the Treasury yield curve.

## Exhibit 2: Comparison of Traditional Approach and Contemporary Approach in Valuing a Bond
### (Each period is six months)

| | Discount (Interest) Rate | | Treasury Security (coupon) | | |
| | Traditional Approach | Contemporary Approach | | | |
| Period | (Treasury rate) | (spot rate) | 12% | 8% | 0% |
|---|---|---|---|---|---|
| 1 | 10-year | 1-period | $60 | $40 | $0 |
| 2 | 10-year | 2-period | 60 | 40 | 0 |
| 3 | 10-year | 3-period | 60 | 40 | 0 |
| 4 | 10-year | 4-period | 60 | 40 | 0 |
| 5 | 10-year | 5-period | 60 | 40 | 0 |
| 6 | 10-year | 6-period | 60 | 40 | 0 |
| 7 | 10-year | 7-period | 60 | 40 | 0 |
| 8 | 10-year | 8-period | 60 | 40 | 0 |
| 9 | 10-year | 9-period | 60 | 40 | 0 |
| 10 | 10-year | 10-period | 60 | 40 | 0 |
| 11 | 10-year | 11-period | 60 | 40 | 0 |
| 12 | 10-year | 12-period | 60 | 40 | 0 |
| 13 | 10-year | 13-period | 60 | 40 | 0 |
| 14 | 10-year | 14-period | 60 | 40 | 0 |
| 15 | 10-year | 15-period | 60 | 40 | 0 |
| 16 | 10-year | 16-period | 60 | 40 | 0 |
| 17 | 10-year | 17-period | 60 | 40 | 0 |
| 18 | 10-year | 18-period | 60 | 40 | 0 |
| 19 | 10-year | 19-period | 60 | 40 | 0 |
| 20 | 10-year | 20-period | 1,060 | 1,040 | 1,000 |

## RISK MEASURES

Investors are not only interested in determining the true value of a fixed income security but also the identification of the risks inherent with investing in a security. There are several types of risk associated with investing in a security. One risk is credit or default risk. This risk can be gauged by the rating assigned by the major commercial rating companies.

Another key risk measure is the price sensitivity of a fixed income security to changes in interest rates. This measure is popularly referred to as *duration*. The duration of any fixed income security is measured by changing interest rates up and down by a small number of basis points and determining how the value of the security changes. To determine what the value of a security would be if interest rates change, it is necessary to have a valuation model. Thus duration is a by-product of a valuation model. If the valuation model used to value a fixed income security is poor, the resulting duration measure will also be a poor measure of the price sensitivity of a security to changes in interest rates.

A drawback of duration is that it is a measure of the price sensitivity of a security assuming the interest rate for all maturities change by the same number of basis points. But as explained earlier, each cash flow should be discounted at its own unique discount rate. Thus, a security's price may be highly sensitive to a change in interest rates that is not the same for all maturity levels. Using a valuation model that recognizes that each cash flow should be discounted at its own unique discount rate, the price sensitivity of a security to changes in interest rates that are not the same for each maturity can be determined.

## OVERVIEW OF BOOK

This foregoing discussion has provided a bird's eye view of the principles of the valuation of fixed income securities. The eight chapters to follow provide more detailed information about the valuation process.

The valuation process begins with estimation of the theoretical Treasury spot rate or zero-coupon rate for each maturity. It is these rates that are the benchmark or minimum interest rate to discount a security's estimated cash flow. Chapter 2 describes this process and shows how the theoretical Treasury spot rates should be used in the valuation of any security.

The theoretical spot rates are related to forward rates. Forward rates are the market's consensus of future interest rates. In Chapter 3 we explain forward rates, how they can be determined, and their relationship to spot rates. Valuing a security using spot rates or forward rates will produce the same value for a security. As we noted, modeling of future interest rates is essential to valuing fixed income securities with embedded options because of the affect that future rates have on cash flows. Most valuation models model short-term rates. This is done by assuming that short rates follow a certain stochastic process. This more technical phase of the valuation process is described in the appendix to Chapter 3.

A by-product of the valuation process is the price sensitivity of a fixed income security to interest rate changes. In Chapter 4 we describe two popular measures of duration, modified duration (or its sister measure, Macaulay duration) and effective duration. We note in that chapter that the former is a worthless measure for security's with embedded options and that investors should avoid the use of this measure.

In Chapter 5, we explain how a fixed income security with an embedded option should be viewed conceptually. There we argue that the value of such securities will depend on the value of the embedded option. Consequently, it is important to understand the factors that affect the value of an option. These factors are described in Chapter 5.

There are two valuation methods that are commonly used to value fixed income securities with embedded options: binomial method and Monte Carlo method. A by-product of these models is the option-adjusted spread (OAS). In Chapter 5 we also explain what this measure is. It is important to note that the OAS is not a new technology for valuing securities. That is, it is not a valuation model as it is often referred to by market participants. Instead, it is a measure that is derived from one of the two valuation methods.

In Chapters 6 and 7 the two valuation methods are explained and illustrated. In Chapter 6 the binomial method is explained and applied to the valuation of corporate bonds. The Monte Carlo method is the subject of Chapter 7. Since this method is commonly used to value mortgage-backed securities, we illustrate this method to value such securities. For each method, the procedure for calculating the OAS and effective duration and effective convexity are explained.

In Chapter 8, we explain the principles for valuing inverse floating rate securities. These securities are quite popular in the collateralized mortgage-backed securities market and in the municipal securities market. In Chapter 9, we explain the state-of-the-art technology for valuing convertible securities.

## KEY POINTS

Here are the key points of this chapter:

1. Valuation is the process of determining the fair value of a financial asset.

2. The fundamental principle of valuation is that the value of any financial asset is the present value of the expected cash flow.

3. The cash flow is the cash that is expected to be received each period from an investment.

4. For any fixed income security in which neither the issuer nor the investor can alter the repayment of the principal before its contractual due date, the cash flow can easily be determined assuming that the issuer does not default.

5. The difficulty in determining the cash flow arises for securities where either the issuer or the investor can alter the cash flow.

6. An embedded option is an option that is part of the structure of a bond, as opposed to bare options, which trade separately from an underlying security.

7. Most non-Treasury securities include an embedded option, a provision that grants the issuer or the investor the right to change the scheduled date or dates when the principal repayment is due.

8. The four most common provisions in fixed income securities that allow for the altering of the principal repayment are call and refunding provisions, accelerated sinking fund provisions, put provisions, and prepayment provisions in mortgage loans.

9. For all but the put provision, the option to alter the principal repayment schedule rests with the issuer/borrower.

10. The cash flow for a floating-rate security is not known because the future value of the reference rate is unknown.

11. The cash flow for a convertible security is unknown because the investor has the right to convert the security into some financial asset or commodity either at any time during the life of the security or only at the maturity date.

12. A key factor that determines whether either the borrower or the investor would exercise an option is the level of interest rates in the future relative to the security's coupon rate.

13. To properly estimate the cash flow of a fixed income security it is necessary to incorporate into the analysis how interest rates can change in the future and how such changes affect the cash flow.

14. The traditional practice in the valuation of a fixed income security has been to discount every period's cash flow by the same interest rate (or discount rate).

15. The fundamental flaw of the traditional approach is that it views each security as the same package of cash flows.

16. The contemporary approach values a bond as a package of cash flows, with each cash flow viewed as a zero-coupon instrument and each cash flow discounted at its own unique discount rate.

17. To implement the contemporary approach it is necessary to determine the theoretical spot rate that the U.S. Treasury would have to pay to issue a zero-coupon instrument for each maturity.

18. A key risk measure is the price sensitivity of a fixed income security to changes in interest rates, referred to as duration.

19. A valuation model is needed to determine what the value of a security would be if interest rates change and therefore to determine a bond's duration.

20. A drawback of duration is that it is a measure of the price sensitivity of a security assuming the interest rate for all maturities changes by the same number of basis points.

# 2

# SPOT RATES AND THEIR ROLE IN VALUATION

As we emphasized in the previous chapter, the key to the valuation of any security is the estimation of its cash flow and the discounting of each cash flow by an appropriate rate. The starting point for the determination of the appropriate rate is the theoretical spot rate on default-free securities. Since Treasury securities are viewed as default-free securities, the theoretical spot rates on these securities are the benchmark rates.

> **The objectives of this chapter are to:**
>
> 1. explain the difference between the Treasury yield curve and the Treasury spot rate curve;
>
> 2. show how the theoretical spot rate curve for Treasury securities can be constructed from the Treasury yield curve;
>
> 3. explain what the discount function is and how it is determined;
>
> 4. demonstrate how the Treasury spot rate curve can be used to price any Treasury security;
>
> 5. show why, based on arbitrage arguments, the price of a Treasury security will not deviate significantly from its theoretical value based on spot rates;

> 6. explain the drawbacks of the traditional (or nominal) yield spread measure;
>
> 7. present a measure called the static spread that is superior to the nominal yield measure, and describe the circumstances under which the two measures will deviate; and,
>
> 8. explain how credit risk should be introduced into the term structure.

## TREASURY YIELD CURVE

The graphical depiction of the relationship between the yield on Treasury securities of different maturities is known as the *yield curve*. The Treasury yield curve is typically constructed from on-the-run Treasury issues. These are the most recently auctioned Treasury securities: 3-month, 6-month, 1-year, 2-year, 4-year, 5-year, 7-year, 10-year, and 30-year.

The first three issues are Treasury bills which are issued as discount securities. These securities are sold at auction at a price below their maturity value and pay no coupon interest. The investor realizes interest by the difference between the maturity value and the price paid. Thus, Treasury bills are zero-coupon securities. In contrast, the six issues that mature after one year are coupon securities. There are no securities issued by the U.S. Department of the Treasury with a maturity greater than one year that are discount or zero-coupon securities. Consequently, the Treasury yield curve is a combination of zero-coupon securities and coupon securities.

In the valuation of securities what is needed is the rate on zero-coupon default-free securities or, equivalently, the rate on zero-coupon Treasury securities. However, as just noted, there are no zero-coupon Treasury securities issued by the U.S. Department of the Treasury with a maturity greater than one year. Our goal is to construct a theoretical rate that the U.S. government would have to offer if it issued zero-coupon securities with a maturity greater than one year.

There are, in fact, zero-coupon Treasury securities with a maturity greater than one year that are created by government dealer firms. These securities are called *stripped Treasury securities*. Prior to 1985, stripped Treasury securities were either created as trademark products by dealer firms such as TIGRs (a Merrill Lynch product) and CATs (a Salomon Brothers product) or Trust Receipts (TRs) not associated with any particular dealer firm. Today, all stripped Treasury securities are created by dealer firms under a Treasury Department program called STRIPS, which stands for Separate Trading of Registered Interest and Principal Securities. The process by which a dealer firm can create these securities is depicted in Exhibit 1.

It would seem logical that the observed yield on stripped Treasury securities could be used to construct an actual spot rate curve rather than go through the procedure we will describe. There are three problems with using the observed rates on stripped Treasury securities. First, the liquidity of the stripped Treasury market is not as great as that of the Treasury coupon market. Thus, the observed rates on stripped Treasury securities reflect a premium for liquidity.

Second, there are maturity sectors of the stripped Treasury securities market that attract specific investors who may be willing to trade off yield in exchange for an attractive feature associated with that particular maturity sector, thereby distorting the term structure relationship. For example, unlike domestic taxable entities, certain foreign governments may grant investors preferential tax treatment on zero-coupon Treasuries. As a result, these foreign investors invest heavily in long-maturity stripped Treasury securities, driving down yields in that maturity sector.

Finally, the tax treatment of stripped Treasury securities is different from that of Treasury coupon securities. Specifically, the accrued interest on stripped Treasury securities is taxed even though no cash is received by the investor. Thus they are negative cash flow securities to taxable entities, and, as a result, their yield reflects this tax disadvantage.

**20** SPOT RATES AND THEIR ROLE IN VALUATION

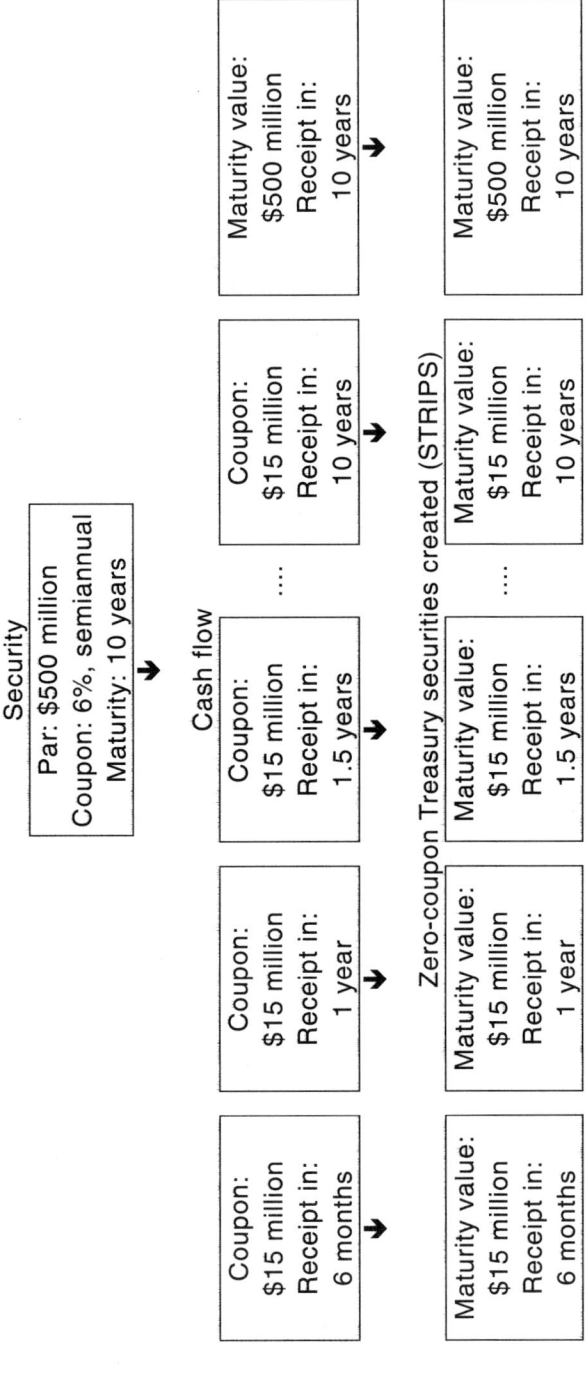

**Exhibit 1: Creating Zero-Coupon Treasury Securities (STRIPS)**
Dealer purchases $500 million par of a 6% 10-year Treasury

## Exhibit 2: Maturity and Yield to Maturity for 20 Hypothetical Treasury Securities

| Period | Years | Yield to maturity (%) | Price | Spot rate (%) | Discount function |
|---|---|---|---|---|---|
| 1  | 0.5  | 3.00 | —      | 3.0000 | 0.9852 |
| 2  | 1.0  | 3.30 | —      | 3.3000 | 0.9678 |
| 3  | 1.5  | 3.50 | 100.00 | 3.5053 | 0.9492 |
| 4  | 2.0  | 3.90 | 100.00 | 3.9164 | 0.9254 |
| 5  | 2.5  | 4.40 | 100.00 | 4.4376 | 0.8961 |
| 6  | 3.0  | 4.70 | 100.00 | 4.7520 | 0.8686 |
| 7  | 3.5  | 4.90 | 100.00 | 4.9622 | 0.8424 |
| 8  | 4.0  | 5.00 | 100.00 | 5.0650 | 0.8187 |
| 9  | 4.5  | 5.10 | 100.00 | 5.1701 | 0.7948 |
| 10 | 5.0  | 5.20 | 100.00 | 5.2772 | 0.7707 |
| 11 | 5.5  | 5.30 | 100.00 | 5.3864 | 0.7465 |
| 12 | 6.0  | 5.40 | 100.00 | 5.4976 | 0.7222 |
| 13 | 6.5  | 5.50 | 100.00 | 5.6108 | 0.6979 |
| 14 | 7.0  | 5.55 | 100.00 | 5.6643 | 0.6764 |
| 15 | 7.5  | 5.60 | 100.00 | 5.7193 | 0.6551 |
| 16 | 8.0  | 5.65 | 100.00 | 5.7755 | 0.6341 |
| 17 | 8.5  | 5.70 | 100.00 | 5.8331 | 0.6134 |
| 18 | 9.0  | 5.80 | 100.00 | 5.9584 | 0.5895 |
| 19 | 9.5  | 5.90 | 100.00 | 6.0863 | 0.5658 |
| 20 | 10.0 | 6.00 | 100.00 | 6.2169 | 0.5421 |

## CONSTRUCTING THE THEORETICAL SPOT RATE CURVE FOR TREASURIES

A default-free theoretical spot rate curve can be constructed from the observed Treasury yield curve. There are several approaches that are used in practice. The approach that we describe below for creating a theoretical spot rate curve is called *bootstrapping*.

To explain this approach, we use the price, annualized yield (yield to maturity), and maturity for the 20 hypothetical Treasury securities shown in Exhibit 2. Our focus is on the first four columns of the exhibit. Our goal is to explain how the values in the last two columns of the exhibit are derived.

Throughout the analysis and illustrations to come, it is important to remember that the basic principle is that the value of the Treasury coupon security should be equal to the value of the package of zero-coupon Treasury securities that duplicates the coupon bond's cash flow.

Consider the six-month Treasury bill in Exhibit 2. Since a Treasury bill is a zero-coupon instrument, its annualized yield of 3.00% is equal to the spot rate. Similarly, for the one-year Treasury, the cited yield of 3.30% is the one-year spot rate. Given these two spot rates, we can compute the spot rate for a theoretical 1.5-year zero-coupon Treasury. The price of a theoretical 1.5-year Treasury should equal the present value of the three cash flows from the 1.5-year coupon Treasury, where the yield used for discounting is the spot rate corresponding to the cash flow. Since all the coupon bonds are selling at par, the yield to maturity for each bond is the coupon rate. Using $100 as par, the cash flow for the 1.5-year coupon Treasury is:

| | | |
|---|---|---|
| 0.5 years | $0.035 \times \$100 \times 0.5$ | = $ 1.75 |
| 1.0 years | $0.035 \times \$100 \times 0.5$ | = $ 1.75 |
| 1.5 years | $0.035 \times \$100 \times 0.5 + 100$ | = $ 101.75 |

The present value of the cash flow is then:

$$\frac{1.75}{(1+z_1)^1} + \frac{1.75}{(1+z_1)^2} + \frac{101.75}{(1+z_3)^3}$$

where:

$z_1$ = one-half the six-month theoretical spot rate,
$z_2$ = one-half the one-year theoretical spot rate, and
$z_3$ = one-half the 1.5-year theoretical spot rate.

Since the six-month spot rate and one-year spot rate are 3.00% and 3.30%, respectively, we know that:

$z_1 = 0.0150$ and $z_2 = 0.0165$

We can compute the present value of the 1.5-year coupon Treasury security as:

$$\frac{1.75}{(1+z_1)^1} + \frac{1.75}{(1+z_1)^2} + \frac{101.75}{(1+z_3)^3}$$

$$= \frac{1.75}{(1.015)^1} + \frac{1.75}{(1.0165)^2} + \frac{101.75}{(1+z_3)^3}$$

Since the price of the 1.5-year coupon Treasury security is par, the following relationship must hold:

$$\frac{1.75}{(1.015)^1} + \frac{1.75}{(1.0165)^2} + \frac{101.75}{(1+z_3)^3} = 100$$

We can solve for the theoretical 1.5-year spot rate as follows:

$$1.7241 + 1.6936 + \frac{101.75}{(1+z_3)^3} = 100$$

$$\frac{101.75}{(1+z_3)^3} = 96.5822$$

$$(1+z_3)^3 = \frac{101.725}{96.5822}$$

$$z_3 = 0.0175265 = 1.7527\%$$

Doubling this yield we obtain the bond-equivalent yield of 3.5053%, which is the theoretical 1.5-year spot rate. That rate is the rate that the market would apply to a 1.5-year zero-coupon Treasury security if, in fact, such a security existed.

Given the theoretical 1.5-year spot rate, we can obtain the theoretical two-year spot rate. The cash flow for the two-year coupon Treasury in Exhibit 2 is:

## SPOT RATES AND THEIR ROLE IN VALUATION

| 0.5 years | $0.039 \times \$100 \times 0.5$ | = $ | 1.95 |
| 1.0 years | $0.039 \times \$100 \times 0.5$ | = $ | 1.95 |
| 1.5 years | $0.039 \times \$100 \times 0.5$ | = $ | 1.95 |
| 2.0 years | $0.039 \times \$100 \times 0.5 + 100$ | = $ | 101.95 |

The present value of the cash flow is then:

$$\frac{1.95}{(1+z_1)^1} + \frac{1.95}{(1+z_2)^2} + \frac{1.95}{(1+z_3)^3} + \frac{101.95}{(1+z_4)^4}$$

where $z_4$ = one-half the two-year theoretical spot rate.

Since the six-month spot rate, one-year spot rate, and 1.5-year spot rate are 3.00%, 3.30%, and 3.5053%, respectively, then:

$$z_1 = 0.0150, \ z_2 = 0.0165, \text{ and } z_3 = 0.0175265$$

Therefore, the present value of the two-year coupon Treasury security is:

$$\frac{1.95}{(1.0150)^1} + \frac{1.95}{(1.0165)^2} + \frac{1.95}{(1.017527)^3} + \frac{101.95}{(1+z_4)^4}$$

Since the price of the two-year coupon Treasury security is par, the following relationship must hold:

$$\frac{1.95}{(1.0150)^1} + \frac{1.95}{(1.0165)^2} + \frac{1.95}{(1.017527)^3} + \frac{101.95}{(1+z_4)^4} = 100$$

We can solve for the theoretical two-year spot rate as follows:

$$\frac{101.95}{(1+z_4)^4} = 94.3392$$

$$(1+z_4)^4 = \frac{101.95}{94.3392}$$

$$z_4 = 0.019582 = 1.9582\%$$

Doubling this yield, we obtain the theoretical two-year spot rate bond-equivalent yield of 3.9164%.

One can follow this approach sequentially to derive the theoretical 2.5-year spot rate from the calculated values of $z_1$, $z_2$, $z_3$, $z_4$ (the six-month-, one-year-, 1.5-year-, and two-year rates), and the price and coupon of the bond with a maturity of 2.5 years. Further, one could derive theoretical spot rates for the remaining 15 half-yearly rates.

The spot rates thus obtained are shown in the next-to-the-last column of Exhibit 2. They represent the term structure of default-free spot rates for maturities up to ten years at the particular time to which the bond price quotations refer.

## THE DISCOUNT FUNCTION

The term structure is represented by the spot rate curve. We also know that the present value of $1 at any future date, n, when discounted at the spot rate for period n is:

$$\frac{\$1}{\left[1+\left(\frac{\text{Spot rate for period n}}{2}\right)\right]^n}$$

For example, the present value of $1 five years from now using the spot rate for 10 periods in Exhibit 2, 5.2772%, is

$$\frac{\$1}{\left[1+\left(\frac{0.052772}{2}\right)\right]^{10}} = 0.7707$$

This value can be viewed as the time value of $1 for a default-free cash flow to be received in 5 years. Equivalently, it shows the price of a zero-coupon default-free security with a maturity of 5 years and a maturity value of $1.

The last column of Exhibit 2 shows the time value of $1 for each period. The set of time values for all periods is called the *discount function*.

## APPLYING THE SPOT RATES TO PRICE A TREASURY COUPON SECURITY

To demonstrate how to use the spot rate curve, suppose that we want to price an 8% 10-year Treasury security. The price of this issue is the present value of the cash flow where each cash flow is discounted at the corresponding spot rate. This is illustrated in Exhibit 3.

The third column shows the cash flow for each period. The fourth column shows the spot rate curve. The corresponding discount function is shown in the next to the last column. Multiplying the value in the discount function column by the cash flow gives the present value of the cash flow. The sum of the present values is equal to 115.2619. This is the theoretical value of this issue.

Exhibit 4 shows how to price a 6% 10-year Treasury issue. As indicated in Exhibit 2, the price of this issue is 100. This agrees with the theoretical value calculated in Exhibit 4.

## WHY TREASURIES MUST BE PRICED BASED ON SPOT RATES

The price of a Treasury security is determined by the spot rates, not the yield to maturity of a Treasury coupon security of the same maturity. We will use an illustration to demonstrate the economic forces that will assure that the actual market price of a Treasury coupon security will not depart significantly from its theoretical value.

## Exhibit 3: Determination of the Theoretical Price of an 8% 10-Year Treasury

| Period | Years | Cash flow | Spot rate (%) | Discount function | Present Value |
|---|---|---|---|---|---|
| 1 | 0.5 | 4.00 | 3.0000 | 0.9852 | 3.9409 |
| 2 | 1.0 | 4.00 | 3.3000 | 0.9678 | 3.8712 |
| 3 | 1.5 | 4.00 | 3.5053 | 0.9492 | 3.7968 |
| 4 | 2.0 | 4.00 | 3.9164 | 0.9254 | 3.7014 |
| 5 | 2.5 | 4.00 | 4.4376 | 0.8961 | 3.5843 |
| 6 | 3.0 | 4.00 | 4.7520 | 0.8686 | 3.4743 |
| 7 | 3.5 | 4.00 | 4.9622 | 0.8424 | 3.3694 |
| 8 | 4.0 | 4.00 | 5.0650 | 0.8187 | 3.2747 |
| 9 | 4.5 | 4.00 | 5.1701 | 0.7948 | 3.1791 |
| 10 | 5.0 | 4.00 | 5.2772 | 0.7707 | 3.0828 |
| 11 | 5.5 | 4.00 | 5.3864 | 0.7465 | 2.9861 |
| 12 | 6.0 | 4.00 | 5.4976 | 0.7222 | 2.8889 |
| 13 | 6.5 | 4.00 | 5.6108 | 0.6979 | 2.7916 |
| 14 | 7.0 | 4.00 | 5.6643 | 0.6764 | 2.7055 |
| 15 | 7.5 | 4.00 | 5.7193 | 0.6551 | 2.6205 |
| 16 | 8.0 | 4.00 | 5.7755 | 0.6341 | 2.5365 |
| 17 | 8.5 | 4.00 | 5.8331 | 0.6134 | 2.4536 |
| 18 | 9.0 | 4.00 | 5.9584 | 0.5895 | 2.3581 |
| 19 | 9.5 | 4.00 | 6.0863 | 0.5658 | 2.2631 |
| 20 | 10.0 | 104.00 | 6.2169 | 0.5421 | 56.3828 |
| | | | | Total | 115.2619 |

To demonstrate this, consider the 8% 10-year Treasury security. Suppose that this Treasury security is priced based on the 6% yield to maturity of the 10-year maturity Treasury coupon security in Exhibit 2. Discounting all of the cash flows of the 8% 10-year Treasury security at 6% gives a present value of 114.88.

The question is, could this security trade at 114.88 in the market? Let's see what would happen if the 8% 10-year Treasury traded at 114.88. Suppose that a dealer firm buys this issue at 114.88 and strips it. By stripping it, we mean creating zero-coupon instruments as depicted in Exhibit 1. By stripping this issue, the dealer firm creates 20 zero-coupon instruments guaranteed by the U.S. Treasury.[1]

---

[1] As shown in Exhibit 1, 21 zero-coupon instruments are created since the last coupon and the maturity value are sold separately. In our illustrations, we do not make any distinction between the last coupon and maturity value.

## Exhibit 4: Determination of the Theoretical Price of a 6%, 10-Year Treasury

| Period | Years | Cash flow | Spot rate (%) | Discount function | Present value |
|---|---|---|---|---|---|
| 1 | 0.5 | 3.00 | 3.0000 | 0.9852 | 2.9557 |
| 2 | 1.0 | 3.00 | 3.3000 | 0.9678 | 2.9034 |
| 3 | 1.5 | 3.00 | 3.5053 | 0.9492 | 2.8476 |
| 4 | 2.0 | 3.00 | 3.9164 | 0.9254 | 2.7761 |
| 5 | 2.5 | 3.00 | 4.4376 | 0.8961 | 2.6882 |
| 6 | 3.0 | 3.00 | 4.7520 | 0.8686 | 2.6057 |
| 7 | 3.5 | 3.00 | 4.9622 | 0.8424 | 2.5271 |
| 8 | 4.0 | 3.00 | 5.0650 | 0.8187 | 2.4560 |
| 9 | 4.5 | 3.00 | 5.1701 | 0.7948 | 2.3843 |
| 10 | 5.0 | 3.00 | 5.2772 | 0.7707 | 2.3121 |
| 11 | 5.5 | 3.00 | 5.3864 | 0.7465 | 2.2396 |
| 12 | 6.0 | 3.00 | 5.4976 | 0.7222 | 2.1667 |
| 13 | 6.5 | 3.00 | 5.6108 | 0.6979 | 2.0937 |
| 14 | 7.0 | 3.00 | 5.6643 | 0.6764 | 2.0292 |
| 15 | 7.5 | 3.00 | 5.7193 | 0.6551 | 1.9654 |
| 16 | 8.0 | 3.00 | 5.7755 | 0.6341 | 1.9024 |
| 17 | 8.5 | 3.00 | 5.8331 | 0.6134 | 1.8402 |
| 18 | 9.0 | 3.00 | 5.9584 | 0.5895 | 1.7686 |
| 19 | 9.5 | 3.00 | 6.0863 | 0.5658 | 1.6973 |
| 20 | 10.0 | 103.00 | 6.2169 | 0.5421 | <u>55.8407</u> |
| | | | | Total | 100.0000 |

How much can the 20 zero-coupon instruments be sold for by the dealer firm? Expressed equivalently, at what yield can each of the zero-coupon instruments be sold? The answer is in Exhibit 2. The yield at which each zero-coupon instrument can be sold is the spot rate shown in the next-to-the-last column.

We can use Exhibit 3 to determine the proceeds that would be received per $100 of par value of the 8% 10-year issue stripped. The last column shows how much would be received for each coupon sold as a zero-coupon instrument. The total proceeds received from selling the zero-coupon Treasury securities created would be $115.2619 per $100 of par value of the Treasury issue purchased by the dealer. Since the dealer purchased the issue for $114.88, this would result in an arbitrage profit of $0.3819 per $100 of the 8% 10-year Treasury issue purchased.

To understand why the dealer has the opportunity to realize this arbitrage profit, look at the last column of Exhibit 3 which shows how much the dealer paid for each cash flow by buying the entire package of cash flows (i.e., by buying the issue). For example, consider the $4 coupon payment in four years. By buying the 10-year Treasury bond priced to yield 6%, the dealer effectively pays a price based on 6% (3% semiannual) for that coupon payment, or, equivalently, $3.1577. Under the assumptions of this illustration, however, investors were willing to accept a lower yield to maturity (the 4-year spot rate), 5.065% (2.5325% semiannual), to purchase a zero-coupon Treasury security with four years to maturity. Thus investors were willing to pay $3.2747. On this one coupon payment, the dealer realizes a profit equal to the difference between $3.2747 and $3.1577 (or $0.117). From all the cash flows, the total profit is $0.3819. In this instance, coupon stripping results in the sum of the parts being greater than the whole.

Suppose that, instead of the observed yield to maturity from Exhibit 2, the yields that investors want are the same as the theoretical spot rates that are shown in the exhibit. As can be seen in Exhibit 3, if we use these spot rates to discount the cash flows, the total proceeds from the sale of the zero-coupon Treasury securities would be equal to $115.2619, making coupon stripping uneconomic since the proceeds from stripping would be the same as the cost of purchasing the issue.

In our illustration of coupon stripping, the price of the Treasury security is less than its theoretical price. Suppose instead that the price of the Treasury coupon security is greater than its theoretical price. In this case, investors can create a portfolio of zero-coupon Treasury securities such that the cash flow of the portfolio replicates the cash flow of the mispriced Treasury coupon security. By doing so, the investor will realize a yield higher than the yield on the Treasury coupon security. For example, suppose that the market price of the 10-year Treasury coupon security we used in our illustration is $116. An investor could buy 20 outstanding zero-coupon stripped Treasury securities with a maturity value identical to the cash flow shown in the third column of Exhibit 3. The cost of purchasing this portfolio of stripped Treasury securities would be $115.1880. Thus, an investor is effectively purchasing a portfolio of stripped Treasury securities that has the same cash flow as an 8% 10-year Treasury coupon security at a cost of $115.1880 instead of $116.

It is the process of coupon stripping and reconstituting that will

# 30  SPOT RATES AND THEIR ROLE IN VALUATION

prevent the market price of Treasury securities from departing significantly from their theoretical value.

## STATIC SPREAD

Traditional analysis of the yield premium for a non-Treasury bond involves calculating the difference between the yield to maturity (or yield to call) of the bond in question and the yield to maturity of a comparable maturity Treasury coupon security. The latter is obtained from the Treasury yield curve. For example, consider the following 10-year bonds:

| Issue | Coupon | Price | Yield to maturity |
|---|---|---|---|
| Treasury | 6% | 100.00 | 6.00% |
| Non-Treasury | 8% | 104.19 | 7.40% |

The yield spread for these two bonds as traditionally computed is 140 basis points (7.4% minus 6%). We refer to this traditional yield spread as the *nominal spread*.

### Drawbacks of the Conventional Yield Spread Measure

The drawbacks of this convention, however, are (1) for both bonds, the yield fails to take into consideration the term structure of the spot rates; and (2) in the case of callable and/or putable bonds, expected interest rate volatility may alter the future cash flow of the non-Treasury bond. Here, we focus only on the first problem: failure to consider the spot rate curve. We will deal with the second problem in Chapters 6 and 7.

### Determination of the Static Spread

The *static spread* is a measure of the spread that the investor would realize over the entire Treasury spot rate curve if (1) the bond is held to maturity and (2) the spot rates do not change. It is not a spread off one point on the Treasury yield curve, as is the nominal yield spread. The static spread is calculated as the spread that will make the present value of the cash flow from the non-Treasury bond, when discounted at the Treasury spot rate plus the spread, equal to the non-Treasury bond's market price. A trial-and-error procedure is required to determine the static spread.

## Exhibit 5: Determination of the Static Spread for the 8%, 10-Year Non-Treasury Issue Selling at 104.19 to Yield 7.4%

| Period | Years | Cash flow | Spot rate (%) | Present value: Spread 100 bp | Present value: Spread 125 bp | Present value: Spread 146 bp |
|---|---|---|---|---|---|---|
| 1 | 0.5 | 4.00 | 3.0000 | 3.9216 | 3.9168 | 3.9127 |
| 2 | 1.0 | 4.00 | 3.3000 | 3.8334 | 3.8240 | 3.8162 |
| 3 | 1.5 | 4.00 | 3.5053 | 3.7414 | 3.7277 | 3.7163 |
| 4 | 2.0 | 4.00 | 3.9164 | 3.6297 | 3.6121 | 3.5973 |
| 5 | 2.5 | 4.00 | 4.4376 | 3.4979 | 3.4767 | 3.4590 |
| 6 | 3.0 | 4.00 | 4.7520 | 3.3742 | 3.3497 | 3.3293 |
| 7 | 3.5 | 4.00 | 4.9622 | 3.2565 | 3.2290 | 3.2061 |
| 8 | 4.0 | 4.00 | 5.0650 | 3.1497 | 3.1193 | 3.0940 |
| 9 | 4.5 | 4.00 | 5.1701 | 3.0430 | 3.0100 | 2.9826 |
| 10 | 5.0 | 4.00 | 5.2772 | 2.9366 | 2.9013 | 2.8719 |
| 11 | 5.5 | 4.00 | 5.3864 | 2.8307 | 2.7933 | 2.7622 |
| 12 | 6.0 | 4.00 | 5.4976 | 2.7255 | 2.6862 | 2.6537 |
| 13 | 6.5 | 4.00 | 5.6108 | 2.6210 | 2.5801 | 2.5463 |
| 14 | 7.0 | 4.00 | 5.6643 | 2.5279 | 2.4855 | 2.4504 |
| 15 | 7.5 | 4.00 | 5.7193 | 2.4367 | 2.3929 | 2.3568 |
| 16 | 8.0 | 4.00 | 5.7755 | 2.3472 | 2.3023 | 2.2652 |
| 17 | 8.5 | 4.00 | 5.8331 | 2.2596 | 2.2137 | 2.1758 |
| 18 | 9.0 | 4.00 | 5.9584 | 2.1612 | 2.1148 | 2.0766 |
| 19 | 9.5 | 4.00 | 6.0863 | 2.0642 | 2.0174 | 1.9790 |
| 20 | 10.0 | 104.00 | 6.2169 | 51.1833 | 49.9638 | 48.9630 |
| | | | Total: | 107.5414 | 105.7165 | 104.2145 * |

* Closest spread to four decimals.

To illustrate how this is done, let's use the non-Treasury bond in our previous illustration and the Treasury yield curve in Exhibit 2. The Treasury spot rates are reproduced in the fourth column of Exhibit 5. The third column in the exhibit is the cash flow for the 8%, 10-year non-Treasury issue. The goal is to determine the spread that when added to all the Treasury spot rates will produce a present value for the cash flow of the non-Treasury bond equal to its market price, 104.19.

Suppose we select a spread of 100 basis points. To each Treasury spot rate shown in the fourth column 100 basis points is added. So, for example, the five-year (period 10) spot rate is 6.2772% (5.2772% plus 1%). The spot rate plus 100 basis points is then used to calculate the present value of 107.5414. Because the present value is not equal to the non-Treasury issue's price (104.19), the static spread is not 100 basis points. If a spread of 125 basis points is tried, it can be seen from the next-to-the-last column of Exhibit 5 that the present value is 105.7165; again, because this is not equal to the non-Treasury issue's price, 125 basis points is not the static spread. The last column of Exhibit 5 shows the present value when a 146 basis point spread is tried. The present value is close to the non-Treasury issue's price. Therefore 146 basis points is the static spread, compared to the nominal yield spread of 140 basis points.

## Divergence Between Static Spread and Nominal Yield Spread

Typically, for standard coupon paying bonds with a bullet maturity (i.e., a single payment of principal) the static spread and the nominal yield spread will not differ significantly. In our example it is only 6 basis points.

For short-term issues, there is little divergence. The main factor causing any difference is the shape of the yield curve. The steeper the yield curve, the greater the difference. To illustrate this, consider the two yield curves shown in Exhibit 6. The yield for the longest maturity of both yield curves is 6%. The first yield curve is steeper than the one used in Exhibit 2; the second yield curve is flat, with all the yield for all maturities equal to 6%.

Exhibit 7 shows the spot rate curve for the first yield curve and that the static spread is 154. Thus, with this steeper yield curve, the difference between the static spread and the nominal yield spread is 14 basis points. Exhibit 8 shows that for the flat yield curve the static spread is 140 basis points, the same as the nominal yield spread. This will always be the case.

The difference between the static spread and the nominal yield spread is greater for issue's in which the principal is repaid over time rather than only at maturity. Thus the difference between the nominal yield spread and the static spread will be considerably greater for sinking fund bonds and mortgage-backed securities in a steep yield curve environment.

### Exhibit 6: Two Hypothetical Yield Curves

| Period | Years | Steep curve (%)' | Flat curve (%) |
|---|---|---|---|
| 1 | 0.5 | 2.00 | 6.00 |
| 2 | 1.0 | 2.40 | 6.00 |
| 3 | 1.5 | 2.80 | 6.00 |
| 4 | 2.0 | 2.90 | 6.00 |
| 5 | 2.5 | 3.00 | 6.00 |
| 6 | 3.0 | 3.10 | 6.00 |
| 7 | 3.5 | 3.30 | 6.00 |
| 8 | 4.0 | 3.80 | 6.00 |
| 9 | 4.5 | 3.90 | 6.00 |
| 10 | 5.0 | 4.20 | 6.00 |
| 11 | 5.5 | 4.40 | 6.00 |
| 12 | 6.0 | 4.50 | 6.00 |
| 13 | 6.5 | 4.60 | 6.00 |
| 14 | 7.0 | 4.70 | 6.00 |
| 15 | 7.5 | 4.90 | 6.00 |
| 16 | 8.0 | 5.00 | 6.00 |
| 17 | 8.5 | 5.30 | 6.00 |
| 18 | 9.0 | 5.70 | 6.00 |
| 19 | 9.5 | 5.80 | 6.00 |
| 20 | 10.0 | 6.00 | 6.00 |

## THE TERM STRUCTURE OF CREDIT SPREADS

Thus far, our focus in this chapter has been on the term structure of U.S. Treasury securities — default-free securities. The Treasury spot rates can then be used to price any default-free security. As we illustrated earlier, failure of Treasury securities to be priced according to the Treasury spot rates creates the opportunity for arbitrage profits or enhanced returns.

For a corporate bond, the theoretical price is not as easy to determine. The price of a corporate bond must reflect not only the spot rate for default-free bonds but also a risk premium to reflect default risk and any options embedded in the issue. For now, we will skip options embedded in bonds, a complexity addressed in later chapters.

## Exhibit 7: Determination of the Static Spread for the 8%, 10-Year Non-Treasury Issue Selling at 104.19 to Yield 7.4% Assuming a Steep Yield Curve

| Period | Years | Cash flow | Spot rate (%) | Spread 154 bp |
|---|---|---|---|---|
| 1 | 0.5 | 4.00 | 2.0000 | 3.9304 |
| 2 | 1.0 | 4.00 | 2.4000 | 3.8469 |
| 3 | 1.5 | 4.00 | 2.8075 | 3.7501 |
| 4 | 2.0 | 4.00 | 2.9081 | 3.6631 |
| 5 | 2.5 | 4.00 | 3.0097 | 3.5745 |
| 6 | 3.0 | 4.00 | 3.1124 | 3.4845 |
| 7 | 3.5 | 4.00 | 3.3216 | 3.3810 |
| 8 | 4.0 | 4.00 | 3.8570 | 3.2326 |
| 9 | 4.5 | 4.00 | 3.9605 | 3.1334 |
| 10 | 5.0 | 4.00 | 4.2898 | 3.0011 |
| 11 | 5.5 | 4.00 | 4.5102 | 2.8820 |
| 12 | 6.0 | 4.00 | 4.6174 | 2.7799 |
| 13 | 6.5 | 4.00 | 4.7267 | 2.6784 |
| 14 | 7.0 | 4.00 | 4.8380 | 2.5775 |
| 15 | 7.5 | 4.00 | 5.0752 | 2.4551 |
| 16 | 8.0 | 4.00 | 5.1904 | 2.3554 |
| 17 | 8.5 | 4.00 | 5.5699 | 2.2088 |
| 18 | 9.0 | 4.00 | 6.1027 | 2.0366 |
| 19 | 9.5 | 4.00 | 6.2242 | 1.9399 |
| 20 | 10.0 | 104.00 | 6.4980 | 47.2910 |
| | | | Total: | 104.2022 |

In practice, the spot rate that has been used to discount the cash flow of a corporate bond is the Treasury spot rate plus a constant credit spread. For example, if the six-month Treasury spot rate is 3%, and the 10-year Treasury spot rate is 6%, and a suitable credit spread is deemed to be 100 basis points, then a 4% spot rate is used to discount a six-month cash flow of a corporate bond and a 7% discount rate to discount a 10-year cash flow.

The drawback of this approach is that there is no reason to expect the credit spread to be the same, whenever the cash flow is expected to be received. Instead, it might be expected that the credit spread increases with the maturity of the corporate bond. That is, there is a term structure for credit spreads.

## Exhibit 8: Determination of the Static Spread for the 8%, 10-Year Non-Treasury Issue Selling at 104.19 to Yield 7.4% Assuming a Flat Yield Curve

| Period | Years | Cash flow | Spot rate (%) | Spread 140 bp |
|---|---|---|---|---|
| 1 | 0.5 | 4.00 | 6.0000 | 3.8573 |
| 2 | 1.0 | 4.00 | 6.0000 | 3.7197 |
| 3 | 1.5 | 4.00 | 6.0000 | 3.5869 |
| 4 | 2.0 | 4.00 | 6.0000 | 3.4590 |
| 5 | 2.5 | 4.00 | 6.0000 | 3.3355 |
| 6 | 3.0 | 4.00 | 6.0000 | 3.2165 |
| 7 | 3.5 | 4.00 | 6.0000 | 3.1018 |
| 8 | 4.0 | 4.00 | 6.0000 | 2.9911 |
| 9 | 4.5 | 4.00 | 6.0000 | 2.8844 |
| 10 | 5.0 | 4.00 | 6.0000 | 2.7815 |
| 11 | 5.5 | 4.00 | 6.0000 | 2.6822 |
| 12 | 6.0 | 4.00 | 6.0000 | 2.5865 |
| 13 | 6.5 | 4.00 | 6.0000 | 2.4942 |
| 14 | 7.0 | 4.00 | 6.0000 | 2.4052 |
| 15 | 7.5 | 4.00 | 6.0000 | 2.3194 |
| 16 | 8.0 | 4.00 | 6.0000 | 2.2367 |
| 17 | 8.5 | 4.00 | 6.0000 | 2.1569 |
| 18 | 9.0 | 4.00 | 6.0000 | 2.0799 |
| 19 | 9.5 | 4.00 | 6.0000 | 2.0057 |
| 20 | 10.0 | 104.00 | 6.0000 | <u>50.2873</u> |
| | | | Total: | 104.1876 |

In practice, the difficulty in estimating a term structure for credit spreads is that unlike Treasury securities in which there is a wide-range of maturities from which to construct a Treasury spot rate curve, there are no issuers that offer a sufficiently wide range of corporate zero-coupon securities to construct a zero-coupon spread curve. Robert Litterman and Thomas Iben of Goldman Sachs describe a procedure to construct a generic zero-coupon spread curve by credit rating and industry using data provided from a trading desk.[2]

---

[2] Robert Litterman and Thomas Iben, "Corporate Bond Valuation and the Term Structure of Credit Spreads," *Journal of Portfolio Management* (Spring 1991), pp. 52-64. The original paper was published by Goldman Sachs in 1988.

## 36  SPOT RATES AND THEIR ROLE IN VALUATION

The basic principle is as follows.[3] Consider four hypothetical zero-coupon securities, two Treasury issues and two securities issued by the same corporation:

| Type | Maturity | Price per $1 par | Yield (%) |
|---|---|---|---|
| Treasury | 1 year | 0.930 | 7.39 |
| Corporate | 1 year | 0.926 | 7.84 |
| Treasury | 2 years | 0.848 | 8.42 |
| Corporate | 2 years | 0.840 | 8.91 |

Focus first on the two issues with one year to maturity. Investors are willing to pay 93.0 cents to receive $1 by purchasing the one-year Treasury and 92.6 cents to receive $1 by purchasing the one-year corporate security. The 4-cent difference produces a credit spread of 45 basis points (7.84% minus 7.39%). The lower price for the corporate security reflects default risk; that is, it reflects the probability that the issuer will default. In this simple illustration it is assumed that if default occurs, the investor does not realize anything. In practice, this is not true and the formulation can be modified to reflect this.

For the same expected return to result by holding either bond, the price of the corporate bond must be equal to the price of the Treasury times the probability of solvency (i.e., not defaulting). Thus,

Price of corporate zero =
Price of Treasury zero × (Probability of solvency)

or equivalently, since the probability of solvency is equal to one minus the probability of default,

Price of corporate zero =
Price of Treasury zero × (1 - Probability of default)

Solving for the probability of default,

---

[3] The numerical example is the one used by Litterman and Iben, pp. 53-54.

$$\text{Probability of default} = 1 - \frac{\text{Price of corporate zero}}{\text{Price of Treasury zero}}$$

In our example,

$$\text{Probability of default} = 1 - \frac{0.926}{0.930} = 0.0043$$

Now let's focus on the two zero-coupon securities that mature two years from now. The two-year corporate zero will pay off $1 in the second year only if the corporation that has issued both one-year and two-year securities does not default in either the first or the second year. The probability of default in the first year has already been determined (0.0043). The next step is to determine the conditional probability of default in the second year, given that the corporation does not default in the first year. Litterman and Iben refer to this probability as the "forward probability of default."

Given the assumption that the expected return from holding a Treasury zero for two years must equal the return from holding a corporate zero for two years times the probability of solvency, the forward probability of default can be calculated. In this example it is .0052. This procedure can be used to determine a term structure of credit spreads for zero-coupon corporates for a given corporate issuer.

Exhibit 9 shows in tabular form a generic zero-coupon spread term structure for industrial corporations for each investment grade credit rating as of September 8, 1993. Notice that the credit spread increases with maturity. This is a typical shape for the term structure of credit spreads. In addition, the shape of the term structure is not the same for all credit ratings. The lower the credit rating, the steeper the term structure.

One implication of an upward-sloping term structure for credit spreads is that it is inappropriate to discount the cash flow from a corporate bond at a constant spread to the Treasury spot rate curve. The short-term cash flows will be undervalued, and the long-term cash flows will be overvalued.

## Exhibit 9: Generic Zero Spread Curves for Industrial Corporations by Credit Quality
### (As of September 8, 1993)

| Credit rating | Maturity (in years) | | | | | | | | |
|---|---|---|---|---|---|---|---|---|---|
| | 2 | 3 | 5 | 7 | 10 | 15 | 20 | 25 | 30 |
| Aaa | 22 | 25 | 28 | 31 | 33 | 37 | 41 | 45 | 48 |
| Aa | 28 | 32 | 36 | 38 | 41 | 49 | 57 | 65 | 71 |
| A | 38 | 47 | 52 | 58 | 63 | 71 | 79 | 88 | 94 |
| Baa | 55 | 71 | 77 | 83 | 89 | 98 | 107 | 116 | 123 |

Source: Goldman Sachs & Co. The author is grateful to Harsh Kumar for providing this information.

## Benchmark Spot Rate Curve

When the generic zero spreads for a given credit quality and in a given industry are added to the default-free spot rates, the resulting credit term structure is used to value bonds of issuers of the same credit quality in the industry sector. This term structure is referred to as the *benchmark spot rate curve* or *benchmark zero-coupon rate curve*.

For example, Exhibit 10 reproduces the default-free spot rate curve in Exhibit 2. Also shown in the exhibit is a hypothetical generic zero spread for AAA industrial bonds. The resulting benchmark spot rate curve is in the next-to-the-last column. It is this spot rate curve that is used to value a AAA industrial bond. This is done in Exhibit 10 for a hypothetical 8% 10-year AAA industrial bond. The theoretical price is 108.4615.

## Static Spread

In the same way that a static spread relative to a default-free spot rate curve can be calculated, a static spread to any benchmark spot rate curve can be calculated. To illustrate, suppose that a hypothetical AAA industrial bond with a coupon rate of 8% and a 10-year maturity is trading at 105.5423. The static spread relative to the AAA industrial term structure is the spread that must be added to that term structure that will make the present value of the cash flow equal to the market price. In our illustration, the static spread relative to this benchmark is 40 basis points, as shown in Exhibit 11.

## Exhibit 10: Calculation of Value of a Hypothetical AAA Industrial 8%, 10-Year Bond Using Benchmark Credit Structure

| Period | Years | Cash flow | Spot rate (%) | Credit spread (%) | Credit structure (%) | Present value |
|---|---|---|---|---|---|---|
| 1 | 0.5 | 4.00 | 3.0000 | 0.20 | 3.2000 | 3.9370 |
| 2 | 1.0 | 4.00 | 3.3000 | 0.20 | 3.5000 | 3.8636 |
| 3 | 1.5 | 4.00 | 3.5053 | 0.25 | 3.7553 | 3.7829 |
| 4 | 2.0 | 4.00 | 3.9164 | 0.30 | 4.2164 | 3.6797 |
| 5 | 2.5 | 4.00 | 4.4376 | 0.35 | 4.7876 | 3.5538 |
| 6 | 3.0 | 4.00 | 4.7520 | 0.35 | 5.1020 | 3.4389 |
| 7 | 3.5 | 4.00 | 4.9622 | 0.40 | 5.3622 | 3.3237 |
| 8 | 4.0 | 4.00 | 5.0650 | 0.45 | 5.5150 | 3.2177 |
| 9 | 4.5 | 4.00 | 5.1701 | 0.45 | 5.6201 | 3.1170 |
| 10 | 5.0 | 4.00 | 5.2772 | 0.50 | 5.7772 | 3.0088 |
| 11 | 5.5 | 4.00 | 5.3864 | 0.55 | 5.9364 | 2.8995 |
| 12 | 6.0 | 4.00 | 5.4976 | 0.60 | 6.0976 | 2.7896 |
| 13 | 6.5 | 4.00 | 5.6108 | 0.65 | 6.2608 | 2.6794 |
| 14 | 7.0 | 4.00 | 5.6643 | 0.70 | 6.3643 | 2.5799 |
| 15 | 7.5 | 4.00 | 5.7193 | 0.75 | 6.4693 | 2.4813 |
| 16 | 8.0 | 4.00 | 5.7755 | 0.80 | 6.5755 | 2.3838 |
| 17 | 8.5 | 4.00 | 5.8331 | 0.85 | 6.6831 | 2.2876 |
| 18 | 9.0 | 4.00 | 5.9584 | 0.90 | 6.8584 | 2.1801 |
| 19 | 9.5 | 4.00 | 6.0863 | 0.95 | 7.0363 | 2.0737 |
| 20 | 10.0 | 104.00 | 6.2169 | 1.00 | 7.2169 | 51.1833 |
| | | | | | Total | 108.4615 |

Thus, when a static spread is cited, it must be cited relative to some benchmark spot rate curve. This is necessary because it indicates the credit and sector risks that are being considered when the static spread was calculated.

## The Term Structure for Municipal Bonds

Unlike the taxable fixed-income market, there is no risk-free interest rate benchmark for the tax-exempt municipal market. Several benchmark curves are used in this market sector. In general, a benchmark yield curve is constructed for AAA quality rated general obligation and revenue bonds. The Delphis Hanover yield curve is a popular yield curve that is often quoted in the municipal market.

## Exhibit 11: Demonstration that the Static Spread is 40 Basis Points

| Period | Years | Cash flow | Spot rate | Credit spread | Spread 40 bp | Present value |
|---|---|---|---|---|---|---|
| 1 | 0.5 | 4.00 | 3.0000 | 0.20 | 3.6000 | 3.9293 |
| 2 | 1.0 | 4.00 | 3.3000 | 0.20 | 3.9000 | 3.8484 |
| 3 | 1.5 | 4.00 | 3.5053 | 0.25 | 4.1553 | 3.7607 |
| 4 | 2.0 | 4.00 | 3.9164 | 0.30 | 4.6164 | 3.6511 |
| 5 | 2.5 | 4.00 | 4.4376 | 0.35 | 5.1876 | 3.5193 |
| 6 | 3.0 | 4.00 | 4.7520 | 0.35 | 5.5020 | 3.3989 |
| 7 | 3.5 | 4.00 | 4.9622 | 0.40 | 5.7622 | 3.2788 |
| 8 | 4.0 | 4.00 | 5.0650 | 0.45 | 5.9150 | 3.1681 |
| 9 | 4.5 | 4.00 | 5.1701 | 0.45 | 6.0201 | 3.0630 |
| 10 | 5.0 | 4.00 | 5.2772 | 0.50 | 6.1772 | 2.9509 |
| 11 | 5.5 | 4.00 | 5.3864 | 0.55 | 6.3364 | 2.8383 |
| 12 | 6.0 | 4.00 | 5.4976 | 0.60 | 6.4976 | 2.7255 |
| 13 | 6.5 | 4.00 | 5.6108 | 0.65 | 6.6608 | 2.6127 |
| 14 | 7.0 | 4.00 | 5.6643 | 0.70 | 6.7643 | 2.5109 |
| 15 | 7.5 | 4.00 | 5.7193 | 0.75 | 6.8693 | 2.4103 |
| 16 | 8.0 | 4.00 | 5.7755 | 0.80 | 6.9755 | 2.3112 |
| 17 | 8.5 | 4.00 | 5.8331 | 0.85 | 7.0831 | 2.2137 |
| 18 | 9.0 | 4.00 | 5.9584 | 0.90 | 7.2584 | 2.1056 |
| 19 | 9.5 | 4.00 | 6.0863 | 0.95 | 7.4363 | 1.9990 |
| 20 | 10.0 | 104.00 | 6.2169 | 1.00 | 7.6169 | 49.2468 |
| | | | | | Total: | 105.5423 |

As in the taxable market, current coupon bonds are used for constructing the yield curve. However, unlike the Treasury market in which current coupon bonds are issued on regular cycles, no such practice is followed in the municipal market. In order to derive an appropriate yield curve, the AAA curve is generally derived from market observations on yields of newly-issued bonds in the associated market sector.

Given the AAA yield curve, a AAA spot rate curve can be constructed using the bootstrapping methodology described earlier. As in the case of corporates, a term structure for municipal credit spreads can be developed and added to the AAA yield curve.

# KEY POINTS

Here are the key points of this chapter:

1. The base interest rate in valuing fixed-income securities is the rate on default-free securities and U.S. Treasury securities are viewed as default-free securities.

2. Because each cash flow of a fixed-income security should be viewed as a zero-coupon instrument, to properly value fixed-income securities, what is needed is the rate on zero-coupon default-free securities or, equivalently, the rate on zero-coupon Treasury securities.

3. The rate on a zero-coupon instrument is called the spot rate.

4. The Treasury yield curve indicates the relationship between the yield on Treasury securities and maturity; however, the securities included are a combination of zero-coupon instruments (that is, Treasury bills) and Treasury coupon securities.

5. Since the U.S. Treasury does not issue zero-coupon securities with a maturity greater than one year, a theoretical spot rate curve must be constructed from the yield curve.

6. The collection of spot rates showing the relationship between theoretical spot rates and maturity is called the spot rate curve or the term structure of interest rates.

7. One approach to constructing the spot rate curve is bootstrapping, the basic principle of which is that the value of the cash flow from an on-the-run Treasury issue when discounted at the spot rates must be equal to the observed market price.

8. The discount function is calculated from the theoretical spot rates and represents the present value of a $1 default-free cash flow or equivalently, the value of a default-free zero-coupon instrument with a $1 maturity value.

9. *From a Treasury spot rate curve or discount function, the value of any default-free security can be determined.*

10. *The economic force that assures that securities will be priced based on spot rates creates the opportunity for government dealers to strip Treasury securities or for investors to risklessly enhance portfolio returns.*

11. *The traditional approach to measuring the yield premium for a non-Treasury bond is to calculate the difference between the yield of the bond in question and the yield of a comparable maturity Treasury coupon security.*

12. *The drawbacks of the traditional approach are that the yield used fails to take into consideration the term structure of interest rates and, in the case of callable and/or putable bonds, the effect of expected interest rate volatility on the cash flow of the non-Treasury bond is ignored.*

13. *To take into consideration the term structure of interest rates, a static spread should be calculated.*

14. *The static spread is a measure of the spread that the investor would realize over the entire Treasury spot rate curve if the bond is held to maturity and the spot rates do not change.*

15. *Unlike the traditional or nominal spread measure, the static spread is not a spread off one point on the Treasury yield curve but is a spread over the entire spot rate curve.*

16. *For bullet bonds, unless the yield curve is very steep, the nominal yield spread will not differ significantly from the static spread; for securities where principal is repaid over time rather than just at maturity there can be a significant difference, particularly in a steep yield curve environment.*

17. *To value a security with credit risk, it is necessary to determine a term structure of credit risk or equivalently a zero-coupon credit spread.*

18. *Evidence suggests that the credit spread increases with maturity and the lower the credit rating, the steeper the curve.*

19. *An implication of an upward-sloping term structure for credit spreads is that it is inappropriate to discount the cash flow from a corporate bond at a constant spread to the Treasury spot rate curve.*

20. *Adding the zero-coupon credit for a particular credit quality within a sector to the Treasury spot rate curve gives the benchmark spot rate curve that should be used to value a security and from which a static spread can be calculated.*

# 3
# FORWARD RATES AND TERM STRUCTURE THEORIES

In the previous chapter, we saw how a default-free theoretical spot rate curve can be extrapolated from the Treasury yield curve. Additional information useful to market participants can be extrapolated from the Treasury yield curve: forward rates. These rates can be viewed as the market's consensus of future interest rates. This view, however, is predicated on a particular theory about the term structure of interest rates.

> **The objectives of this chapter are to:**
>
> 1. explain what is meant by forward rates;
>
> 2. demonstrate how forward rates can be calculated;
>
> 3. show the relationship between spot rates and forward rates;
>
> 4. explain the various theories of the term structure of interest rates and what they suggest about forward rates; and,
>
> 5. review the models used to explain the behavior of interest rates.

## FORWARD RATES

Market participants typically have different views about what they expect future interest rates to be. Under a certain theory of the term structure of interest rates described later in this chapter and based on arbitrage arguments, the market's consensus of future interest rates can be extrapolated from the Treasury yield curve. These rates are called *forward rates*.

Examples of forward rates that can be calculated from the Treasury yield curve are the:

- six-month forward rate six months from now
- six-month forward rate three years from now
- one-year forward rate one year from now
- three-year forward rate two years from now
- five-year forward rate three years from now

Since the forward rates are extrapolated from the Treasury yield curve, these rates are sometimes referred to as *implicit forward rates*.

To illustrate how forward rates are derived, we begin with the derivation of six-month forward rates. The six-month forward rates are sometimes referred to as *short forward rates*. The structure of short forward rates is called the *forward rate curve*.

## Deriving Six-Month Forward Rates

To illustrate the process of extrapolating six-month forward rates, we will use the yield curve and corresponding spot rate curve from Exhibit 1 of the previous chapter. These are reproduced in Exhibit 1.

Consider an investor who has a one-year investment horizon and is faced with the following two alternatives:

**Alternative 1:** buy a one-year Treasury bill, or
**Alternative 2:** buy a six-month Treasury bill, and when it matures in six months buy another six-month Treasury bill.

The investor will be indifferent toward the two alternatives if they produce the same return over the one-year investment horizon. The investor knows the spot rate on the six-month Treasury bill and the one-year Treasury bill. However, he does not know what yield will be available on a six-month Treasury bill that will be purchased six months from now. That is, he does not know the six-month forward rate six months from now. Given the spot rates for the six-month Treasury bill and the one-year Treasury bill, the forward rate on a six-month Treasury bill is the rate that equalizes the dollar return between the two alternatives.

## Exhibit 1: Hypothetical Treasury Yield Curve and Resulting Spot Rate Curve

| Period | Years | Yield to maturity (%) | Spot rate (%) |
|---|---|---|---|
| 1 | 0.5 | 3.00 | 3.0000 |
| 2 | 1.0 | 3.30 | 3.3000 |
| 3 | 1.5 | 3.50 | 3.5053 |
| 4 | 2.0 | 3.90 | 3.9164 |
| 5 | 2.5 | 4.40 | 4.4376 |
| 6 | 3.0 | 4.70 | 4.7520 |
| 7 | 3.5 | 4.90 | 4.9622 |
| 8 | 4.0 | 5.00 | 5.0650 |
| 9 | 4.5 | 5.10 | 5.1701 |
| 10 | 5.0 | 5.20 | 5.2772 |
| 11 | 5.5 | 5.30 | 5.3864 |
| 12 | 6.0 | 5.40 | 5.4976 |
| 13 | 6.5 | 5.50 | 5.6108 |
| 14 | 7.0 | 5.55 | 5.6643 |
| 15 | 7.5 | 5.60 | 5.7193 |
| 16 | 8.0 | 5.65 | 5.7755 |
| 17 | 8.5 | 5.70 | 5.8331 |
| 18 | 9.0 | 5.80 | 5.9584 |
| 19 | 9.5 | 5.90 | 6.0863 |
| 20 | 10.0 | 6.00 | 6.2169 |

To see how that rate can be determined, suppose that an investor purchased a six-month Treasury bill for $X. At the end of six months, the value of this investment would be:

$$X(1 + z_1)$$

where $z_1$ is one-half the bond-equivalent yield (BEY) of the theoretical six-month spot rate.

Let f represent one-half the forward rate (expressed as a BEY) on a six-month Treasury bill available six months from now. If the investor were to renew his investment by purchasing that bill at that time, then the future dollars available at the end of one year from the $X investment would be:

## Exhibit 2: Graphical Depiction of the Six-Month Forward Rate Six Months from Now

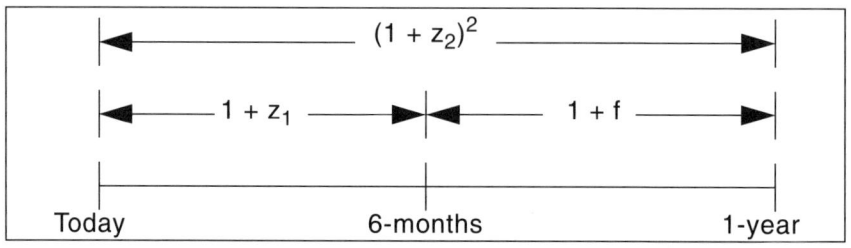

X (1 + $z_1$) (1 + f)

Now consider the alternative of investing in a one-year Treasury bill. If we let $z_2$ represent one-half the BEY of the theoretical one-year spot rate, then the future dollars available at the end of one year from the $X investment would be:

X (1 + $z_2$)$^2$

This is depicted in Exhibit 2

Now, we are prepared to analyze the investor's choices and what this says about forward rates. The investor will be indifferent toward the two alternatives confronting him if he makes the same dollar investment ($X) and receives the same future dollars from both alternatives at the end of one year. That is, the investor will be indifferent if:

X (1 + $z_1$) (1 + f) = X (1 + $z_2$)$^2$

Solving for f, we get:

$$f = \frac{(1+z_2)^2}{(1+z_1)} - 1$$

Doubling f gives the BEY for the six-month forward rate six months from now.

We can illustrate the use of this formula with the theoretical spot rates shown in Exhibit 1. From that exhibit, we know that:

six-month bill spot rate = 0.030, therefore $z_1$ = 0.0150
one-year bill spot rate = 0.033, therefore $z_2$ = 0.0165

Substituting into the formula, we have:

$$f = \frac{(1.0165)^2}{(1.0150)} - 1 = 0.0180 = 1.8\%$$

Therefore, the forward rate on a six-month Treasury security is 3.6% (1.8% × 2) BEY.

Let's confirm our results. If $X is invested in the six-month Treasury bill at 1.5% and the proceeds then reinvested at the six-month forward rate of 1.8%, the total proceeds from this alternative would be:

X (1.015) (1.018) = 1.03327 X

Investment of $X in the one-year Treasury bill at one-half the one-year rate, 1.0165%, would produce the following proceeds at the end of one year:

X $(1.0165)^2$ = 1.03327 X

Both alternatives have the same payoff if the six-month Treasury bill yield six months from now is 1.8% (3.6% on a BEY). This means that, if an investor is guaranteed a 1.8% yield (3.6% BEY) on a six-month Treasury bill six months from now, he will be indifferent toward the two alternatives.

The same line of reasoning can be used to obtain the six-month forward rate beginning at any time period in the future. For example, the following can be determined:

- the six-month forward rate three years from now
- the six-month forward rate five years from now

The notation that we use to indicate six-month forward rates is $_1f_m$ where the subscript 1 indicates a one-period (six-month) rate and the subscript m indicates the period beginning m periods from now. When m is equal to zero, this means the current rate. Thus, the first six-month forward rate is simply the current six-month spot rate. That is,

$$_1f_0 = z_1$$

The general formula for determining a six-month forward rate is:

$$_1f_m = \frac{(1+z_{m+1})^{m+1}}{(1+z_m)^m} - 1$$

For example, suppose that the six-month forward rate four years (8 six-month periods) from now is sought. In terms of our notation, m is 8 and we seek $_1f_8$. The formula is then:

$$_1f_8 = \frac{(1+z_9)^9}{(1+z_8)^8} - 1$$

From Exhibit 1, since the 4-year spot rate is 5.065% and the 4.5-year spot rate is 5.1701%, $z_8$ is 2.5325% and $z_9$ is 2.58505%. Then,

$$_1f_8 = \frac{(1.0258505)^9}{(1.025325)^8} - 1 = 3.005\%$$

Doubling this rate gives a six-month forward rate four years from now of 6.01%

Exhibit 3 shows all of the six-month forward rates for the Treasury yield curve and corresponding spot rate curve shown in Exhibit 1. The set of these forward rates is the short-term forward-rate curve.

## Exhibit 3: Six-Month Forward Rates:
### The Short-Term Forward Rate Curve

| Notation | Forward Rate |
|---|---|
| $_1f_0$ | 3.00 |
| $_1f_1$ | 3.60 |
| $_1f_2$ | 3.92 |
| $_1f_3$ | 5.15 |
| $_1f_4$ | 6.54 |
| $_1f_5$ | 6.33 |
| $_1f_6$ | 6.23 |
| $_1f_7$ | 5.79 |
| $_1f_8$ | 6.01 |
| $_1f_9$ | 6.24 |
| $_1f_{10}$ | 6.48 |
| $_1f_{11}$ | 6.72 |
| $_1f_{12}$ | 6.97 |
| $_1f_{13}$ | 6.36 |
| $_1f_{14}$ | 6.49 |
| $_1f_{15}$ | 6.62 |
| $_1f_{16}$ | 6.76 |
| $_1f_{17}$ | 8.10 |
| $_1f_{18}$ | 8.40 |
| $_1f_{19}$ | 8.72 |

## Relationship between Spot Rates and Short-Term Forward Rates

Suppose an investor invests $X in a three-year zero-coupon Treasury security. The total proceeds three years (six periods) from now would be:

$$X (1 + z_6)^6$$

**52** FORWARD RATES AND TERM STRUCTURE THEORIES

The investor could instead buy a six-month Treasury bill and reinvest the proceeds every six months for three years. The future dollars or dollar return will depend on the six-month forward rates. Suppose that the investor can actually reinvest the proceeds maturing every six months at the calculated six-month forward rates shown in Exhibit 3. At the end of three years, an investment of $X would generate the following proceeds:

$$X(1+z_1)(1+{}_1f_1)(1+{}_1f_2)(1+{}_1f_3)(1+{}_1f_4)(1+{}_1f_5)$$

Since the two investments must give the same proceeds at the end of four years, the two previous equations can be equated:

$$X(1+z_6)^6 = X(1+z_1)(1+{}_1f_1)(1+{}_1f_2)(1+{}_1f_3)(1+{}_1f_4)(1+{}_1f_5)$$

Solving for the three year (six period) spot rate, we have:

$$z_6 = [(1+z_1)(1+{}_1f_1)(1+{}_1f_2)(1+{}_1f_3)(1+{}_1f_4)(1+{}_1f_5)]^{1/6} - 1$$

This equation tells us that the three-year spot rate depends on the current six-month spot rate and the five six-month forward rates. In fact, the right-hand side of this equation is a geometric average of the current six-month spot rate and the five six-month forward rates.

Let's use the values in Exhibits 1 and 3 to confirm this result. Since the six-month spot rate in Exhibit 1 is 3%, $z_1$ is 1.5% and therefore

$$z_6 = [(1.015)(1.018)(1.0196)(1.02575)(1.0327)(1.03165)]^{1/6} - 1$$
$$= 0.023761 = 2.3761\%$$

Doubling this rate gives 4.7522%. This agrees with the spot rate shown in Exhibit 1.

In general, the relationship between a T-period spot rate, the current six-month spot rate, and the six-month forward rates is as follows:

$$z_T = [(1+z_1)(1+{}_1f_1)(1+{}_1f_2) \ldots (1+{}_1f_{T-1})]^{1/T} - 1$$

## Exhibit 4: Graphical Depiction of Forward Rates

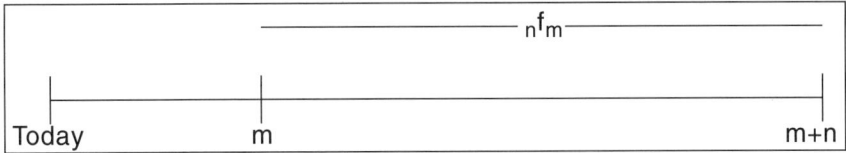

Therefore, discounting at the forward rates will give the same present value as discounting at spot rates. This means that calculating the static spread over the Treasury spot rate curve is the same as calculating the static spread over the Treasury forward rate curve.

## Forward Rates for Any Periods

We can take the analysis of forward rates much further. It is not necessary to limit ourselves to six-month forward rates. The Treasury yield curve can be used to calculate the forward rate for any time in the future for any investment horizon.

To demonstrate how this is done, we must redefine our earlier notation. Before we defined $_1f_m$ as the one-period (or six-month) forward rate m periods from now. We will now let $_nf_m$ be the forward rate for an investment of n periods beginning m periods from now. This is depicted in Exhibit 4. For example, $_4f_6$ is the four-period forward rate beginning six periods from now.

Now let's see how the spot rates can be used to calculate forward rates for a period greater than six months. We assume in the illustration that there are zero-coupon Treasury securities available. The existence of these securities is not necessary for determination of the forward rates. The assumption just simplifies the presentation.

Suppose that an investor with a five-year investment horizon is considering the following two alternatives:

*Alternative 1:* Buy a five-year (ten-period) zero-coupon Treasury security
*Alternative 2:* Buy a three-year (six-period) zero-coupon Treasury security, and when it matures in three years buy a two-year zero-coupon Treasury security

By investing $X in a five-year zero-coupon Treasury today, the investor will have the following at the end of five years:

$$X(1 + z_{10})^{10}$$

where $z_{10}$ is one-half the BEY of the theoretical 10-period spot rate.

With the second alternative, the amount available at the end of three years from investing $X in a three-year zero-coupon Treasury security would be:

$$X(1 + z_6)^6$$

The amount at the end of five years depends on the forward rate for a two-year investment beginning three years from now. In terms of our formula, it depends on $_4f_6$. The amount at the end of five years would then be:

$$X(1 + z_6)^6 (1 + {_4f_6})^4$$

The investor will be indifferent toward the two alternatives confronting him if he makes the same dollar investment ($X) and receives the same future dollars from both alternatives at the end of five years. That is, the investor will be indifferent if:

$$X(1 + z_{10})^{10} = X(1 + z_6)^6 (1 + {_4f_6})^4$$

Solving for $_4f_6$, we get:

$$_4f_6 = \left[\frac{(1+z_{10})^{10}}{(1+z_6)^6}\right]^{1/4} - 1$$

Doubling $_4f_6$ gives the BEY for the two-year forward rate three years from now.

We can illustrate the use of this formula with the theoretical spot rates shown in Exhibit 1. From that exhibit, we know that the:

five-year spot rate = 5.2772%, therefore $z_{10}$ = 0.026386
three-year spot rate = 4.7520%, therefore $z_6$ = 0.023760

Substituting these into the formula, we have:

$$_4f_6 = \left[\frac{(1.026386)^{10}}{(1.023769)^6}\right]^{1/4} - 1 = 0.03034 = 3.034\%$$

Therefore, the two-year forward rate three years from now is 6.068% (3.3034% × 2) on a BEY.

In general, the formula for any forward rate is:

$$_nf_m = \left[\frac{(1+z_{m+n})^{m+n}}{(1+z_n)^m}\right]^{1/n} - 1$$

## THEORIES OF THE TERM STRUCTURE OF INTEREST RATES

If we plot the term structure — the yield to maturity, or the spot rate, at successive maturities against maturity — what is it likely to look like?

Exhibit 5 shows four shapes that have appeared with some frequency over time. Panel A shows an upward-sloping yield curve; that is, yield rises steadily as maturity increases. This shape is commonly referred to as a "normal" or "positive" yield curve. Panel B shows a downward-sloping or "inverted" yield curve, where yields decline as maturity increases. Panel C shows a "humped" yield curve. Finally, panel D shows a "flat" yield curve. Two major theories have evolved to account for these observed shapes of the yield curve: the *expectations theory* and the *market segmentation theory*.

## Exhibit 5: Four Hypothetical Yield Curves

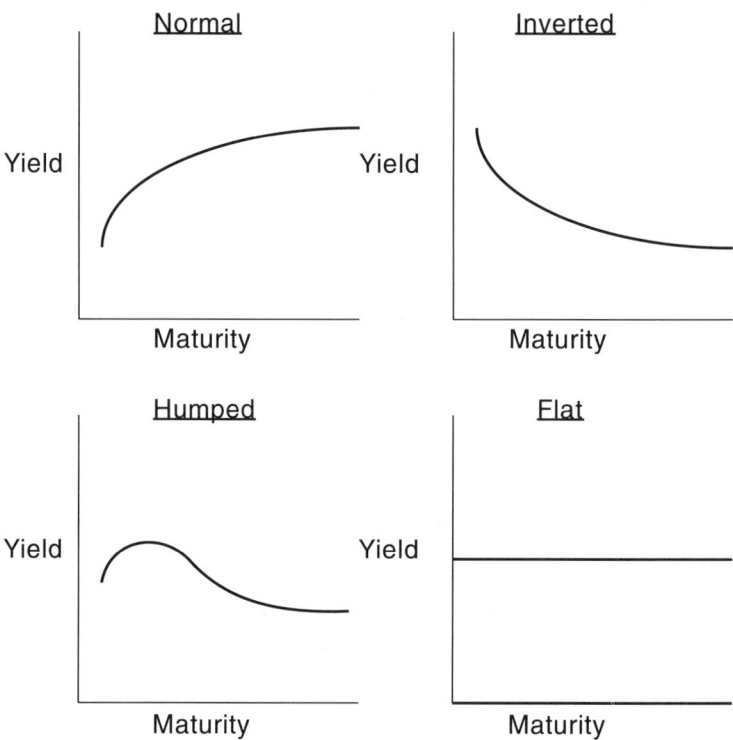

There are several forms of the expectations theory — the *pure expectations theory*, the *liquidity theory*, and the *preferred habitat theory*. All share a hypothesis about the behavior of short-term forward rates and also assume that the forward rates in current long-term bonds are closely related to the market's expectations about future short-term rates. These three theories differ, however, on whether other factors also affect forward rates, and how. The pure expectations theory postulates that no systematic factors other than expected future short-term rates affect forward rates; the liquidity theory and the preferred habitat theory assert that there are other factors. Accordingly, the last two forms of the expectations theory are sometimes referred to as *biased expectations theories*. The relationship among the various theories is described below and summarized in Exhibit 6.

Chapter 3

**Exhibit 6: Term Structure Theories**

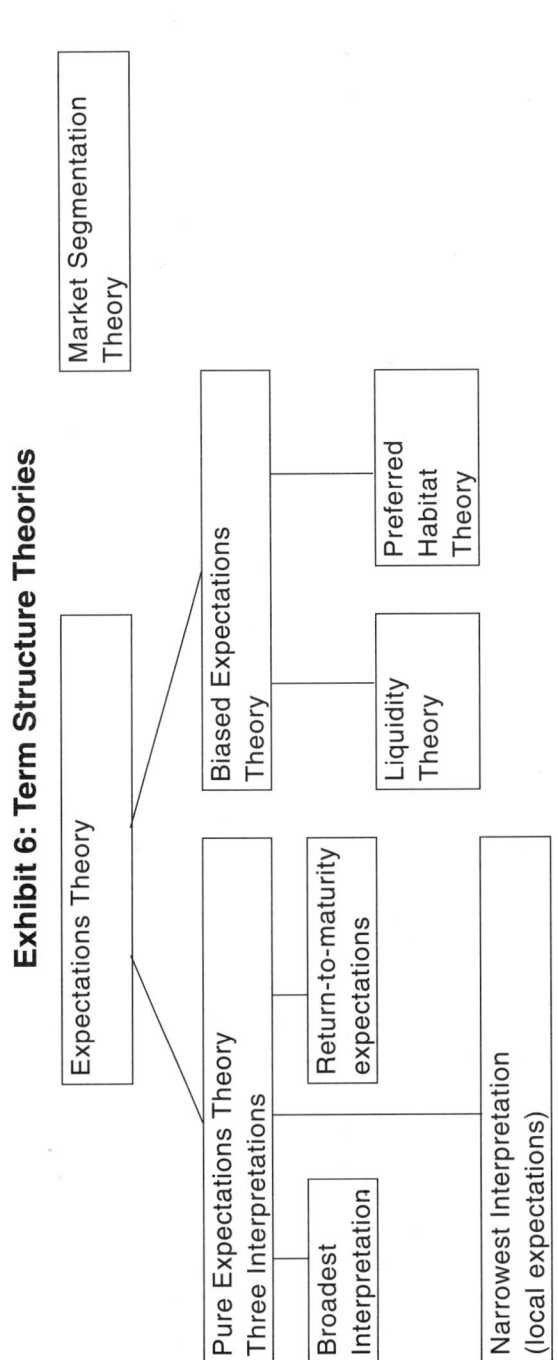

## The Pure Expectations Theory

According to the pure expectations theory, the forward rates exclusively represent the expected future rates. Thus, the entire term structure at a given time reflects the market's current expectations of the family of future short-term rates. Under this view, a rising term structure, as in Panel A of Exhibit 5, must indicate that the market expects short-term rates to rise throughout the relevant future. Similarly, a flat term structure reflects an expectation that future short-term rates will be mostly constant, while a falling term structure must reflect an expectation that future short-term rates will decline steadily.

The pure expectations theory suffers from one shortcoming, which, qualitatively, is quite serious. It neglects the risks inherent in investing in bonds. If forward rates were perfect predictors of future interest rates, then the future prices of bonds would be known with certainty. The return over any investment period would be certain and independent of the maturity of the instrument acquired. However, with the uncertainty about future interest rates and, therefore, about future prices of bonds, these instruments become risky investments in the sense that the return over some investment horizon is unknown.

***Drawbacks of the Theory:*** There are two risks that cause uncertainty about the return over some investment horizon. The first is the uncertainty about the price of the bond at the end of the investment horizon. For example, an investor who plans to invest for five years might consider the following three investment alternatives: (1) invest in a five-year bond and hold it for five years; (2) invest in a 12-year bond and sell it at the end of five years; and, (3) invest in a 30-year bond and sell it at the end of five years. The return that will be realized for the second and third alternatives is not known because the price of each long-term bond at the end of five years is unknown. In the case of the 12-year bond, the price will depend on the yield on seven-year bonds five years from now; and the price of the 30-year bond will depend on the yield on 25-year bonds five years from now. Since forward rates implied in the current term structure for a seven-year bond five years from now and a 25-year bond five years from now are not perfect predictors of the actual future rates, there is uncertainty about the price for both bonds five years from now. Thus, there is price risk; that is, the price of the bond may be lower than currently expected at the end of the investment horizon. As explained in the next chapter, an important feature of the interest rate risk is that it increases with the length of the bond's maturity.

The second risk involves the uncertainty about the rate at which the proceeds from a bond that matures prior to the maturity date can be reinvested until the maturity date, that is, reinvestment risk. For example, an investor who plans to invest for five years might consider the following three alternative investments: (1) invest in a five-year bond and hold it for five years; (2) invest in a six-month instrument and, when it matures, reinvest the proceeds in six-month instruments over the entire five-year investment horizon; and, (3) invest in a two-year bond and, when it matures, reinvest the proceeds in a three-year bond. The risk in the second and third alternatives is that the return over the five-year investment horizon is unknown because rates at which the proceeds can be reinvested until maturity are unknown.

***Interpretations of the Theory:*** There are several interpretations of the pure expectations theory that have been put forth by economists. These interpretations are not exact equivalents nor are they consistent with each other, in large part because they offer different treatments of the two risks associated with realizing a return that we have just explained.[1]

The broadest interpretation of the pure expectations theory suggests that investors expect the return for any investment horizon to be the same, regardless of the maturity strategy selected.[2] For example, consider an investor who has a six-month investment horizon. According to this theory, it makes no

---

[1] These formulations are summarized by John Cox, Jonathan Ingersoll, Jr., and Stephen Ross, "A Re-examination of Traditional Hypotheses About the Term Structure of Interest Rates," *Journal of Finance* (September 1981), pp. 769-799.
[2] F. Lutz, "The Structure of Interest Rates," *Quarterly Journal of Economics* (1940-41), pp. 36-63.

difference if a 5-year, 12-year, or 30-year bond is purchased and held for five years since the investor expects the return from all three bonds to be the same over the five-year investment horizon. A major criticism of this very broad interpretation of the theory is that, because of price risk associated with investing in bonds with a maturity greater than the investment horizon, the expected returns from these three very different bond investments should differ in significant ways.[3]

A second interpretation, referred to as the *local expectations* form of the pure expectations theory, suggests that the return will be the same over a short-term investment horizon starting today. For example, if an investor has a six-month investment horizon, buying a five-year, 10-year or 20-year bond will produce the same six-month return.

This is illustrated in Exhibit 7 for a six-month investment horizon for three of the bonds in Exhibit 1 — the one-year, five-year, and 10-year issues. For the six-month issue in Exhibit 1, the total return is the six-month spot rate of 3%. Panel A of Exhibit 7 shows the cash flow for the one-year issue six months from now. If the short-term forward is realized, the six-month forward rate is 3.6% as indicated in Exhibit 3. The price of the one-year issue six months from now when discounted at the six-month forward rate is shown in Exhibit 7. Adding this price to the coupon rate and dividing by the initial price of 100 gives a six-month total return of 1.5% and a one-year total return of 3%. This is the same total return as the six-month issue. Panels B and C of Exhibit 7 show the same calculations for the five-year and ten-year issues assuming that the six-month forward rates shown in Exhibit 3 are realized six-months from now. As can be seen, the total return is 3%. Thus, in each case, the total return over a six-month horizon is the same and it is equal to the current six-month spot rate.

It has been demonstrated that the local expectations formulation, which is narrow in scope, is the only interpretation of the pure expectations theory that can be sustained in equilibrium.[4]

---

[3] Cox, Ingersoll and Ross, pp. 774-775.
[4] Cox, Ingersoll, and Ross.

## Exhibit 7: Total Return Over Six-Month Investment Horizon if Six-Month Forward Rates Are Realized

| Panel A: Total return on 1-year issue if forward rates are realized | | | |
|---|---|---|---|
| Period | Cash flow | Six-month forward rate | Price at horizon |
| 1 | 101.650 | 3.60 | 99.85265 |

Price at horizon: 99.85265
Coupon: 1.65
Total proceeds: 101.5027
Total return: 3.00%

| Panel B: Total return on 5-year issue if forward rates are realized | | | |
|---|---|---|---|
| Period | Cash flow | Six-month forward rate | Present value |
| 1 | 2.600 | 3.60 | 2.55403 |
| 2 | 2.600 | 3.92 | 2.50493 |
| 3 | 2.600 | 5.15 | 2.44205 |
| 4 | 2.600 | 6.54 | 2.36472 |
| 5 | 2.600 | 6.33 | 2.29217 |
| 6 | 2.600 | 6.23 | 2.22293 |
| 7 | 2.600 | 5.79 | 2.16039 |
| 8 | 2.600 | 6.01 | 2.09736 |
| 9 | 102.600 | 6.24 | 80.26096 |
| | | Total: | 98.89954 |

Price at horizon: 98.89954
Coupon: 2.60
Total proceeds: 101.4995
Total return: 3.00%

## 62 FORWARD RATES AND TERM STRUCTURE THEORIES

| Panel C: Total return on 10-year issue if forward rates are realized ||||
|---|---|---|---|
| Period | Cash flow | Six-month forward rate | Present value |
| 1 | 3.000 | 3.60 | 2.94695 |
| 2 | 3.000 | 3.92 | 2.89030 |
| 3 | 3.000 | 5.15 | 2.81775 |
| 4 | 3.000 | 6.54 | 2.72853 |
| 5 | 3.000 | 6.33 | 2.64482 |
| 6 | 3.000 | 6.23 | 2.56492 |
| 7 | 3.000 | 5.79 | 2.49275 |
| 8 | 3.000 | 6.01 | 2.42003 |
| 9 | 3.000 | 6.24 | 2.34681 |
| 10 | 3.000 | 6.48 | 2.27316 |
| 11 | 3.000 | 6.72 | 2.19927 |
| 12 | 3.000 | 6.97 | 2.12520 |
| 13 | 3.000 | 6.36 | 2.05970 |
| 14 | 3.000 | 6.49 | 1.99497 |
| 15 | 3.000 | 6.62 | 1.93105 |
| 16 | 3.000 | 6.76 | 1.86791 |
| 17 | 3.000 | 8.10 | 1.79521 |
| 18 | 3.000 | 8.40 | 1.72285 |
| 19 | 103.000 | 8.72 | 56.67989 |
|  |  | Total: | 98.50208 |

Price at horizon: 98.50208
Coupon: 3.00
Total proceeds: 101.5021
Total return: 3.00%

The third and final interpretation of the pure expectations theory suggests that the return that an investor will realize by rolling over short-term bonds to some investment horizon will be the same as holding a zero-coupon bond with a maturity that is the same as that investment horizon. (A zero-coupon bond has no reinvestment risk, so that future interest rates over the investment horizon do not affect the return.) This variant is called the *return-to-maturity expectations* interpretation. For example, let's once again assume that an investor has a five-year investment horizon. By buying a five-year zero-coupon bond and holding it to maturity, the investor's return is the difference between the maturity value and the price of the bond, divided by the price of the bond. According to the return-to-maturity expectations, the same return will be realized by buying a six-month instrument and rolling it over for five years. At this time, the validity of this interpretation is subject to considerable doubt.

## Biased Expectations Theories

There are two forms of the biased expectations theory: the liquidity theory and the preferred habitat theory.

***The Liquidity Theory:*** We have explained that the drawback of the pure expectations theory is that it does not consider the risks associated with bond investments. Nonetheless, we have just shown that there is indeed risk in holding a long-term bond for one period, and that risk increases with the bond's maturity because maturity and price volatility are directly related.

Given this uncertainty, and considering that investors typically do not like uncertainty, some economists and financial analysts have suggested a different theory. This theory states that investors will hold longer-term maturities if they are offered a long-term rate higher than the average of expected future rates by a risk premium that is positively related to the term to maturity.[5] Put differently, the forward rates should reflect both interest rate expectations and a "liquidity" premium (really a risk premium), and the premium should be higher for longer maturities.

According to this theory, which is called the *liquidity theory of the term structure*, the implied forward rates will not be an unbiased estimate of the market's expectations of future interest rates because they embody a liquidity premium. Thus, an upward-sloping yield curve may reflect expectations that future interest rates either (1) will rise, or (2) will be unchanged or even fall, but with a liquidity premium increasing fast enough with maturity so as to produce an upward-sloping yield curve.

---

[5] John R. Hicks, *Value and Capital* (London: Oxford University Press, 1946), second ed., pp. 141-145.

***The Preferred Habitat Theory:*** Another theory, known as the preferred habitat theory, also adopts the view that the term structure reflects the expectation of the future path of interest rates as well as a risk premium. However, the preferred habitat theory rejects the assertion that the risk premium must rise uniformly with maturity.[6] Proponents of the preferred habitat theory say that the latter conclusion could be accepted if all investors intend to liquidate their investment at the shortest possible date while all borrowers are anxious to borrow long. This assumption can be rejected since institutions have holding periods dictated by the nature of their liabilities.

The preferred habitat theory asserts that if there is an imbalance between the supply and demand for funds within a given maturity range, investors and borrowers will not be reluctant to shift their investing and financing activities out of their preferred maturity sector to take advantage of any imbalance. However, to do so, investors must be induced by a yield premium in order to accept the risks associated with shifting funds out of their preferred sector. Similarly, borrowers can only be induced to raise funds in a maturity sector other than their preferred sector by a sufficient cost savings to compensate for the corresponding funding risk.

Thus, this theory proposes that the shape of the yield curve is determined by both expectations of future interest rates and a risk premium, positive or negative, to induce market participants to shift out of their preferred habitat. Clearly, according to this theory, yield curves sloping up, down, flat, or humped are all possible.

## Market Segmentation Theory

The market segmentation theory also recognizes that investors have preferred habitats dictated by the nature of their liabilities. This theory also proposes that the major reason for the shape of the yield curve lies in asset/liability management constraints (either regulatory or self-imposed) and/or creditors (borrowers) restricting their lending (financing) to specific maturity sectors.[7] However, the market seg-

---

[6] Franco Modigliani and Richard Sutch, "Innovations in Interest Rate Policy," *American Economic Review* (May 1966), pp. 178-197.

[7] This theory was suggested in J.M. Culbertson, "The Term Structure of Interest Rates," *Quarterly Journal of Economics* (November 1957), pp. 489-504.

mentation theory differs from the preferred habitat theory in that it assumes that neither investors nor borrowers are willing to shift from one maturity sector to another to take advantage of opportunities arising from differences between expectations and forward rates. Thus, for the segmentation theory, the shape of the yield curve is determined by supply of and demand for securities within each maturity sector.

## MODELS DESCRIBING THE BEHAVIOR OF INTEREST RATES

Term structure theory is concerned with the behavior of interest rates; it identifies the factors that are expected to explain the movement of interest rates. Whatever the factors are, they are random in nature. That is, the future value of a factor that is expected to explain the movement of interest rates is not known with certainty. Thus, it is necessary to specify a statistical process that describes the behavior of these factors and is a reasonable characterization of their actual behavior.

The most common model used to describe the behavior of interest rates is the one which assumes that short-term rates follow some statistical process and that other interest rates in the term structure are related to short-term rates. The short rate is the only one that is assumed to drive the rates of all other maturities. Hence, these models are referred to as *one-factor models*. The other rates are not randomly determined once the short rate is specified. Using arbitrage arguments, the equilibrium rate for all other maturities is determined. Three formulations of the one factor model are described in the appendix to this chapter.

There are also two-factor models that have been proposed. One factor in all these models is the short rate. The different models specify a second factor. In the model proposed by Brennan and Schwartz, the second factor is a long-term rate.[8] In the two-factor developed by Fong and Vasicek, the second factor is the volatility of short rates.[9]

---

[8] Michael J. Brennan and Eduardo S. Schwartz, "A Continuous Time Approach to the Pricing of Bonds," *Journal of Banking and Finance* (July 1979), pp. 133-155.
[9] H. Gifford Fong and Oldrich A. Vasicek, "Fixed-Income Volatility Management," *Journal of Portfolio Management* (Summer 1991), pp. 41-46.

## KEY POINTS

Here are the key points of this chapter:

1. Using arbitrage arguments, the market's consensus of future interest rates can be extrapolated from the Treasury yield curve or equivalently, the spot rate curve.

2. These rates are called forward rates or implied forward rates and the set of short-term (six-month) forward rates is the short forward rate curve.

3. The spot rate for a given period is related to the forward rates, specifically, the spot rate is a geometric average of the current six-month spot rate and the subsequent six-month forward rates.

4. Because of the relationship between spot and forward rates, discounting at the forward rates will give the same value for a security as discounting at the spot rates.

5. This means that calculating the static spread over the Treasury spot rate curve is the same as calculating the static spread over the Treasury forward rate curve.

6. Historically, different shapes have been observed for the Treasury yield curve: a normal or positive yield curve, a downward-sloping or inverted yield curve, a humped yield curve, and a flat yield curve.

7. The two major theories for explaining these observed shapes of the yield curve are the expectations theory and the market segmentation theory.

8. The three forms of the expectations theory (the pure expectations theory, the liquidity theory, and the preferred habitat theory) assume that the forward rates in current long-term bonds are closely related to the market's expectations about future

short-term rates.

9. The three forms of the expectations theory differ on whether other factors also affect forward rates, and how.

10. The pure expectations theory postulates that no systematic factors other than expected future short-term rates affect forward rates.

11. Because forward rates are not perfect predictors of future interest rates, the pure expectations theory suffers from one shortcoming: it neglects the risks (interest rate risk and reinvestment risk) associated with investing in bonds.

12. The broadest interpretation of the pure expectations theory suggests that investors expect the return for any investment horizon to be the same, regardless of the maturity strategy selected.

13. The local expectations form of the pure expectations theory suggests that the return will be the same over a short-term investment horizon starting today and it is this narrow interpretation that economists have demonstrated is the only interpretation that can be sustained in equilibrium.

14. The return-to-maturity expectations interpretation of the pure expectations theory suggests that the return that an investor will realize by rolling over short-term bonds to some investment horizon will be the same as holding a zero-coupon bond with a maturity that is the same as that investment horizon.

15. The liquidity theory and the preferred habitat theory assert that there are other factors that affect forward rates and these two theories are therefore referred to as biased expectations theories.

16. The liquidity theory states that investors will hold longer-term maturities only if they are offered a risk premium and there-

fore forward rates should reflect both interest rate expectations and a liquidity risk premium.

17. The preferred habitat theory in addition to adopting the view that forward rates reflect the expectation of the future path of interest rates as well as a risk premium argues that the risk premium need not reflect a liquidity premium but the demand and supply of funds in a given maturity range.

18. The market segmentation theory also recognizes that investors have preferred maturity sectors dictated by the nature of their liabilities but it goes further than the preferred habitat theory by assuming that neither investors nor borrowers are willing to shift from one maturity sector to another to take advantage of opportunities arising from differences between expectations and forward rates.

19. To model the term structure, it is necessary to identify the factors that affect the behavior of interest rates and to specify a statistical process that describes the behavior of those factors and is a reasonable characterization of their actual behavior.

20. The one-factor model which assumes that changes in the short rate determines the term structure is the most commonly used model.

# APPENDIX

# ONE-FACTOR MODELS OF THE TERM STRUCTURE

One factor models of the term structure are formulated in terms of how they describe the dynamics of the short rate; that is, they specify how the short rate changes for small changes in the underlying variables that affect its value. In this appendix, we discuss the various formulations of the one-factor model.

# SOME BASICS

To introduce the term structure dynamic models, some basic concepts from probability theory must be explained.

## Random Variable

In one-factor models, the short rate is a *random* or *stochastic variable* because its value over time changes in an uncertain way. A random variable is defined as a variable which can have more than one possible future outcome.

A random variable can be classified as either a *continuous variable* or a *discrete variable*. A continuous variable is one that has no break. For example, consider the random variable of interest, the short rate. Suppose that the short rate can be between 0% and 25% and that it can take on any value within this range of probable outcomes. Thus, in moving from, say, 3% to 4%, the short rate can take on a value of 3.79217%. A discrete variable, by contrast, has breaks or jumps. For example, if in moving from 3% to 4% the short rate is restricted to taking on only values in 20 basis point increments (i.e., 3.2%, 3.4%, 3.6%, and 3.8%) it would be classified as a discrete variable. In the development of the models in this chapter, we assume that the random variables are continuous.

## Stochastic Process

While the value of the short rate at some future time is uncertain, the pattern by which it changes over time can be assumed. In statistical terminology, this pattern or behavior is called a *stochastic process* or *probability distribution*. Thus, when we say that it is necessary to describe the dynamics of the short rate, we mean that it is necessary to specify the stochastic process that describes the movement of the short rate.

***Discrete-Time Versus Continuous-Time Stochastic Processes:*** Stochastic processes can be classified according to when the value of the random variable can change. When the value of the random variable can change at only fixed points in time, the stochastic process that describes the random process is called a *discrete-time stochastic process*. If, however, the random variable can change at any point in time (no matter how small the time interval), the stochastic process is called a *continuous-time stochastic process*.

In the models that we describe in this appendix, we assume a continuous-time stochastic process; that is, we assume continuous trading. The assumption that the random variable is continuous and that the stochastic process is a continuous-time stochastic process allows the use of calculus to derive important results.

***Standard Weiner Process:*** There are several types of continuous-time stochastic processes. A simple stochastic process for describing the dynamics of the short rate is a *standard Wiener process* and is expressed in equation form as follows:

$$dr = b \, dt + \sigma \, dx \qquad (1)$$

where

$dr$ = change in the short rate;
$b$ = expected direction of rate change
$dt$ = length of time interval
$\sigma$ = standard deviation of changes in the short rate
$dx$ = random process

Equation (1) states that the change in the short rate (dr) over a very small interval of time (dt) depends on: (1) the expected direction of the change in the short rate (b) and (2) a random process (dx).

The expected direction of the change in the short rate (b) is called the *drift rate*. The random nature of the change in the short rate comes from the random variable x in equation (1).

In a standard Wiener process it is assumed that the random variable x over a very small time interval is normally distributed with a mean of zero and a standard deviation of one.[10] The change in the short rate will then be proportional to the value of the random variable, the proportionality depending on the standard deviation of the change in the short rate ($\sigma$). It is also assumed that the change in the short rate for any two different short intervals of time are independent.

Given the above assumptions, two properties of the standard Wiener process follow:

**Property 1:** The expected value of the change in the short rate is equal to the drift rate (b). If the drift rate is assumed to be equal to zero, this means that the expected value of the change in the short rate is zero and therefore the expected value for the short rate is its current value.

**Property 2:** The variance of the change in the short rate over some interval of T is equal to T and its standard is the square root of T.

**Ito Process:** A special case of the standard Wiener process is to assume that both the drift rate and the standard deviation of the change in the short rate is a function of (i.e., depends on) the level of the short rate and time. This is expressed as follows:

$$dr = b(r,t)\, dt + \sigma(r,t)\, dx \qquad (2)$$

All of the symbols are the same as in equation (1).

The notation b(r,t) means that the drift rate depends on the

---

[10] Statistically, this means that x is drawn from a standardized normal distribution.

short rate r and time t. Similarly, σ(r,t) means that the standard deviation of the change in the short rate depends on the short rate and time. This special case of the standard Wiener process as formulated in equation (2) is called an *Ito process*.

## ALTERNATIVE SPECIFICATIONS OF THE ONE-FACTOR MODELS

It is the Ito process that is used in modelling the short-term rate. To describe the dynamics of the short rate it is necessary to specify the dynamics of the two terms in the Ito process:

(1) dynamics of the drift term, b(r,t), and
(2) dynamics of the variance or volatility term, σ(r,t)

It is the specification of the variance term that characterizes a model of the term structure as a *one-factor model*.

### Dynamics of the Drift Term

In the Ito process to describe changes in the short rate over time, one formulation is to assume that the drift rate follows a *mean-reversion process* as described below:

$$b(r, t) = \alpha(\bar{r} - r)$$

where

$\alpha$ = the speed of adjustment
$\bar{r}$ = the long-run stable mean of the short rate

The mean-reverting process in the drift term drives the short rate to converge toward its long-run stable mean with the appropriate speed of adjustment ($\alpha$).

### Dynamics of the Variance Term

Three alternative specifications of the variance term have been suggested in the financial economics literature.[11] In each formulation, the variance term does not depend on time. Because of this, the resulting term structure model is called a one-factor model. That is, each formulation has the following form:

$$\sigma(r,t) = \sigma(r)$$

which means that the variance rate is independent of t.

**Vasicek Specification:**[12] The first specification, suggested by Oldrich Vasicek in 1977, is

$$\sigma(r,t) = \sigma$$

This means that volatility is independent of both the level of the short-term rate and time.

**Dothan Specification:**[13] In 1978, Uri Dothan suggested the following specification for volatility:

$$\sigma(r,t) = \sigma r$$

This specification assumes that volatility is related to the level of the short rate, but independent of time. Thus, the higher the level of the short rate, the greater the volatility of rates.

**Cox-Ingersoll-Ross Specification:**[14] In 1985, John Cox, Jonathan

---

[11] For a discussion of other formulations and empirical evidence on their relative performance, see K.C. Chan, G. Andrew Karolyi, Francis A. Longstaff, and Anthony B. Sanders, "An Empirical Comparison of Alternative Models of the Short-Term Interest Rate," *Journal of Finance* (July 1992), pp. 1209-1227.

[12] Oldrich A. Vasicek, "An Equilibrium Characterization of the Term Structure," *Journal of Financial Economics* (1977), pp. 177-188.

[13] L. Uri Dothan, "On the Term Structure of Interest Rates," *Journal of Financial Economics* (1978), pp. 59-69.

[14] John C. Cox, Jonathan E. Ingersoll, Jr, and Stephen A. Ross. "A Theory of the Term Structure of Interest Rates," *Econometrica* (1985), pp. 385-407.

Ingersoll, and Stephen Ross (CIR) suggested the following specification which has subsequently been used in most sophisticated models of the term structure of interest rates:

$$\sigma(rt) = \sigma\sqrt{r}$$

The CIR model, also called the *square-root model*, indicates that (1) volatility increases with the short rate and (2) negative interest rates cannot occur.

## Mean-Reverting Square Root Diffusion Model

A popular formula for describing a one-factor model is to assume that the drift rate is mean reverting as described earlier and the variance rate follows the CIR or square-root model. The resulting stochastic process for the short rate is then:

$$dx = \alpha(\bar{r} - r)\,dt + \sigma\sqrt{r}\,dx \tag{3}$$

This model is sometimes referred to as the *mean-reverting square-root diffusion process*. This assumed stochastic process of the short rate has shown to be a reasonable approximation of interest rate behavior.

# 4
# MEASURING PRICE SENSITIVITY TO INTEREST RATE CHANGES

While the focus of this book is on the valuation of fixed income securities, investors are also concerned with how the value of a security will change when interest rates change. The responsiveness of a security's price to interest rate changes is popularly referred to as *duration*.

**The objectives of this chapter are to:**

1. review the relationship between the price and the yield of a fixed income security;

2. illustrate the price volatility properties of an option-free bond;

3. explain why the calculation of the duration of a security requires a valuation model;

4. provide a general formula that can be used to calculate the duration of any security assuming a parallel shift in the yield curve;

5. explain why the traditional duration measure, modified duration, is of limited value in determining the duration of a security with an embedded option;

6. distinguish between modified duration and effective duration;

> 7. explain what the convexity measure of a bond is; and,
>
> 8. distinguish between modified convexity and effective convexity.

## PRICE VOLATILITY CHARACTERISTICS OF OPTION-FREE BONDS

A fundamental principle of an option-free bond (that is, a bond that does not have any embedded options) is that the price of the bond changes in the opposite direction from a change in the bond's yield. Exhibit 1 illustrates this property for four hypothetical bonds, where the bond prices are shown assuming a par value of $100.

When the price/yield relationship for any option-free bond is graphed, it exhibits the shape shown in Exhibit 2. Notice that as the yield rises, the price of the option-free bond declines. However, this relationship is not linear (that is, it is not a straight line). The shape of the price/yield relationship for any option-free bond is referred to as *convex*. The price/yield relationship that we have discussed refers to an instantaneous change in yield.

### Properties of Option-Free Bonds

Exhibit 3 uses the four hypothetical bonds in Exhibit 1 to show the percentage change in each bond's price for various changes in the yield, assuming that the initial yield for all four bonds is 6%. An examination of Exhibit 3 reveals several properties concerning the price volatility of an option-free bond.

***Property 1:*** Although the prices of all option-free bonds move in the opposite direction from the change in yield, the percentage price change is not the same for all bonds.

***Property 2:*** For small changes in yield, the percentage price change for a given bond is roughly the same, whether the yield increases or decreases.

## Exhibit 1: Price/Yield Relationship for Four Hypothetical Bonds

|  | *Percent Price Change* | | | |
| ---: | ---: | ---: | ---: | ---: |
| New Yield (%) | 6%/5 year | 6%/20year | 9%/5 year | 9%/20year |
| 4.00 | 108.9826 | 127.3555 | 122.4565 | 168.3887 |
| 5.00 | 104.3760 | 112.5514 | 117.5041 | 150.2056 |
| 5.50 | 102.1600 | 106.0195 | 115.1201 | 142.1367 |
| 5.90 | 100.4276 | 101.1651 | 113.2556 | 136.1193 |
| 5.99 | 100.0427 | 100.1157 | 112.8412 | 134.8159 |
| 6.00 | 100.0000 | 100.0000 | 112.7953 | 134.6722 |
| 6.01 | 99.9574 | 99.8845 | 112.7494 | 134.5287 |
| 6.10 | 99.5746 | 98.8535 | 112.3373 | 133.2472 |
| 6.50 | 97.8944 | 94.4479 | 110.5280 | 127.7605 |
| 7.00 | 95.8417 | 89.3225 | 108.3166 | 121.3551 |
| 8.00 | 91.8891 | 80.2072 | 104.0554 | 109.8964 |

## Exhibit 2: Price/Yield Relationship for an Option-Free Bond

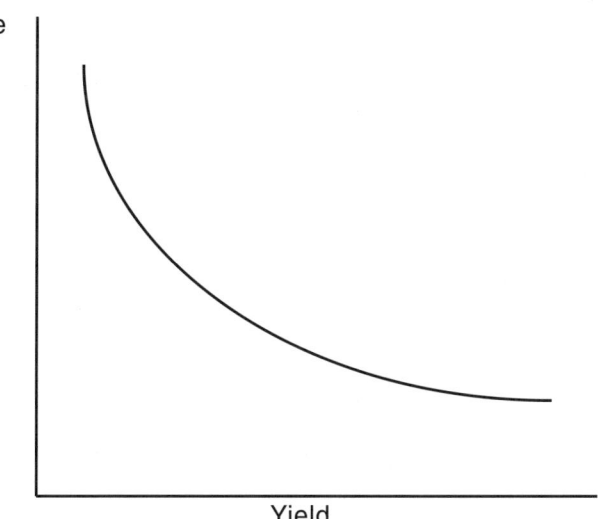

## Exhibit 3: Instantaneous Percentage Price Change for Four Hypothetical Bonds

**(Initial yield for all four bonds is 6%)**

| New Yield (%) | *Percent Price Change* | | | |
|---|---|---|---|---|
| | 6%/5 year | 6%/20year | 9%/5 year | 9%/20year |
| 4.00 | 8.98 | 27.36 | 8.57 | 25.04 |
| 5.00 | 4.38 | 12.55 | 4.17 | 11.53 |
| 5.50 | 2.16 | 6.02 | 2.06 | 5.54 |
| 5.90 | 0.43 | 1.17 | 0.41 | 1.07 |
| 5.99 | 0.04 | 0.12 | 0.04 | 0.11 |
| 6.01 | -0.04 | -0.12 | -0.04 | -0.11 |
| 6.10 | -0.43 | -1.15 | -0.41 | -1.06 |
| 6.50 | -2.11 | -5.55 | -2.01 | -5.13 |
| 7.00 | -4.16 | -10.68 | -3.97 | -9.89 |
| 8.00 | -8.11 | -19.79 | -7.75 | -18.40 |

***Property 3:*** For large changes in yield, the percentage price change is not the same for an increase in yield as it is for a decrease in yield.

***Property 4:*** For a given change in basis points, the percentage price increase is greater than the percentage price decrease.

The implication of Property 4 is that if an investor is long a bond, the price appreciation that will be realized if the yield decreases is greater than the capital loss that will be realized if the yield rises by the same number of basis points. For an investor who is short a bond, the reverse is true: the potential capital loss is greater than the potential capital gain if the yield changes by a given number of basis points.

An explanation for these four properties of bond price volatility lies in the convex shape of the price/yield relationship.

## Characteristics of a Bond that Affect its Price Volatility

There are two characteristics of an option-free bond that determine its price volatility that can be verified by examining Exhibit 3: coupon and term to maturity.

***Characteristic 1:*** For a given term to maturity and initial yield, the lower the coupon rate the greater the price volatility of a bond.

***Characteristic 2:*** For a given coupon rate and initial yield, the longer the term to maturity, the greater the price volatility.

An implication of the second characteristic is that investors who want to increase a portfolio's price volatility because they expect interest rates to fall, all other factors being constant, should hold bonds with long maturities in the portfolio. To reduce a portfolio's price volatility in anticipation of a rise in interest rates, bonds with shorter-term maturities should be held in the portfolio.

## The Effects of Yield to Maturity

We cannot ignore the fact that credit considerations cause different bonds to trade at different yields, even if they have the same coupon and maturity. How, then, holding other factors constant, does the yield to maturity affect a bond's price volatility? As it turns out, the higher the yield to maturity that a bond trades at, the lower the price volatility.

To see this, we can compare a 6% 20-year bond initially selling at a yield of 6%, and a 6% 20-year bond initially selling at a yield of 10%. The former is initially at a price of 100, and the latter carries a price of 65.68. Now, if the yields on both bonds increase by 100 basis points, the first bond trades down by 10.68 points (10.68%). After the assumed increase in yield, the second bond will trade at a price of 59.88, for a price decline of only 5.80 (or 8.83%). Thus, we see that the bond that trades at a lower yield is more volatile in both percentage price change and absolute price change, as long as the other bond characteristics are the same.

A possibly more relevant comparison of bond price volatility is that of comparing bonds that trade at different yields but starting them all on the same footing (e.g., by comparing only bonds trading at par). For par bonds trading at different yields but with the same maturity, the lower yielding bonds still exhibit both greater percentage price changes for a given change in yield.

An implication of this is that, for a given change in yields, price volatility is lower when yield levels in the market are high, and price volatility is higher when yield levels are low.

## MEASURING INTEREST RATE RISK

Now we know that coupon and maturity affect a security's price volatility when yield changes, and that the level of interest rates affects price volatility. What is needed is a measure that encompasses these three factors that affect a security's price volatility when yields change. The most obvious way to measure the price sensitivity of a security to changes in interest rates is to change rates by a small number of basis points and calculate how the value of a security will change.

To do this, we introduce the following notation. Let

$\Delta y$ = change in rate used to calculate new values
$V_+$ = price if yield is increased by $\Delta y$
$V_-$ = price if yield is decreased by $\Delta y$
$V_0$ = initial price (per $100 of par value)

There are two key points to keep in mind in the foregoing discussion. First, the change in yield referred to above is the same change in yield for all maturities. This assumption is commonly referred to as a *parallel yield curve shift assumption*. Thus, the foregoing discussion about the price sensitivity of a security to interest rate changes is limited to parallel shifts in the yield curve. Later in this chapter we will address the case where the yield curve shifts in a nonparallel manner.

Second, the notation refers to the estimated value of the security. This value is obtained from a valuation model. Consequently, the resulting measure of the price sensitivity of a security to interest rates changes is only as good as the valuation model employed to obtain the estimated value of the security.

Now let's focus on the measure of interest. We are interested in the percentage change in the price of a security when interest rates change by a small number of basis points. Using a given decline in yield ($\Delta y$), the percentage price is obtained as follows:

$$\frac{V_- - V_0}{V_0}$$

The percentage change in price per change in basis points is found by dividing the percentage price change by the number of basis points. That is:

$$\frac{V_- - V_0}{V_0 (\Delta y)}$$

Similarly, the percentage change in price for an increase in yield of $\Delta y$ is:

$$\frac{V_0 - V_+}{V_+ (\Delta y)}$$

As explained earlier, the percentage price change for an increase and decrease in interest rates will not be the same. Consequently, the average percentage price change per basis point change in yield can be calculated. This is done as follows:

$$\frac{1}{2}\left[\frac{V_- - V_0}{V_0 (\Delta y)} + \frac{V_0 - V_+}{V_0 (\Delta y)}\right]$$

or equivalently,

$$\frac{V_- - V_+}{2V_0 (\Delta y)}$$

The name popularly used to refer to the approximate percentage price change is *duration*. Thus,

$$\text{Duration} = \frac{V_- - V_+}{2V_0 (\Delta y)} \qquad (1)$$

To illustrate this formula, consider the following option-free bond: a 9% coupon 20-year bond trading to yield 6%. The initial price or value ($V_0$) is 134.6722. Suppose the yield is changed by 20 basis points. If the yield is decreased to 5.8%, the value of this bond ($V_-$) would be

137.5888. If the yield is increased to 6.2%, the value of this bond ($V_+$) would be 131.8439.

Thus,

$$\Delta y = 0.0020$$
$$V_+ = 131.8439$$
$$V_- = 137.5888$$
$$V_0 = 131.8439$$

Substituting these values into the duration formula,

$$\text{Duration} = \frac{137.5888 - 131.8439}{2\,(134.6722)\,(0.002)} = 10.66$$

*The duration of a security can be interpreted as the approximate percentage change in price for a 100 basis point parallel shift in the yield curve.* Thus a bond with a duration of 4.8 will change by approximately 4.8% for a 100 basis point parallel shift in the yield curve. For a 50 basis point parallel shift in the yield curve, the bond's price will change by approximately 2.4%; for a 25 basis point parallel shift in the yield curve, 1.2%, etc.

## Modified Duration Versus Effective Duration

A popular form of duration that is used by practitioners is *modified duration*. Modified duration is the approximate percentage change in a bond's price for a 100 basis point parallel shift in the yield curve assuming that the bond's cash flow does *not* change when the yield curve shifts. What this means is that in calculating the values of $V_-$ and $V_+$ in equation (1), the cash flow used to calculate $V_0$ is used. Therefore, the change in the bond's price when the yield curve is shifted by a small number of basis points is due solely to discounting at the new yield level.

The assumption that the cash flow will not change when the yield curve shifts in a parallel fashion makes sense for option-free bonds such as noncallable Treasury securities. This is because the payments made by the U.S. Department of the Treasury to a holder of its obligations does not change when the yield curve changes. However, the same can not be said for callable and putable bonds and mortgage-backed securities. For these securities, a change in yield will alter the expected cash flow.

## Exhibit 4: Modified Duration Versus Effective Duration

| Duration |
|---|
| Interpretation: Generic description of the sensitivity of a bond's price (as a percentage of initial price) to a parallel shift in the yield curve |

| Modified Duration | Effective Duration |
|---|---|
| Duration measure in which it is assumed that yield changes do not change the expected cash flow | Duration in which recognition is given to the fact that yield changes may change the expected cash flow |

The valuation models that we will describe in Chapters 6 and 7 take into account how shifts in the yield curve will affect cash flow. Thus, when $V_-$ and $V_+$ are the values produced from these valuation models, the resulting duration takes into account both the discounting at different interest rates and how the cash flow changes. When duration is calculated in this manner, it is referred to as *effective duration* or *option-adjusted duration*. Exhibit 4 summarizes the distinction between modified duration and effective duration.

The difference between modified duration and effective duration for fixed income securities with an embedded option can be quite dramatic. For example, a callable corporate bond could have a modified duration of 7 but an effective duration of only 2. For certain collateralized mortgage obligations, the modified duration could be 7 and the effective duration 40! Thus, using modified duration as a measure of the price sensitivity of a security to a parallel shift in the yield curve would be misleading. The more appropriate measure for any security with an embedded option is effective duration.

Before leaving this topic, it is worth comparing the modified duration formula presented above to that commonly found in the literature. It is common in the literature to find the following formula for modified duration:[1]

---

[1] More specifically, this is the formula for modified duration for a bond on a coupon anniversary date.

$$\frac{1}{(1+\text{yield}/k)} \left[ \frac{1\text{PVCF}_1 + 2\text{PVCF}_2 + 3\text{PVCF}_3 + \ldots + n\text{PVCF}_n}{k \times \text{Price}} \right] \quad (2)$$

where

- $k$ = number of periods, or payments, per year (e.g., $k = 2$ for semiannual pay bonds and $k = 12$ for monthly pay bonds)
- $n$ = number of periods until maturity (i.e., number of years to maturity times k)
- yield = yield to maturity of the bond
- $\text{PVCF}_t$ = present value of the cash flow in period t discounted at the yield to maturity

The expression in the bracket for the modified duration formula in equation (2) is a measure formulated in 1938 by Frederick Macaulay.[2] This measure is popularly referred to as *Macaulay duration*. Thus, modified duration is commonly expressed as:

$$\text{Modified duration} = \frac{\text{Macaulay duration}}{(1+\text{yield}/k)}$$

The general formulation for duration as given by equation (1) provides a short-cut procedure for determining a bond's modified duration. Because it is easier to calculate the modified duration using the short-cut procedure, many vendors of analytical software will use equation (1) rather than equation (2) to reduce computation time. But, once again, it must be emphasized that modified duration is a flawed measure of a bond's price sensitivity to interest rate changes for a bond with an embedded option.

## Price Sensitivity to Non-Parallel Yield Curve Shifts

Both modified duration and effective duration assume that any

---

[2] Frederick Macaulay, *Some Theoretical Problems Suggested by the Movement of Interest Rates, Bond Yields, and Stock Prices in the U.S. Since 1856* (New York: National Bureau of Economic Research, 1938).

change in interest rates is the result of a parallel shift in the yield curve. For some fixed income securities, the price sensitivity to most nonparallel shifts will be very close to the estimated price sensitivity for a parallel shift in the yield curve. This is generally true for option-free bonds with a bullet maturity. However, for sinking-fund bonds and bonds with embedded options, particularly mortgage-backed securities, the price sensitivity to a nonparallel shift in the yield curve can be quite different from that estimated for a parallel shift.

Several measures have been proposed in the literature to estimate the price sensitivity of a bond to nonparallel yield curve shifts.[3] A discussion of these measures is beyond the scope of this chapter. However, the valuation models described in Chapters 6 and 7 can be used to determine the price sensitivity to specific nonparallel yield curve shifts assumed by an investor.

## CONVEXITY

Notice that the duration measure indicates that regardless of whether the yield curve is shifted up or down, the approximate percentage price change is the same. However, this does not agree with the properties of a bond's price volatility described earlier in this chapter. Specifically, Property 2 states that for small changes in yield the percentage price change will be the same for an increase or decrease in yield. Property 3 states that for large changes in yield this is not true. This suggests that duration is only a good approximation of the percentage price change for a small change in yield.

---

[3] See, for example, Thomas E. Klaffky, Y.Y. Ma, and Ardavan Nozari, "Managing Yield Curve Exposure: Introducing Reshaping Durations," *Journal of Fixed Income* (December 1992), pp. 5-15; Robert R. Reitano, "Non-Parallel Yield Curve Shifts and Immunization," *Journal of Portfolio Management* (Spring 1992), pp. 36-43; Thomas Y. Ho, "Key Rate Durations: Measures of Interest Rate Risk," *Journal of Fixed Income* (September 1992), pp. 29-44; Brian D. Johnson and Kenneth R. Meyer, "Managing Yield Curve Risk in an Index Environment," *Financial Analysts Journal* (November/December 1989), pp. 51-59; and Chapter 3 in Frank J. Fabozzi and H. Gifford Fong, *Advanced Fixed Income Portfolio Management* (Chicago: Probus Publishing, forthcoming 1994).

To see this, consider once again the 9%, 20-year bond selling to yield 6% with a duration of 10.66. If yields increase instantaneously by 10 basis points (from 6% to 6.1%), then using duration the approximate percentage price change would be -1.066% (-10.66% divided by 10, remembering that duration is the percentage price change for a 100 basis point change in yield). Notice from Exhibit 3 that the actual percentage price change is -1.07%. Similarly, if the yield decreases instantaneously by 10 basis points (from 6.00% to 5.90%), then the percentage change in price would be +1.066%. From Exhibit 3, the actual percentage price change would be +1.07%. This example illustrates that for small changes in yield, duration does an excellent job of approximating the percentage price change.

Instead of a small change in yield, let's assume that yields increase by 200 basis points, from 6% to 8%. The approximate percentage change is -21.32% (-10.66% times 2). As can be seen from Exhibit 3, the actual percentage change in price is only -18.40%. Moreover, if the yield decreased by 200 basis points from 6% to 4%, the approximate percentage price change based on duration would be +21.32%, compared to an actual percentage price change of +25.04%. Thus, the approximation is not as good for a 200 basis point change in yield.

Duration is in fact a first approximation for a small parallel shift in the yield curve. The approximation can be improved by using a second approximation. This approximation is referred to as a bond's *convexity*.[4] The use of this term in the industry is unfortunate since the term convexity is also used to describe the shape or curvature of the price/yield relationship, as explained earlier in this chapter. The convexity measure of a security is the approximate change in price that is not explained by duration.

---

[4] Mathematically, any function can be estimated by a series of approximations referred to as a Taylor series. Each approximation or term of the Taylor series is based on the corresponding derivative. For a bond, duration is the first approximation to price and is related to the first derivative of the bond's price. The convexity measure is the second approximation and related to the second derivative of the bond's price. It turns out that in general the first two approximations do a good job of estimating the bond's price so no additional derivatives are needed. The derivation is provided in Chapter 4 of Frank J. Fabozzi, *Bond Markets, Analysis, and Strategies* (Englewood Cliffs, N.J.: Prentice Hall, 1993).

## Measuring Convexity

The convexity of any bond can be approximated using the following formula:

$$\text{Convexity} = \frac{V_+ + V_- - 2V_0}{2V_0(\Delta y)^2}$$

For our hypothetical 9%, 20-year bond selling to yield 6%, we know that

$\Delta y = 0.0020$
$V_+ = 131.8439$
$V_- = 137.5888$
$V_0 = 131.8439$

Substituting these values into the convexity formula,

$$\text{Convexity} = \frac{137.5888 + 131.8439 - 2(134.6722)}{2(134.6722)(0.002)^2} = 81.96$$

## Percentage Price Change Due to Convexity

Given the convexity measure, the approximate percentage change in price due to the bond's convexity that is not explained by duration is:

$$\text{Convexity} \times (\Delta y)^2$$

For example, for the 9% coupon bond maturing in 20 years, the approximate percentage price change due to convexity if the yield increases from 6% to 8% is

$$81.96 \times (0.02)^2 = 0.0328 = 3.28\%$$

If the yield decreases from 6% to 4%, the approximate percentage price change due to convexity would also be 3.28%.

The approximate percentage price change based on both duration and convexity is found by simply adding the two estimates. So, for example, if yields change from 6% to 8%, the estimated percentage price change would be:

$$\text{Duration} = -21.32\%$$
$$\text{Convexity} = +3.28\%$$
$$\text{Total} = -18.04\%$$

The actual percentage price change is -18.40%. For a decrease of 200 basis points, from 6% to 4% the approximate percentage price change would be as follows:

$$\text{Duration} = +21.32\%$$
$$\text{Convexity} = +3.28\%$$
$$\text{Total} = +24.60\%$$

The actual percentage price change is +25.04%. Thus, both duration and convexity together do a good job of estimating the sensitivity of a bond's price change to large changes in yield.

While it is easy to interpret what duration means, it is more difficult to interpret the convexity measure because it is multiplied by the square of the change in yield. Basically, convexity is the rate of change of duration when yields change.[5]

## Modified Convexity and Effective Convexity

The prices used in equation (3) to calculate convexity can be obtained by either assuming that when the yield curve shifts in a parallel way the expected cash flow does not change or it does change. In the former case, the resulting convexity is referred to as *modified convexity*.[6] Actually, in the industry, convexity is not qualified by the adjective modified. Thus, in practice the term convexity typically means the cash flow is

---

[5] More specifically, convexity is the rate of change of a bond's dollar price change (or dollar duration).

[6] The formula for modified convexity is

$$\frac{1(2)\,PVCF_1 + 2(3)\,PVCF_2 + 3(4)\,PVCF_3 + \ldots + n(n+1)\,PVCF_n}{(1+\text{yield}/k)^2 \; k^2 \; \text{Price}}$$

Using this formula, the modified convexity for the 9%, 20-year bond selling to yield 6% is 82.04. While this number is slightly different from that obtained using equation (3), when we use this measure to obtain the approximate percentage price change due to convexity, the result will be the same.

assumed not to change when yields change. *Effective convexity* or *option-adjusted convexity*, in contrast, assumes that the cash flow does change when yields change. This is the same distinction made for duration.

As with duration, for bonds with embedded options there could be quite a difference between the calculated modified convexity and effective convexity. In fact, for all option-free bonds, either convexity measure will have a positive value. For callable bonds and mortgage-backed securities, the calculated effective convexity can be negative when the calculated modified convexity gives a positive value.

## KEY POINTS

Here are the key points of this chapter:

1. The price of an option-free bond moves inversely with a change in yield.

2. The price/yield relationship for an option-free bond is convex.

3. A property of an option-free bond is that for a small change in yield, the percentage price change is roughly the same, whether the yield increases or decreases.

4. A property of an option-free bond is that for a large change in yield, the percentage price change is not the same for an increase in yield as it is for a decrease in yield.

5. A property of an option-free bond is that for a given change in basis points, the percentage price increase is greater than the percentage price decrease.

6. The coupon and maturity of an option-free bond affect its price volatility.

7. For a given term to maturity and initial yield, the lower the coupon rate the greater the price volatility of a bond.

8. For a given coupon rate and initial yield, the longer the term to maturity, the greater the price volatility.

9. For a given change in yield, price volatility is less when yield levels in the market are high than when yield levels are low.

10. The percentage price change of a bond can be estimated by changing the yield by a small number of basis points and observing how the price changes.

11. The duration of a bond measures the approximate percentage price change for a 100 basis point change in yield, assuming a parallel shift in the yield curve.

12. Modified duration is the approximate percentage change in a bond's price for a 100 basis point parallel shift in the yield curve assuming that the bond's cash flow does not change when the yield curve shifts.

13. Modified duration is not a useful measure of the price sensitivity for securities with embedded options.

14. Effective duration or option-adjusted duration is the approximate percentage price change of a bond for a 100 basis point parallel shift in the yield curve allowing for the cash flow to change as a result of the change in yield.

15. The difference between modified duration and effective duration for fixed income securities with an embedded option can be quite dramatic.

16. Both modified duration and effective duration assume that any change in interest rates is the result of a parallel shift in the yield curve.

17. There are duration measures that allow for a nonparallel shift in the yield curve.

18. The estimate of the price sensitivity of a bond based on duration can be improved by using a bond's convexity.

19. The convexity of a bond measures how quickly its duration changes as yield changes.

20. As with duration, the convexity of a bond can be measured assuming that the cash flow does not change when yield changes (modified convexity) or assuming that it does change when yield changes (effective convexity).

# 5
# OVERVIEW OF THE VALUATION OF BONDS WITH EMBEDDED OPTIONS

Thus far, our discussion of bond valuation has been limited to bonds in which neither the issuer nor the bondholder has the option to alter a bond's cash flows. In the remaining chapters of this book, we look at how to value bonds with embedded options.

> **The objectives of this chapter are to:**
>
> 1. explain the disadvantages of the call feature from a bondholder's perspective and therefore why potential investors want to receive compensation for the risk that the issue might be called;
>
> 2. review the traditional methodology used to evaluate callable bonds;
>
> 3. provide a conceptual framework for thinking about how to value bonds with embedded options;
>
> 4. review the factors that affect the value of an option;
>
> 5. explain what is meant by the option-adjusted spread; and,
>
> 6. describe what modeling risk is.

## DISADVANTAGES OF CALLABLE BONDS

The holder of a callable bond has given the issuer the right to call the issue prior to the expiration date. A mortgage-backed security is also a callable security since the homeowner has the right to pay off all or part of the mortgage loan balance at any time.

The presence of a call option results in two disadvantages to the bondholder. First, callable bonds expose bondholders to reinvestment risk since an issuer will call a bond when the yield on bonds in the market is lower than the issue's coupon rate. For example, if the coupon rate on a callable corporate bond is 13% and prevailing market yields are 7%, the issuer will find it economical to call the 13% issue and refund it with a 7% issue. From the investor's perspective, the proceeds received will have to be reinvested at a lower interest rate.

Second, the price appreciation potential for a callable bond in a declining interest rate environment is limited. The price of the callable bond will not rise as much as an otherwise comparable noncallable bond. This can be seen in Exhibit 1. The price/yield relationship for an option-free (i.e., noncallable/nonputable) bond is convex. The convex curve a-a' shows the price/yield relationship. The exhibit also shows the price/yield relationship for an otherwise equivalent callable bond as depicted by the unusual shape of the curve denoted by a-b.

The reason for the shape of the price/yield relationship for the callable bond is as follows. When the prevailing market yield for comparable bonds is higher than the coupon rate on the bond, it is unlikely that the issuer will call the bond. For example, if the coupon rate on a bond is 7% and the prevailing yield on comparable bonds is 13%, it is highly improbable that the issuer will call the outstanding issue. Since the bond is unlikely to be called, the callable bond will have the same price/yield relationship as a noncallable bond. However, even when the coupon rate is just below the market yield, investors may not pay the same price for the callable bond had it been noncallable because there is still the chance that the market yield may drop further making it beneficial for the issuer to call the bond.

## Exhibit 1: Price/Yield Relationship for an Option-Free Bond and a Callable Bond

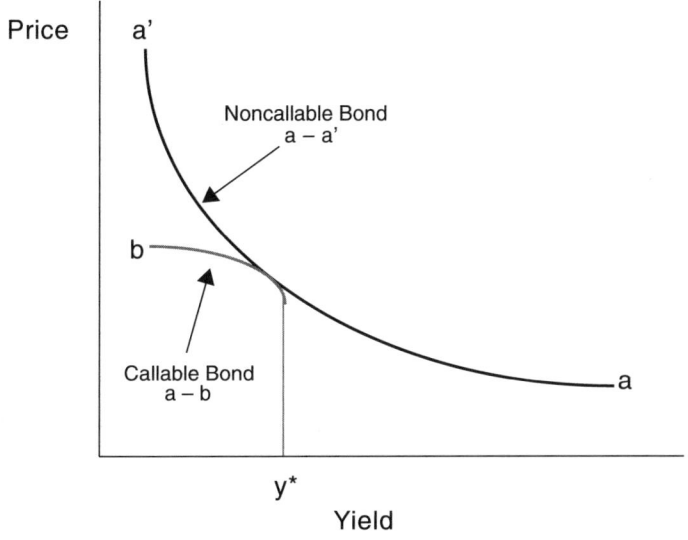

The exact yield level at which investors begin to view the issue likely to be called may not be known, but we do know that there is some level. In Exhibit 1, at yield levels below y*, the price/yield relationship for the callable bond departs from the price/yield relationship for the noncallable bond. If, for example, the market yield is such that a noncallable bond would be selling for 109, but as the callable bond would be called at 104, investors would not pay 109. If they did and the bond is called, investors would receive 104 (the call price) for a bond they purchased for 109. Notice that for a range of yields below y*, there is price compression — that is, there is limited price appreciation as yields decline. The portion of the callable bond price/yield relationship below y* is said to be *negatively convex*.

*Negative convexity means that the price appreciation will be less than the price depreciation for a large change in yield of a given number of basis points.* For a bond that is option-free and exhibits positive convexity, the price appreciation will be greater than the price depreciation for a large change in yield of a given number of basis points. The price changes resulting from bonds exhibiting positive convexity and negative convexity can be expressed as follows:

| Change in interest rates | Absolute value of percentage price change for: | |
| --- | --- | --- |
| | Positive Convexity | Negative Convexity |
| -100 basis points | X% | less than Y% |
| +100 basis points | less than X% | Y% |

Since an investor is exposed to reinvestment risk and truncated price appreciation potential due to negative convexity, he must be compensated for these risks. The key in valuing callable bonds is to adjust the price to reflect these risks. Or equivalently, the key is to adjust the price for the value of the call option that creates these risks.

## STATIC VALUATION METHODOLOGY

The traditional approach to valuing callable bonds has been in terms of the yield to worst. This yield measure is found by calculating the yield to maturity and the yield to call for every call date, and then selecting the lowest of all of the calculated yields.

### Drawbacks of Traditional Valuation Methodology

There are several drawbacks of this approach. First, it assumes that the issue will be called on the date used in the yield to worst calculation. Second, it gives no recognition to the volatility of interest rates which would affect future interest rates and therefore whether the issue will be called in the future. Thus, the traditional valuation analysis can best be described as static valuation analysis since only a single interest rate scenario, usually assuming that the yield curve remains unchanged, is used.

Another pitfall of the traditional valuation approach is that in the valuation of bonds only one yield, the yield to worst, is used to discount all cash flows to the assumed call or maturity date. As we noted in previous chapters, the appropriate discount rates are based on the theoretical spot rates.

To resolve this pitfall, a static spread can be calculated. As explained in Chapter 2, the static spread is defined as the constant spread that is added to the issuer's spot rate curve that will make the present value of the cash flow to either the assumed call or maturity equal to the market price. It is called a static spread since it assumes a static interest rate scenario; that is, it assumes no volatility of interest rates in the future.

The static spread therefore is a spread over the entire theoretical spot rate curve of the issuer, not a single point on the issuer's on-the-run yield curve. As shown in Chapter 2, the magnitude of the difference between the traditional or nominal yield spread and the static yield spread depends on the steepness of the yield curve: the steeper the curve, the greater the difference between the two values. In a relatively flat interest rate environment, the difference between the traditional yield spread and the static spread will be small.

## THE COMPONENTS OF A BOND WITH AN EMBEDDED OPTION

To develop an analytical framework for valuing a bond with an embedded option, it is necessary to decompose a bond into its component parts. A callable bond is a bond in which the bondholder has sold the issuer an option (more specifically, a call option) that allows the issuer to repurchase the contractual cash flows of the bond from the bond's call date until the maturity date.

Consider the following two bonds: (1) a callable bond with an 8% coupon, 20 years to maturity and callable in five years at 104 and (2) a 10-year 9% coupon bond callable immediately at par. For the first bond, the bondholder owns a 5-year noncallable bond and has sold a call option granting the issuer the right to call away from the bondholder 15 years of cash flows 5 years from now for a price of 104. The investor who owns the second bond has a 10-year noncallable bond and has sold a call option granting the issuer the right to immediately call the entire 10-year contractual cash flows, or any cash flows remaining at the time the issue is called, for 100.

Effectively, the owner of a callable bond is entering into two separate transactions. First, he buys a noncallable bond from the issuer for which he pays some price. Then, he sells the issuer a call option for which he receives the option price. Therefore, we can summarize the position of a callable bondholder as follows:

long a callable bond = long a noncallable bond + short a call option

In terms of price, the price of a callable bond is therefore equal to the price of the two components parts. That is,

price of a callable bond = price of a noncallable bond − price of a call option

The reason the call option price is subtracted from the price of the noncallable bond is that when the bondholder sells a call option, he receives the option price. Graphically, this can be seen in Exhibit 1. The difference between the price of the noncallable bond and the callable bond at any given yield is the value of the embedded call option.

Actually, the position is more complicated than we just described. The issuer may be entitled to call the bond at the first call date and anytime thereafter, or at the first call date and any subsequent coupon anniversary. Thus the investor has effectively sold an American-type call option to the issuer but the call price may vary with the date the call option is exercised. This is because the call schedule for a bond may have a different call price depending on the call date. Moreover, the underlying bond for the call option is the remaining coupon payments that would have been made by the issuer had the bond not been called. For exposition purposes, it is easier to understand the principles associated with the investment characteristics of callable bonds by describing the investor's position as long a noncallable bond and short a call option.

The same logic applies to putable bonds. In the case of a putable bond, the bondholder has the right to sell the bond to the issuer at a designated price and time. A putable bond can be broken into two separate transactions. First, the investor buys a nonputable bond. Second, the investor buys a put option from the issuer that allows the investor to sell the bond to the issuer. Therefore, the position of a putable bondholder can be described as:

long a putable bond = long a nonputable bond + long a put option

The price of a putable bond is then

price of a putable bond = price of a nonputable bond + price of a put option

## Factors Affecting the Value of an Option

Now that we know that the value of a bond is affected by the value of any embedded option, it would be helpful to know what factors affect the value of an option.

***Intrinsic Value:*** The option value is a reflection of the option's *intrinsic value* and any additional amount over its intrinsic value. The premium over intrinsic value is often referred to as the *time value*. The intrinsic value of an option is its economic value if it is exercised immediately. If no positive economic value would result from exercising the option immediately, then the intrinsic value is zero.

For a call option, the intrinsic value is positive if the current price of the underlying security is greater than the strike (or exercise) price. The intrinsic value is then the difference between the two prices. If the strike price of a call option is greater than or equal to the current price of the security, the intrinsic value is zero. For example, if the strike price for a call option is 100 and the current price for the security is 105, the intrinsic value is 5. That is, an option buyer exercising the option and simultaneously selling the underlying security would realize 105 from the sale of the security, which would be covered by acquiring the security from the option writer for $100, thereby netting a $5 gain.

When an option has intrinsic value, it is said to be *in the money*. When the strike price of a call option exceeds the current price of the security, the call option is said to be *out of the money*; it has no intrinsic value. An option for which the strike price is equal to the current price of the security is said to be *at the money*. Both at-the-money and out-of-the-money options have an intrinsic value of zero because they not profitable to exercise.

For a put option, the intrinsic value is equal to the amount by which the current price of the security is below the strike price. For example, if the strike price of a put option is 100 and the current price of the security is 92, the intrinsic value is 8. The buyer of the put option who exercises the put option and simultaneously sells the underlying security will net 8 by exercising this option since the security will be sold to the writer for 100 and purchased in the market for 92. The intrinsic value is zero if the strike price is less than or equal to the current market price.

For our put option with a strike price of 100, the option would be: (1) in the money when the security's price is less than 100, (2) out of the money when the security's price exceeds 100, and (3) at the money when the security's price is equal to 100.

The relations above are summarized in Exhibit 2.

***Time Value:*** The time value of an option is the amount by which the option price exceeds its intrinsic value. The option buyer hopes that, at some time prior to expiration, changes in the market price of the underlying security will increase the value of the rights conveyed by the option. For this prospect, the option buyer is willing to pay a premium above the intrinsic value.

For example, if the price of a call option with a strike price of 100 is 9 when the current price of the security is 105, the time value of this option is 4 (9 minus its intrinsic value of 5). Had the current price of the security been 90 instead of 105, then the time value of this option would be the entire 9 because the option has no intrinsic value.

## Factors that Influence an Option's Value

There are six factors that influence the value of an option in which the underlying security is a fixed-income instrument:

1. *current price of the underlying security;*

2. *strike price;*

3. *time to expiration of the option;*

4. *expected interest rate volatility over the life of the option;*

5. *short-term risk-free interest rate over the life of the option;* and

6. *coupon interest payment over the life of the option.*

The impact of each of these factors may depend on whether (1) the option is a call or a put, and (2) the option is an American option or a European option. A summary of the effect of each factor on American put and call option prices is presented in Exhibit 3.

## Exhibit 2: Relationship Between Security Price, Strike Price, and Intrinsic Value

| | Call option | Put Option |
|---|---|---|
| If Security price > Strike price | | |
| Intrinsic value | Security price - Strike price | Zero |
| Jargon | In-the-money | Out-of-the money |
| | Call option | Put Option |
| If Security price < Strike price | | |
| Intrinsic value | Zero | Security price - Stock price |
| Jargon | Out-of-the money | In-the-money |
| | Call option | Put Option |
| If Security price = Strike price | | |
| Intrinsic value | Zero | Zero |
| Jargon | At-the money | At-the money |

## Exhibit 3: Summary of Factors that Affect the Price of an American Option

| | Effect of an Increase of Factor on: | |
|---|---|---|
| Factor | Call Price | Put Price |
| Current price of underlying security | increase | decrease |
| Strike price | decrease | increase |
| Time to expiration of option | increase | increase |
| Expected interest rate volatility | increase | increase |
| Short-term interest rate | increase | decrease |
| Coupon payments | decrease | increase |

***Current Price of the Underlying Security.*** The option price will change as the price of the underlying security changes. For a call option, as the price of the underlying security increases (holding all other factors constant), the option price increases. The opposite holds for a put option: as the price of the underlying security increases, the price of a put option decreases.

***Strike Price.*** All other factors equal, the lower the strike price, the higher the price of a call option. For put options, the higher the strike price, the higher the option price.

***Time to Expiration of the Option.*** An option is a "wasting asset." That is, after the expiration date passes the option has no value. Holding all other factors equal, the longer the time to expiration of the option, the greater the option price. This is because, as the time to expiration decreases, less time remains for the underlying security's price to rise (for a call buyer) or to fall (for a put buyer) — that is, to compensate the option buyer for any time value paid — and, therefore, the probability of a favorable price movement decreases. Consequently, for American options, as the time remaining until expiration decreases, the option price approaches its intrinsic value.

***Expected Interest Volatility Over the Life of the Option.*** All other factors equal, the greater the expected interest rate volatility (as measured by the standard deviation or variance) of the interest rate, the more an investor would be willing to pay for the option, and the more an option writer would demand for it. This is because the greater the expected volatility, the greater the probability that the price of the underlying security will move in favor of the option buyer at some time before expiration.

***Short-term Risk-Free Interest Rate Over the Life of the Option.*** Buying the underlying security ties up one's money. Buying an option on the same quantity of the underlying security makes the difference between the security price and the option price available for investment at the risk-free rate. All other factors constant, the higher the short-term risk-free interest rate, the greater the cost of buying the underlying security and carrying it to the expiration date of the call option. Hence, the higher the short-term risk-free interest rate, the more attractive the call option will be relative to the direct purchase of the underlying security. As a result, the higher the short-term risk-free interest rate, the greater the price of a call option.

***Coupon Payments Over the Life of the Option.*** Coupon interest payments on the underlying security tend to decrease the price of a call option because they make it more attractive to hold the underlying security than to hold the option. For put options, coupon interest payments on the underlying security tend to increase their price.

## VALUATION METHODOLOGIES

There are two main approaches to the valuation of bonds with embedded options. These are:

1. the binomial lattice method, or simply, binomial method, and

2. the Monte Carlo simulation method, or simply, Monte Carlo method.

There are two things that are common to both methods. First, each begins with an assumption as to the statistical process that is assumed to generate the term structure of interest rates. Second, each method is based on the principle that arbitrage profits cannot be generated.

In the next two chapters, we discuss each method. For now, here is a quick overview. In the binomial method, an interest rate tree is "grown." The tree is then used to determine whether the embedded option will be exercised at a node and what the value will be at each node. In the Monte Carlo simulation method, interest rate paths are generated. On each interest rate path, a cash flow is determined taking into consideration the possible exercise of the embedded option. The present value of the cash flow on each interest rate path is then calculated. The average of the present value over all the interest rate paths is the value of the bond.

## Option-Adjusted Spread

What an investor seeks to do is to buy securities whose value is greater than their market price. A valuation model such as the two described above allows an investor to estimate the value of a security, which at this point would be sufficient to determine the fairness of the price of the security. That is, the investor can say that this bond is 1 point cheap or 2 points cheap, and so on.

A valuation model need not stop here, however. Instead, it can convert the divergence between the price observed in the market for the security and the value derived from the model into a yield spread measure. This step is necessary since most market participants find it more convenient to think about yield spread than about price differences.

The *option-adjusted spread* (OAS) was developed as a measure of the yield spread that can be used to convert dollar differences between value and price. Thus, basically, the OAS is used to reconcile value with market price. But what is it a "spread" over? As we shall see when we describe the two valuation methodologies, the OAS is a spread over the issuer's spot rate curve or benchmark. The spot rate curve itself is not a single curve, but a series of spot rate curves that allow for changes in forward rates.

The reason that the resulting spread is referred to as "option-adjusted" is because the cash flows of the security whose value we seek are adjusted to reflect any embedded options. In contrast, the static spread does not consider how the cash flows will change when interest rates change in the future. That is, the static spread assumes that interest rate volatility is zero. Consequently, the static spread is also referred to as the *zero volatility OAS*.

While the product of a valuation model is the OAS, the process can be worked in reverse. For a specified OAS, the valuation model can determine the theoretical value of the security that is consistent with that OAS. This is depicted in Exhibit 4.

## Option Cost

The implied cost of the option embedded in any security can be obtained by calculating the difference between the OAS at the assumed volatility of interest rates and the static spread. That is,

$$\text{Option cost} = \text{Static spread} - \text{Option-adjusted spread}$$

## Exhibit 4: Bond Valuation Model and OAS

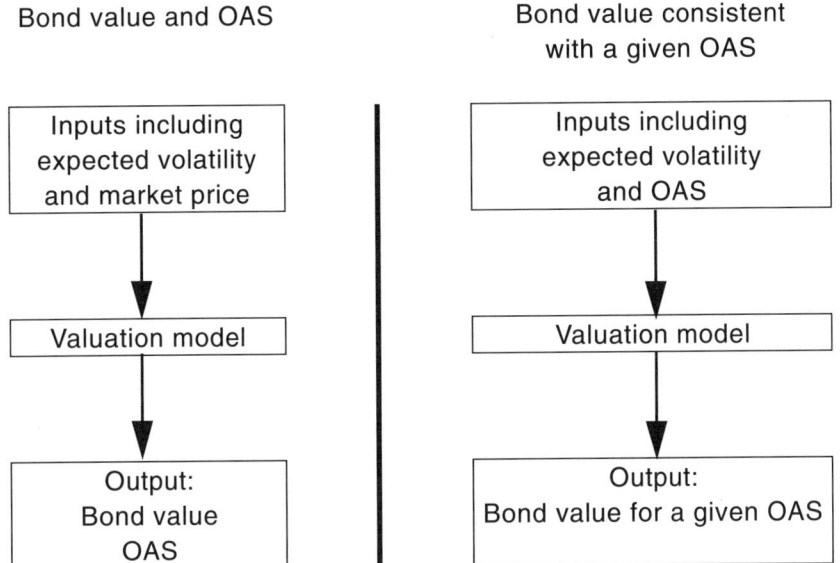

The reason that the option cost is measured in this way is as follows. In an environment of no interest rate changes, the investor would earn the static spread. When future interest rates are uncertain, the spread is different because of any embedded option; the OAS reflects the spread after adjusting for this option. Therefore, the option cost is the difference between the spread that would be earned in a static interest rate environment (the static spread, or equivalently, the zero volatility OAS) and the spread after adjusting for any embedded option (the OAS).

For callable bonds and mortgage passthrough securities, the option cost is positive. This is because the borrower's ability to alter the cash flow will result in an OAS that is less than the static spread. In the case of a putable bond, the OAS is greater than the static spread so that the option cost is negative. This occurs because of the investor's ability to alter the cash flow.

In general, when the option cost is positive, this means that the investor has sold or is short an option. This is true for callable bonds and mortgage passthrough securities. A negative value for the option cost means that the investor has purchased or is long an option. A putable bond is an example of this negative option cost. There are certain securities in the mortgage-backed securities market that also have an option cost that is negative.

The relationships are summarized below:

| Sign of option cost | Interpretation |
|---|---|
| Positive | Investor has sold or is short an option |
| Negative | Investor has purchased or is long an option |

While the option cost as described above is measured in basis points, it can be translated into a dollar price.

## Modeling Risk

The user of any valuation model is exposed to *modeling risk*. This is the risk that the output of the model is incorrect because the assumptions upon which it is based are incorrect. Consequently, it is imperative that the results of a valuation model be stress-tested for modeling risk by altering the assumptions.

## KEY POINTS

Here are the key points of this chapter:

1. It is necessary to have a framework for the analysis of bonds with embedded options.

2. The potential investor in a callable bond must be compensated for the risk that the issuer will call the bond prior to the stated maturity date.

3. The two risks faced by a potential investor are reinvestment risk and truncated price appreciation when yields decline (that is, negative convexity).

4. The traditional methodology for valuing bonds with embedded options relies on the yield to worst.

5. One drawback of the traditional methodology is that it assumes a static environment for interest rates in the future and is therefore referred to as a static valuation methodology.

6. Another drawback of the traditional methodology is that it fails to recognize the term structure of interest rates.

7. To value a bond with an embedded option it is necessary to understand that the bond can be decomposed into an option-free component and an option component.

8. Because of the embedded option component, it is necessary to understand what factors affect the value of an option.

9. The value of an option can be decomposed into intrinsic value and time value.

10. The six factors that affect the value of an option are the current price of the underlying security, strike price, time to expiration of the option, expected interest rate volatility over the

*life of the option, short-term risk-free interest rate over the life of the option, and coupon interest payment over the life of the option.*

11. There are two valuation methodologies that are being used today to value bonds with embedded options: the binomial lattice model and the Monte Carlo simulation model.

12. The two methodologies seek to determine the fair or theoretical value of the bond.

13. The option-adjusted spread (OAS) converts the cheapness or richness of a bond into a spread over the future possible spot rate curves.

14. The spread is option adjusted because it allows for future interest rate volatility to affect the cash flows.

15. The cost of the embedded option is measured as the difference between the static spread and the option-adjusted spread.

16. The static spread is also referred to as the zero volatility OAS.

17. The user of a valuation model is exposed to modeling risk and should test the sensitivity of the model to alternative assumptions.

# 6

# BINOMIAL METHOD

The binomial method is a popular technique for valuing not only callable and putable bonds but also options on bonds and swaptions. Our focus in this chapter is the application of the binomial method to value callable and putable bonds.

> **The objectives of this chapter are to:**
>
> 1. explain what is meant by a binomial interest rate tree;
>
> 2. explain how a binomial interest rate tree is constructed to be consistent with the prices for the on-the-run issues of an issuer and a given volatility assumption;
>
> 3. demonstrate how a binomial interest rate tree can be used to value an option-free bond and a bond with an embedded option;
>
> 4. explain how the value of the embedded option is determined;
>
> 5. explain how the option-adjusted spread is calculated using the binomial method; and,
>
> 6. show how effective duration and effective convexity are calculated using the binomial method.

## VALUING OPTION-FREE BONDS: A REVIEW

To illustrate this, we start with the on-the-run yield curve for the particular issuer whose bonds we want to value. The starting point is the Treasury's on-the-run yield curve. To obtain a particular issuer's on-the-run yield curve, an appropriate credit spread is added to each on-the-run Treasury issue. The credit spread need not be constant for all maturities. For example, the credit spread may increase with maturity.

In our illustration, we use the following hypothetical on-the-run issue for an issuer:

| Maturity | Yield to maturity | Market Price |
|---|---|---|
| 1 year | 3.5% | 100 |
| 2 years | 4.2% | 100 |
| 3 years | 4.7% | 100 |
| 4 years | 5.2% | 100 |

Each bond is trading at par value (100) so the coupon rate is equal to the yield to maturity. We will simplify the illustration by assuming annual-pay bonds.

Using the bootstrapping methodology explained in Chapter 2, the spot rates are given below:

| Year | Spot Rate |
|---|---|
| 1 | 3.5000% |
| 2 | 4.2147% |
| 3 | 4.7345% |
| 4 | 5.2707% |

The corresponding one-year forward rates are:

| | |
|---|---|
| Current one-year forward rate | 3.500% |
| One-year forward rate one year from now | 4.935% |
| One-year forward rate two years from now | 5.784% |
| One-year forward rate three years from now | 6.893% |

Now consider an option-free bond with three years remaining to maturity and a coupon rate of 6.5%. The value of this bond can be calculated in one of two ways, both producing the same value. First, the cash flow can be discounted at the spot rates as shown below:

$$\frac{\$6.5}{(1.035)^1} + \frac{\$6.5}{(1.042147)^2} + \frac{\$6.5}{(1.047345)^3} + \frac{\$100 + \$6.5}{(1.052707)^4} = \$104.643$$

The second way is to discount by the one-year forward rates as shown below:

$$\frac{\$6.5}{(1.035)} + \frac{\$6.5}{(1.035)(1.04935)} + \frac{\$6.5}{(1.035)(1.04935)(1.05784)} +$$
$$\frac{\$100 + \$6.5}{(1.035)(1.04935)(1.05784)(1.06893)} = \$104.643$$

## INTRODUCING INTEREST RATE VOLATILITY

Once we allow for embedded options, consideration must be given to interest rate volatility. This can be done by introducing a *binomial interest rate tree*. This tree is nothing more than a graphical depiction of the one-period or short rates over time based on some assumption about interest rate volatility. How this tree is constructed is illustrated next.

## BINOMIAL INTEREST RATE TREE[1]

Exhibit 1 shows an example of a binomial interest rate tree. In this tree, each node (bold circle) represents a time period that is equal to one year from the node to its left. Each node is labeled with an N, representing node, and a subscript that indicates the path that the one-year rate took to get to that node. L represents the lower of the two one-year rates and H represents the higher of the two one-year rates. For example, node $N_{HH}$ means to get to that node the following path for one-year rates occurred: the one-year rate realized is the higher of the two rates in the first year and then the higher of the one-year rates in the second year.[2]

---

[1] The model described in this chapter was presented in Andrew J. Kalotay, George O. Williams, and Frank J. Fabozzi, "A Model for the Valuation of Bonds and Embedded Options," *Financial Analysts Journal* (May-June 1993), pp. 35-46.

[2] Note that NHL is equivalent to NLH in the second year and that in the third year NHHL is equivalent to NHLH and NLHH and that NHLL is equivalent to NLLH. We have simply selected one label for a node rather than clutter up the figure with unnecessary information.

## Exhibit 1: Four-Year Binomial Interest Rate Tree

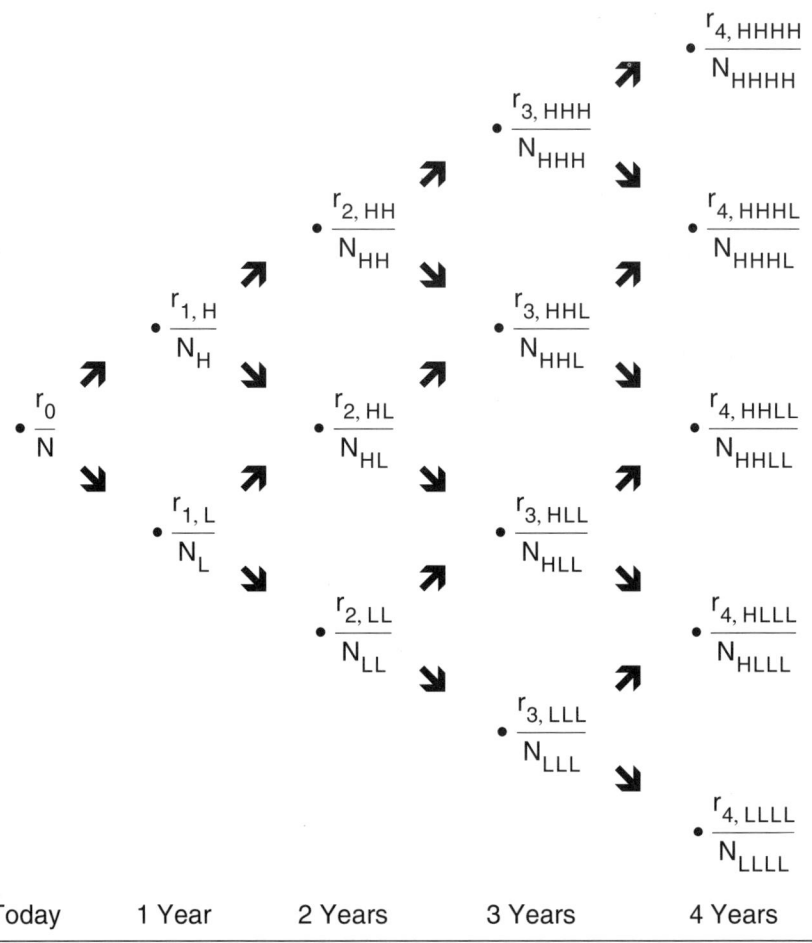

| Today | 1 Year | 2 Years | 3 Years | 4 Years |

Look first at the point denoted by just N in Exhibit 1. This is the root of the tree and is nothing more than the current one-year spot rate, or equivalently the current one-year rate, which we denote by $r_0$. What we have assumed in creating this tree is that the one-year rate can take on two possible values the next period and the two rates have the same probability of occurring. One rate will be higher than the other. It is assumed that the one-year rate can evolve over time based on a random process called a lognormal random walk with a certain volatility.

We use the following notation to describe the tree in the first year.

# Chapter 6

Let

$\sigma$ = assumed volatility of the one-year rate
$r_{1,L}$ = the lower one-year rate one year from now
$r_{1,H}$ = the higher one-year rate one year from now

The relationship between $r_{1,L}$ and $r_{1,H}$ is as follows:

$$r_{1,H} = r_{1,L}(e^{2\sigma})$$

where e is the base of the natural logarithm 2.71828.

For example, suppose that $r_{1,L}$ is 4.4448% and $\sigma$ is 10% per year, then:

$$r_{1,H} = 4.4448\% \, (e^{2 \times 0.10}) = 5.4289\%$$

In the second year, there are three possible values for the one-year rate, which we will denote as follows:

$r_{2,LL}$ = one-year rate in second year assuming the lower rate in the first year and the lower rate in the second year
$r_{2,HH}$ = one-year rate in second year assuming the higher rate in the first year and the higher rate in the second year
$r_{2,HL}$ = one-year rate in second year assuming the higher rate in the first year and the lower rate in the second year or equivalently the lower rate in the first year and the higher rate in the second year.

The relationship between $r_{2,LL}$ and the other two one-year rates is as follows:

$$r_{2,HH} = r_{2,LL}(e^{4\sigma}) \text{ and } r_{2,HL} = r_{2,LL}(e^{2\sigma})$$

So, for example, if $r_{2,LL}$ is 4.6958%, then assuming once again that $\sigma$ is 10%, then

$$r_{2,HH} = 4.6958\% \, (e^{4 \times 0.10}) = 7.0053\%$$

and $r_{2,HL} = 4.6958\% \, (e^{2 \times 0.10}) = 5.7354\%$

In the third year there are four possible values for the one-year rate, which are denoted as follows: $r_{3,HHH}$, $r_{3,HHL}$, $r_{3,HLL}$, and $r_{3,LLL}$, and whose first three values are related to the last as follows:

$$r_{3,HHH} = (e^{6\sigma}) \, r_{3,LLL}$$
$$r_{3,HHL} = (e^{4\sigma}) \, r_{3,LLL}$$
$$r_{3,HLL} = (e^{2\sigma}) \, r_{3,LLL}$$

Exhibit 1 shows the notation for a 4-year binomial interest rate tree. We can simplify the notation by letting $r_t$ be the one-year rate t years from now for the lower rate since all the other short rates t years from now depend on that rate. Exhibit 2 shows the interest rate tree using this simplified notation.

Before we go on to show how to use this binomial interest rate tree to value bonds, let's focus on two issues here. First, what does the volatility parameter σ represent? Second, how do we find the value of the bond at each node?

## Volatility and the Standard Deviation

It can be shown that the standard deviation of the one-year rate is equal to $r_0\sigma$.[3] The standard deviation is a statistical measure of volatility. It is important to see that the process that we assumed generates the binomial interest rate tree (or equivalently the short rates), implies that volatility is measured relative to the current level of rates. For example, if σ is 10% and the one-year rate ($r_0$) is 4%, then the standard deviation of the one-year rate is 4% x 10% =.4% or 40 basis points. However, if the current one-year rate is 12%, the standard deviation of the one-year rate would be 12% x 10% or 120 basis points.

---

[3] This can be seen by noting that $e^{2\sigma} \cong 1 + 2\sigma$. Then the standard deviation of one-period rate is $\dfrac{re^{2\sigma} - r}{2} \cong \dfrac{r + 2\sigma r - r}{2} = \sigma r$.

## Exhibit 2: Four-Year Binomial Interest Rate Tree with One-Year Rates*

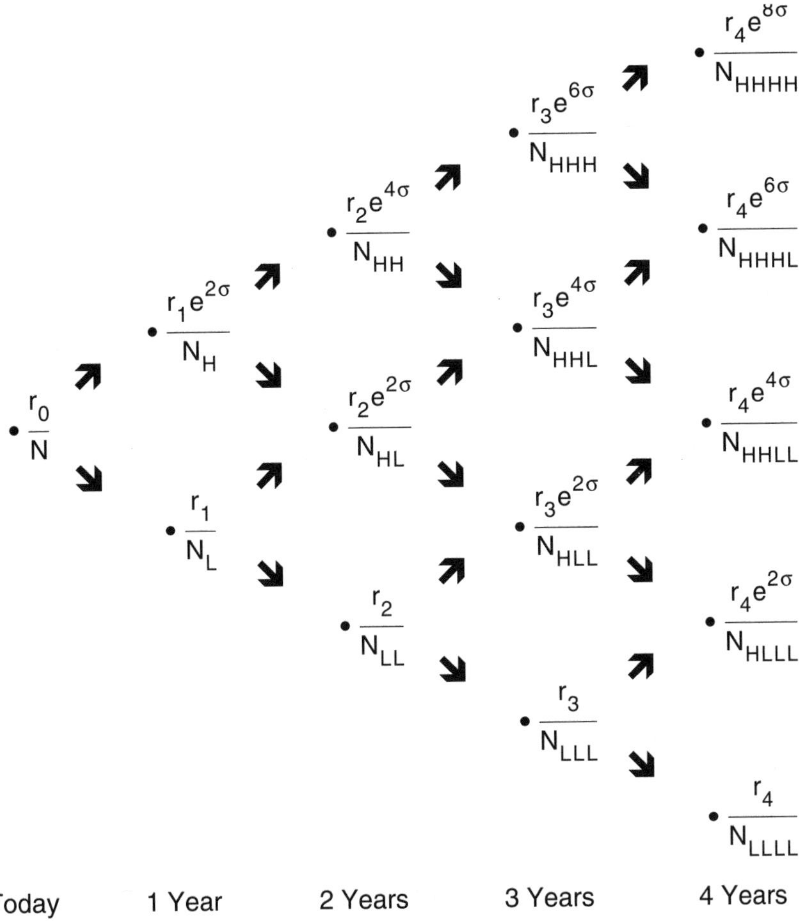

$$\begin{array}{c} \cdot \dfrac{r_4 e^{8\sigma}}{N_{HHHH}} \\ \cdot \dfrac{r_3 e^{6\sigma}}{N_{HHH}} \\ \cdot \dfrac{r_2 e^{4\sigma}}{N_{HH}} \qquad \cdot \dfrac{r_4 e^{6\sigma}}{N_{HHHL}} \\ \cdot \dfrac{r_1 e^{2\sigma}}{N_{H}} \qquad \cdot \dfrac{r_3 e^{4\sigma}}{N_{HHL}} \\ \cdot \dfrac{r_0}{N} \qquad \cdot \dfrac{r_2 e^{2\sigma}}{N_{HL}} \qquad \cdot \dfrac{r_4 e^{4\sigma}}{N_{HHLL}} \\ \cdot \dfrac{r_1}{N_L} \qquad \cdot \dfrac{r_3 e^{2\sigma}}{N_{HLL}} \\ \cdot \dfrac{r_2}{N_{LL}} \qquad \cdot \dfrac{r_4 e^{2\sigma}}{N_{HLLL}} \\ \cdot \dfrac{r_3}{N_{LLL}} \\ \cdot \dfrac{r_4}{N_{LLLL}} \end{array}$$

| Today | 1 Year | 2 Years | 3 Years | 4 Years |

\* $r_t$ equals forward one-year lower rate.

## Determining the Value at a Node

To find the value of the bond at a node, we first calculate the bond's value at the two nodes to the right of the node we are interested in. For example, in Exhibit 2, suppose we want to determine the bond's value at node $N_H$. The bond's value at node $N_{HH}$ and $N_{HL}$ must be determined. Hold aside for now how we get these two values because as we will see the process involves starting from the last year in the tree and working backwards to get the final solution we want, so these two values will be known.

# 116    BINOMIAL METHOD

Effectively what we are saying is that if we are at some node, then the value at that node will depend on the future cash flows. In turn, the future cash flows depend on (1) the bond's value one year from now and (2) the coupon payment one year from now. The latter is known. The former depends on whether the one-year rate is the higher or lower rate. The bond's value depending on whether the rate is the higher or lower rate is reported at the two nodes to the right of the node that is the focus of our attention. So, the cash flow at a node will be either (1) the bond's value if the short rate is the higher rate plus the coupon payment, or (2) the bond's value if the short rate is the lower rate plus the coupon payment. For example, suppose that we are interested in the bond's value at $N_H$. The cash flow will be either the bond's value at $N_{HH}$ plus the coupon payment, or the bond's value at $N_{HL}$ plus the coupon payment.

To get the bond's value at a node we follow the fundamental rule for valuation: the value is the present value of the expected cash flows. The appropriate discount rate to use is the one-year rate at the node. Now there are two present values in this case: the present value if the one-year rate is the higher rate and one if it is the lower rate. Since it is assumed that the probability of both outcomes is equal, an average of the two present values is computed. This is illustrated in Exhibit 3 for any node assuming that the one-year rate is $r_*$ at the node where the valuation is sought and letting:

$V_H$ = the bond's value for the higher one-year rate
$V_L$ = the bond's value for the lower one-year rate
$C$ = coupon payment

Using our notation, the cash flow at a node is either:

$V_H + C$ for the higher one-year rate
$V_L + C$ for the lower one-year rate

The present value of these two cash flows using the one-year rate at the node, $r_*$, is:

$$\frac{V_H + C}{(1 + r_*)} = \text{present value for the higher one-year rate}$$

## Exhibit 3: Calculating a Value at a Node

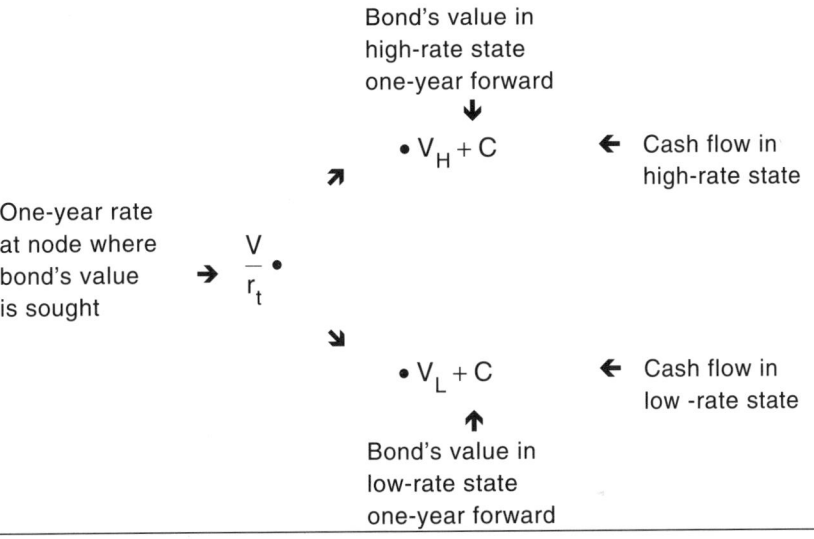

$$\frac{V_L + C}{(1 + r_*)} = \text{present value for the lower one-year rate}$$

Then, the value of the bond at the node is found as follows:

$$\text{Value at a node} = \frac{1}{2}\left[\frac{V_H + C}{(1 + r_*)} + \frac{V_L + C}{(1 + r_*)}\right]$$

## CONSTRUCTING THE BINOMIAL INTEREST RATE TREE

To see how to construct the binomial interest rate tree, let's use the assumed on-the-run yields we used earlier. We will assume that volatility, $\sigma$, is 10% and construct a two-year tree using the two-year bond with a coupon rate of 4.2%.

Exhibit 4 shows a more detailed binomial interest rate tree with the cash flow shown at each node. We'll see how all the values reported in the exhibit are obtained. The root rate for the tree, $r_0$, is simply the current one-year rate, 3.5%.

## Exhibit 4: The One-Year Rates for Year 1 Using the Two-Year 4.2% On-the-Run Issue: First Trial

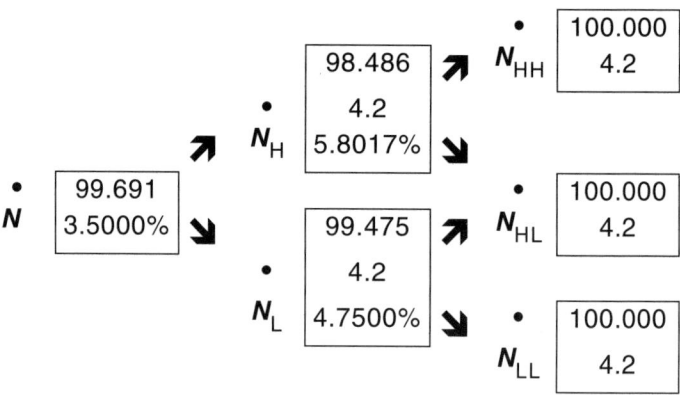

In the first year there are two possible one-year rates, the higher rate and the lower rate. What we want to find is the two one-year rates that will be consistent with the volatility assumption, the process that is assumed to generate the short rates, and the observed market value of the bond. There is no simple formula for this. It must be found by an iterative process (i.e., trial-and-error). The steps are described and illustrated below.

**Step 1:** Select a value for $r_1$. Recall that $r_1$ is the lower one-year rate. In this first trial, we *arbitrarily* selected a value of 4.75%.

**Step 2:** Determine the corresponding value for the higher one-year rate. As explained earlier, this rate is related to the lower one-year rate as follows: $r_1 e^{2\sigma}$. Since $r_1$ is 4.75%, the higher one-year rate is 5.8017% (= 4.75% $e^{2 \times .10}$). This value is reported in Exhibit 4 at node $N_H$.

**Step 3:** Compute the bond value's one year from now. This value is determined as follows:

    3a. Determine the bond's value two years from now. In our example, this is simple. Since we are using a two-year bond, the bond's value is its maturity value ($100) plus its final coupon payment ($4.2). Thus, it is $104.2.

    3b. Calculate the present value of the bond's value found in 3a for the higher rate in the second year. The appropriate discount rate is the higher one-year rate, 5.8017% in our example. The present value is $98.456 (= $104.2/1.058017)$. This is the value of $V_H$ that we referred to earlier.

3c. Calculate the present value of the bond's value assumed in 3a for the lower rate. The discount rate assumed for the lower one-year rate is 4.75%. The present value is $99.475 (= $104.2/1.0475)$ and is the value of $V_L$.

3d. Add the coupon to both $V_H$ and $V_L$ to get the cash flow at $N_H$ and $N_L$, respectively. In our example we have $102.686 for the higher rate and $103.675 for the lower rate.

3e. Calculate the present value of the two values using the one-year rate $r_*$. At this point in the valuation, $r_*$ is the root rate, 3.50%. Therefore,

$$\frac{V_H + C}{1 + r_*} = \frac{\$102.686}{1.035} = \$99.213$$

and

$$\frac{V_L + C}{1 + r_*} = \frac{\$103.675}{1.035} = \$100.169$$

**Step 4:** Calculate the average present value of the two cash flows in Step 3. This is the value we referred to earlier as

$$\text{Value at a node} = \frac{1}{2}\left[\frac{V_H + C}{(1+r_*)} + \frac{V_L + C}{(1+r_*)}\right]$$

In our example, we have

$$\text{Value at a node} = \frac{1}{2}[\$99.213 + \$100.169] = \$99.691$$

**Step 5:** Compare the value in Step 4 to the bond's market value. If the two values are the same, then the $r_1$ used in this trial is the one we seek. This is the one-year rate that would then be used in the binomial interest rate tree for the lower rate and the corresponding higher rate. If, instead, the value found in step 4 is not equal to the market value of the bond, this means that the value $r_1$ in this trial is not the one-year rate that is consistent with (1) the volatility assumption, (2) the process assumed to generate the one-year rate, and (3) the observed market value of the bond. In this case, the five steps are repeated with a different value for $r_1$.

When $r_1$ is 4.75%, a value of $99.691 results in Step 4 which is less than the observed market price of $100. Therefore, 4.75% is too large and the five steps must be repeated trying a lower rate for $r_1$.

Let's jump right to the correct rate for $r_1$ in this example and rework steps 1 through 5. This occurs when $r_1$ is 4.4448%. The corresponding binomial interest rate tree is shown in Exhibit 5.

**Step 1:** In this trial we select a value of 4.4448% for $r_1$, the lower one-year rate.
**Step 2:** The corresponding value for the higher one-year rate is 5.4289% ($= 4.4448\% \ e^{2 \times .10}$).
**Step 3:** The bond's value one year from now is determined as follows:
  3a. The bond's value two years from now is $104.2, just as in the first trial.
  3b. The present value of the bond's value found in 3a for the higher one-year rate, $V_H$, is $98.834 (= $104.2/1.054289).
  3c. The present value of the bond's value found in 3a for the lower one-year rate, $V_L$, is $99.766 (= $104.2/1.044448).
  3d. Adding the coupon to $V_H$ and $V_L$, we get $103.034 as the cash flow for the higher rate and $103.966 as the cash flow for the lower rate.
  3e. The present value of the two cash flows using the one-year rate at the node to the left, 3.5%, gives

$$\frac{V_H + C}{1 + r_*} = \frac{\$103.034}{1.035} = \$99.550$$

and,

$$\frac{V_L + C}{1 + r_*} = \frac{\$103.966}{1.035} = \$100.450$$

**Step 4:** The average present value is $100, which is the value at the node.
**Step 5:** Since the average present value is equal to the observed market price of $100, $r_1$ or $r_{1,L}$ is 4.4448% and $r_{1,H}$ is 5.4289%.

## Exhibit 5: The One-Year Rates for Year 1 Using the Two-Year 4.2% On-the-Run Issue

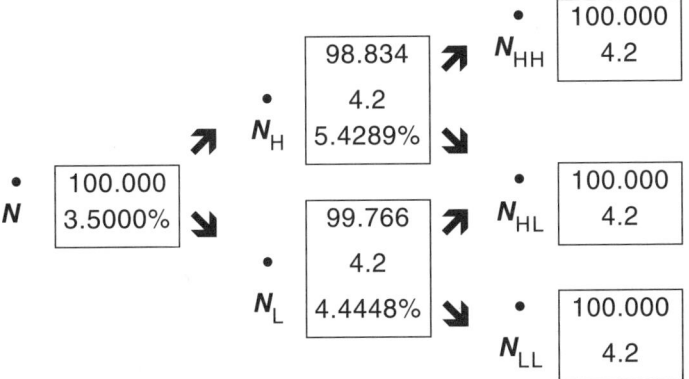

We can "grow" this tree for one more year by determining $r_2$. Now we will use the three-year on-the-run issue, the 4.7% coupon bond, to get $r_2$. The same five steps are used in an iterative process to find the one-year rates in the tree two years from now. Our objective is now to find the value of $r_2$ that will produce a bond value of $100 (since the three-year on-the-run issue has a market price of $100) and is consistent with (1) a volatility assumption of 10%, (2) a current one-year rate of 3.5%, and (3) the two rates one year from now of 4.4448% (the lower rate) and 5.4289%(the higher rate).

We explain how this is done using Exhibit 6. Let's look at how we get the information in the exhibit. The maturity value and coupon payment are shown in the boxes at the four nodes three years from now. Since the three-year on-the-run issue has a maturity value of $100 and a coupon payment of $4.7, these values are the same in the box shown at each node. For the three nodes two years from now the coupon payment of $4.7 is shown. Unknown at these three nodes are (1) the three rates two years from now and (2) the value of the bond two years from now. For the two nodes one year from now, the coupon payment is known, as are the one-year rates one year from now. These are the rates found earlier. The value of the bond, which depends on the bond values at the nodes to the right, are unknown at these two nodes. All of the unknown values are indicated by a question mark.

## Exhibit 6: Information for Deriving the One-Year Rates for Year 2 Using the Three-Year 4.7% On-the-Run Issue

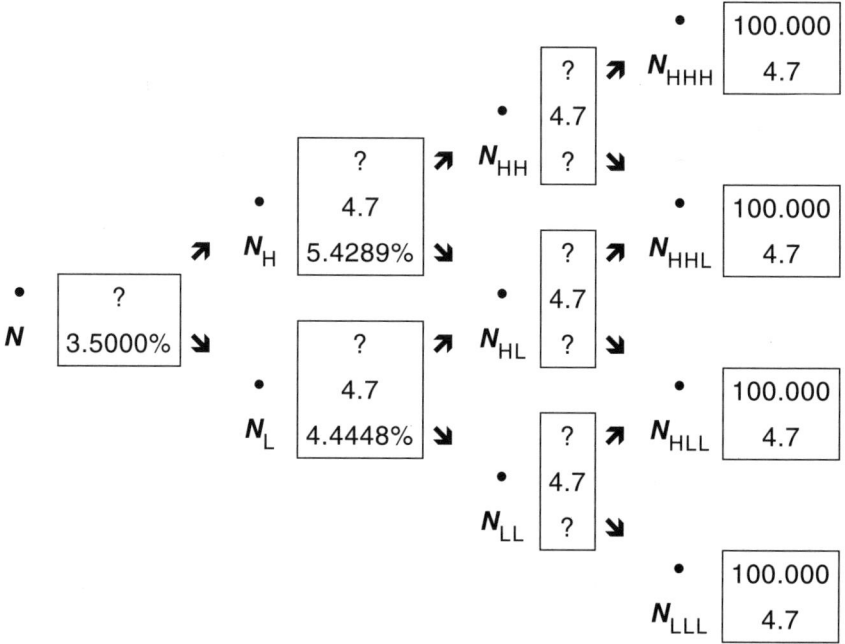

Exhibit 7 is the same as Exhibit 6 complete with the values previously unknown. As can be seen from Exhibit 7, the value of $r_2$, or equivalently $r_{2,LL}$, which will produce the desired result is 4.6958%. We showed earlier that the corresponding rates $r_{2,HL}$ and $r_{2,HH}$ would be 5.7354% and 7.0053%, respectively. To verify that these are the one-year rates two years from now, work backwards from the four nodes at the right of the tree in Exhibit 7. For example, the value in the box at $N_{HH}$ is found by taking the value of $104.7 at the two nodes to its right and discounting at 7.0053%. The value is $97.846. (Since it is the same value for both nodes to the right, it is also the average value.) Similarly, the value in the box at $N_{HL}$ is found by discounting $104.70 by 5.7354% and at $N_{LL}$ by discounting at 4.6958%. The same procedure used in Exhibits 4 and 5 is used to get the values at the other nodes.

## Exhibit 7: The One-Year Rates for Year 2 Using the Three-Year 4.5% On-the-Run Issue

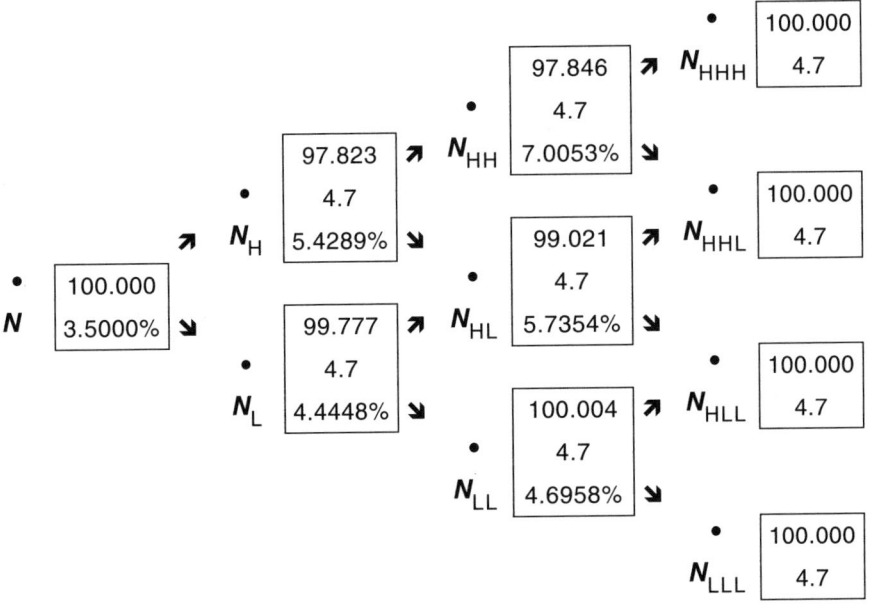

## VALUING AN OPTION-FREE BOND WITH THE TREE

Exhibit 8 shows the one-year rates or binomial interest rate tree that can then be used to value any bond for this issuer with a maturity up to four years. To illustrate how to use the binomial interest rate tree, consider a 6.5% option-free corporate bond with three years remaining to maturity. Also assume that the issuer's on-the-run yield curve is the one given earlier and hence the appropriate binomial interest rate tree is the one in Exhibit 8. Exhibit 9 shows the various values in the discounting process, and produces a bond value of $104.643.

It is important to note that this value is identical to the bond value found earlier when we discounted at either the spot rates or the one-year forward rates. We should expect to find this result since our bond is option free. This clearly demonstrates that the valuation model is consistent with the standard valuation model for an option-free bond.

## Exhibit 8: Binomial Interest Rate Tree for Valuing Up to a Four-Year Bond for Issuer
### (10% Volatility Assumed)

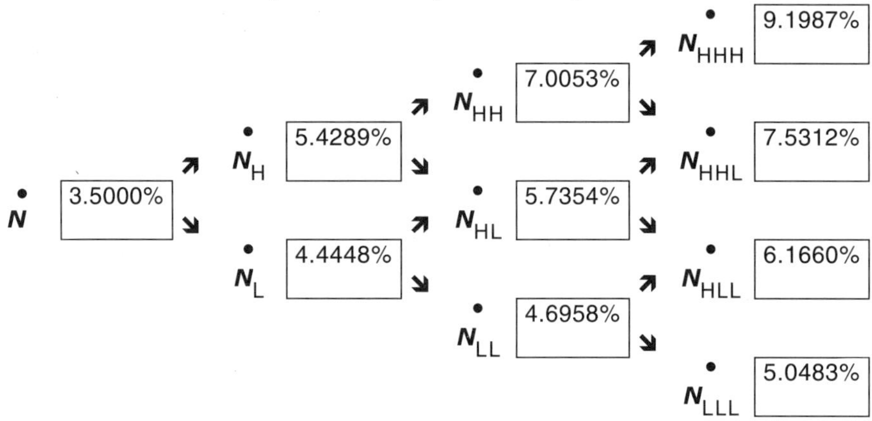

- N  3.5000%
- $N_H$  5.4289%
- $N_L$  4.4448%
- $N_{HH}$  7.0053%
- $N_{HL}$  5.7354%
- $N_{LL}$  4.6958%
- $N_{HHH}$  9.1987%
- $N_{HHL}$  7.5312%
- $N_{HLL}$  6.1660%
- $N_{LLL}$  5.0483%

## VALUING A CALLABLE CORPORATE BOND

Now we will demonstrate how the binomial interest rate tree can be applied to value a callable corporate bond. The valuation process proceeds in the same fashion as in the case of an option-free bond, but with one exception: when the call option may be exercised by the issuer, the bond value at a node must be changed to reflect the lesser of its values if it is not called (i.e., the value obtained by applying the recursive valuation formula described above) and the call price.

For example, consider a 6.5% corporate bond with four years remaining to maturity that is callable in one year at $100. Exhibit 10 shows two values at each node of the binomial interest rate tree. The discounting process explained above is used to calculate the first of the two values at each node. The second value is the value based on whether the issue will be called. For simplicity, let's assume that this issuer calls the issue if it exceeds the call price. Then, in Exhibit 10 at nodes $N_L$, $N_H$, $N_{LL}$, $N_{HL}$, $N_{LLL}$, and $N_{HLL}$, the values from the recursive valuation formula are $101.968, $100.032, $101.723, $100.270, $101.382, and $100.315. These values exceed the assumed call price ($100) and therefore the second value is $100 rather the calculated value. It is the second value that is used in subsequent calculations. The root of the tree indicates that the value for this callable bond is $102.899.

Chapter 6 125

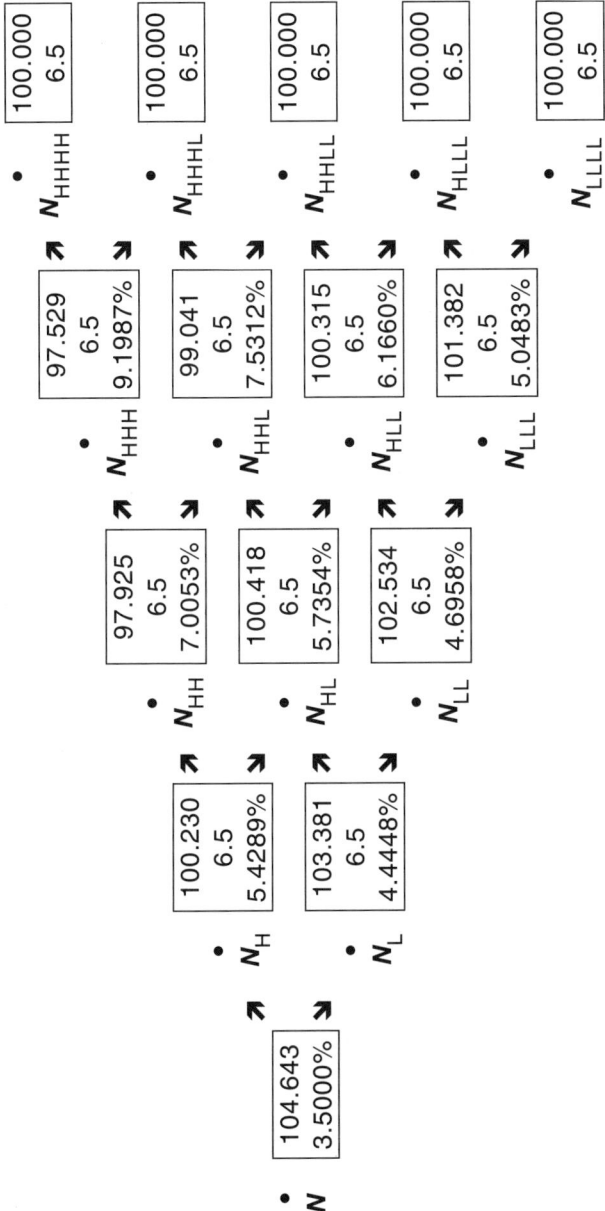

**Exhibit 9: Valuing an Option-Free Corporate Bond with Four Years to Maturity and a Coupon Rate of 6.5% (10% Volatility Assumed)**

**Exhibit 10: Valuing a Callable Corporate Bond with Four Years to Maturity, a Coupon Rate of 6.5%, and Callable in One Year at 100 (10% Volatility Assumed)**

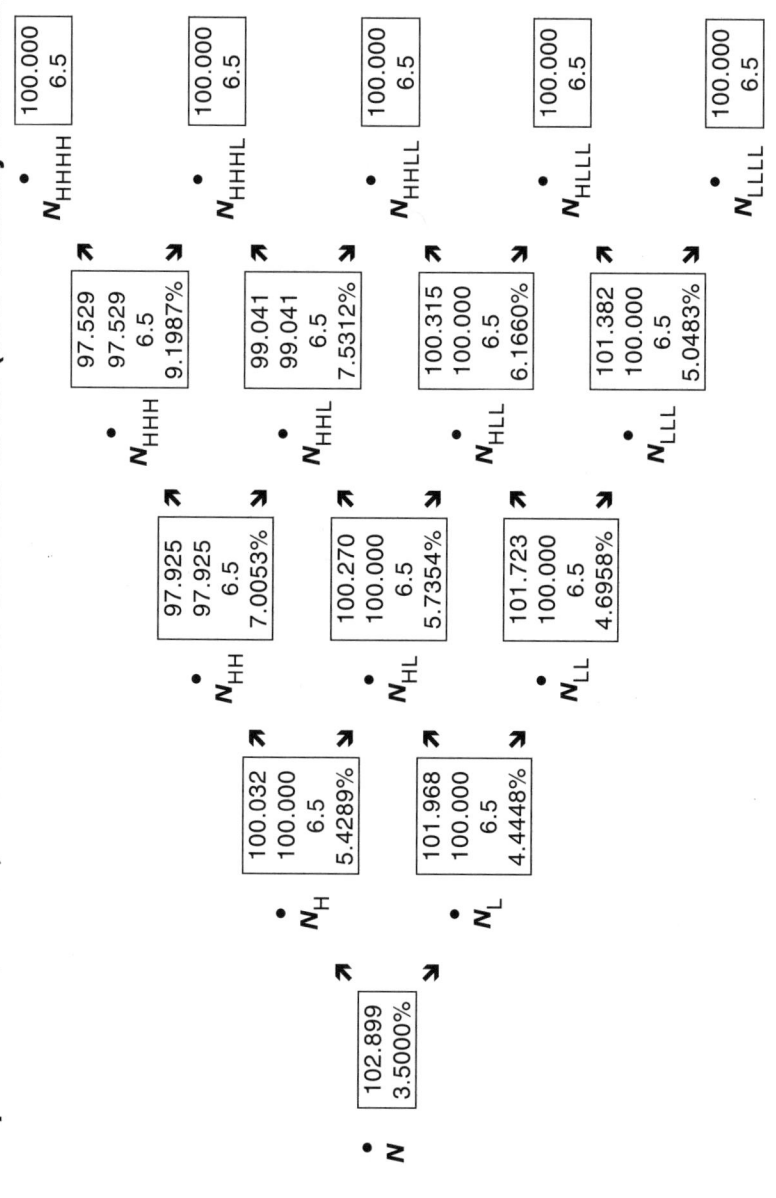

The question that we have not addressed in our illustration, which is nonetheless important, is the circumstances under which the issuer will call the bond. A detailed explanation of the call rule is beyond the scope of this chapter. Basically, it involves determining when it would be economic for the issuer on an after-tax basis to call the issue.

Suppose instead that the call price schedule is 102 in year 1, 101 in year 2, and 100 in year 3. Also assume that the bond will not be called unless it exceeds the call price for that year. Exhibit 11 shows the value at each node and the value of the callable bond. The call price schedule results in a greater value for the callable bond, $103.942 compared to $102.899 when the call price is 100 in each year.

## Determining the Call Option Value

As explained in Chapter 5, the value of a callable bond is equal to the value of an option-free bond minus the value of the call option. This means that:

Value of a call option =
Value of an option-free bond − Value of a callable bond

We have just seen how the value of an option-free bond and the value of a callable bond can be determined. The difference between the two values is therefore the value of the call option.

In our illustration, the value of the option-free bond is $104.643. If the call price is $100 in each year and the value of the callable bond is $102.899, the value of the call option is $1.744 (= $104.634 − $102.899).

## EXTENSION TO OTHER EMBEDDED OPTIONS

The bond valuation framework presented here can be used to analyze other embedded options such as put options, caps and floors on floating-rate notes, and the optional accelerated redemption granted to an issuer in fulfilling its sinking fund requirement. For example, let's consider a putable bond. Suppose that a 6.5% corporate bond with four years remaining to maturity is putable in one year at par ($100). Also assume that the appropriate binomial interest rate tree for this issuer is the one in Exhibit 8.

## Exhibit 11: Valuing a Callable Corporate Bond with Four Years to Maturity, a Coupon Rate of 6.5%, and with a Call Price Schedule (10% Volatility Assumed)

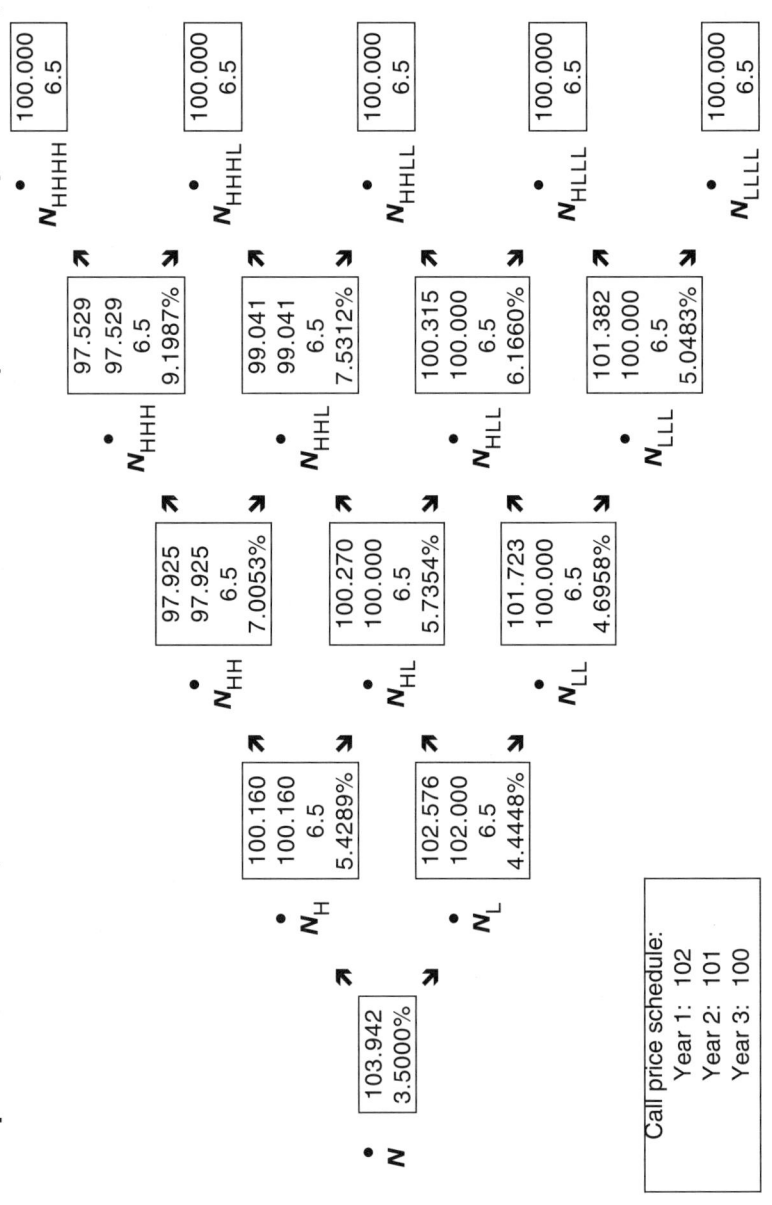

Exhibit 12 shows the binomial interest rate tree with the bond value altered at three nodes ($N_{HH}$, $N_{HHH}$, and $N_{HHL}$) because the bond value at these nodes is less than $100, the assumed value at which the bond can be put. The value of this putable bond is $105.327.

Since the value of an option-free bond can be expressed as the value of a putable bond minus the value of a put option on that bond, this means that:

Value of a put option =
Value of an option-free bond − Value of a putable bond

In our example, since the value of the putable bond is $105.327 and the value of the corresponding option-free bond is $104.643, the value of the put option is −$0.684. The negative sign indicates the issuer has sold the option, or equivalently, the investor has purchased the option.

The framework can also be used to value a bond with multiple or interrelated embedded options. The bond values on each node are altered based on whether one of the options is exercised.

## VOLATILITY AND THE THEORETICAL VALUE

In our illustration, interest rate volatility was assumed to be 10%. The volatility assumption has an important impact on the theoretical value. More specifically, the higher the expected volatility, the higher the value of an option. The same is true for an option embedded in a bond. Correspondingly, this affects the value of the bond with an embedded option.

For example, for a callable bond, a higher interest rate volatility assumption means that the value of the call option increases and, since the value of the option-free bond is not affected, the value of the callable bond must be lower. For a putable bond, higher interest rate volatility means that its value will be higher.

We will demonstrate this using the on-the-run yield curve in our previous illustrations. In the previous illustrations, we assumed interest rate volatility of 10%. To show the effect of higher volatility, we will assume volatility of 20%. Exhibit 13 gives the corresponding binomial interest rate tree. Exhibit 14 verifies that the binomial interest rate tree provides the same value for the option-free bond, $104.643.

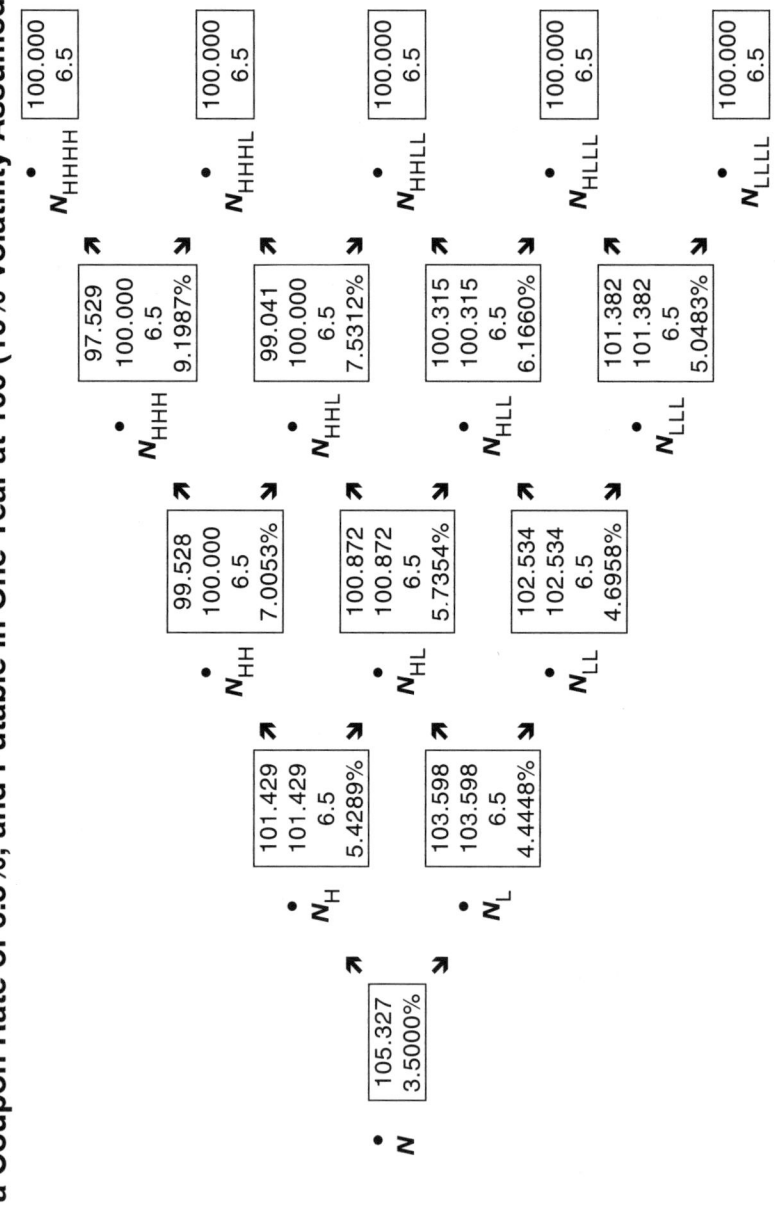

**Exhibit 12: Valuing a Putable Corporate Bond with Four Years to Maturity, a Coupon Rate of 6.5%, and Putable in One Year at 100 (10% Volatility Assumed)**

## Exhibit 13: Binomial Interest Rate Tree for Valuing Up to a Four-Year Bond for Issuer (20% Volatility Assumed)

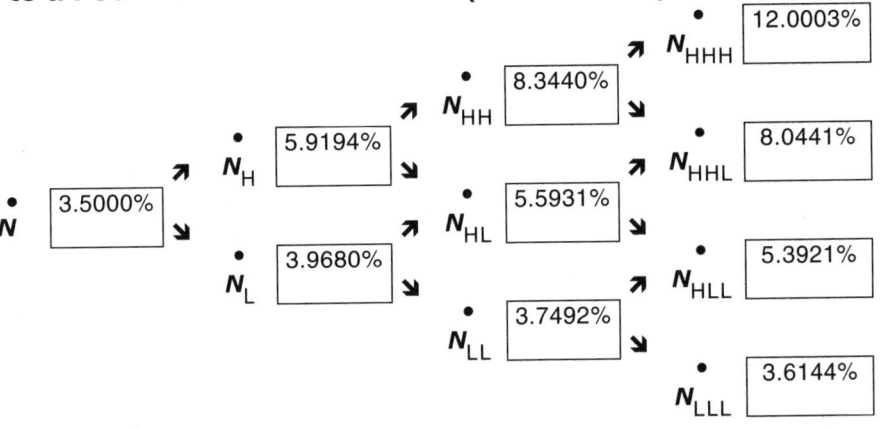

Exhibits 15 and 16 show the calculation for the callable bond and putable bond, respectively, assuming interest rate volatility of 20%. For the callable bond it is assumed that the issue is callable at par beginning in year 1. The value of the callable bond is $102.108 if volatility is assumed to be 20% compared to $102.899 if volatility is assumed to be 10%. The putable bond at 20% volatility has a value of $106.010 compared to $105.327 at 10% volatility.

In the construction of the binomial interest rate, it was assumed that volatility is the same for each year. The methodology can be extended to incorporate a term structure of volatility.

### Option-Adjusted Spread

Suppose the market price of the three-year, 6.5% callable bond is $102.218 and the theoretical value assuming 10% volatility is $102.899. This means that this bond is cheap by $0.681 according to the valuation model. As explained in the previous chapter, bond market participants prefer to think not in terms of a bond's price being cheap or expensive in dollar terms but rather in terms of a yield spread — a cheap bond trades at a higher yield spread and an expensive bond at a lower yield spread.

132  BINOMIAL METHOD

**Exhibit 14: Valuing an Option-Free Corporate Bond with Four Years to Maturity and a Coupon Rate of 6.5% (20% Volatility Assumed)**

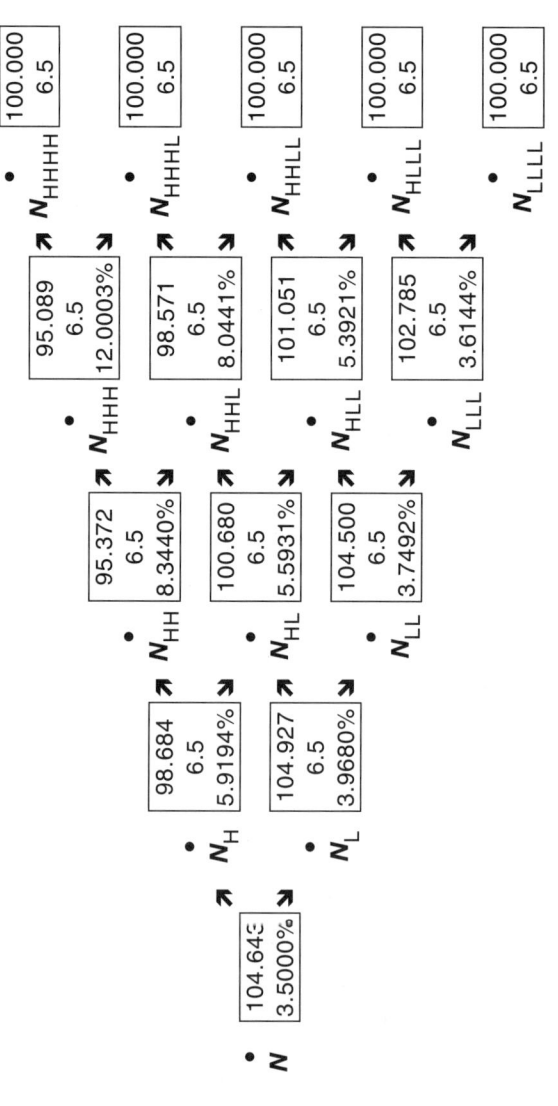

Chapter 6    133

**Exhibit 15: Valuing a Callable Corporate Bond with Four Years to Maturity, a Coupon Rate of 6.5%, and Callable in One Year at 100 (20% Volatility Assumed)**

$N_{HHHH}$ • → 100.000 / 6.5

$N_{HHH}$ • 95.089 / 95.089 / 6.5 / 12.0003%

$N_{HHHL}$ • → 100.000 / 6.5

$N_{HH}$ • 95.372 / 95.372 / 6.5 / 8.3440%

$N_{HHL}$ • 98.571 / 98.571 / 6.5 / 8.0441%

$N_{HHLL}$ • → 100.000 / 6.5

$N_H$ • 98.364 / 98.364 / 6.5 / 5.9194%

$N_{HL}$ • 100.182 / 100.000 / 6.5 / 5.5931%

$N_{HLL}$ • 101.051 / 100.000 / 6.5 / 5.3921%

$N_{HLLL}$ • → 100.000 / 6.5

$N$ • 102.108 / 3.5000%

$N_L$ • 102.435 / 100.000 / 6.5 / 3.9679%

$N_{LL}$ • 102.651 / 100.000 / 6.5 / 3.7492%

$N_{LLL}$ • 102.785 / 100.000 / 6.5 / 3.6144%

$N_{LLLL}$ • → 100.000 / 6.5

**Exhibit 16: Valuing a Putable Corporate Bond with Four Years to Maturity, a Coupon Rate of 6.5%, and Putable in One Year at 100 (20% Volatility Assumed)**

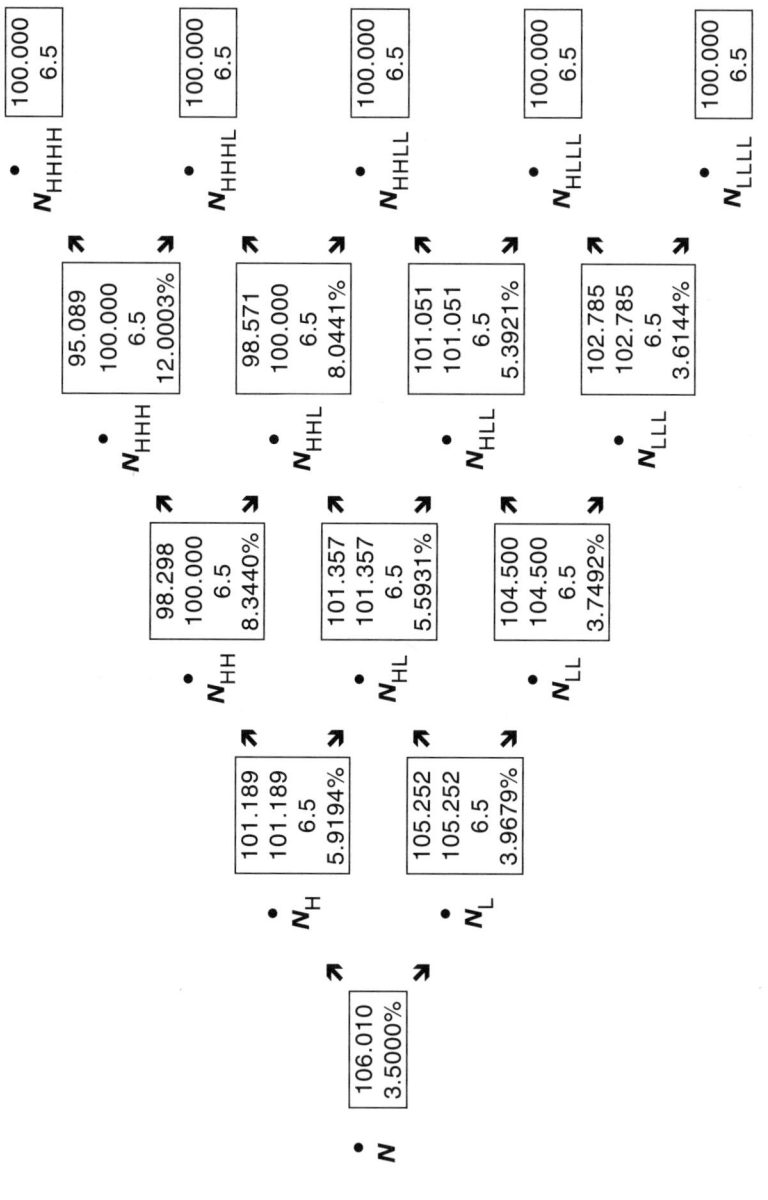

The option-adjusted spread is the constant spread that when added to all the one-year rates on the binomial interest rate tree will make the theoretical value equal to the market price. In our illustration, if the market price is $102.218, the OAS would be the constant spread added to every rate in Exhibit 8 that will make the theoretical value equal to $102.218. The solution in this case would be 35 basis points. This can be verified in Exhibit 17 which shows the value of this issue by adding 35 basis points to each rate.

As with the value of a bond with an embedded option, the OAS will depend on the volatility assumption. For a given bond price, the higher the interest rate volatility assumed, the lower the OAS for a callable bond and the higher the OAS for a putable bond. For example, if volatility is 20% rather than 10%, the OAS would be −11 basis points as can be seen from Exhibit 18.

This illustration clearly demonstrates the importance of the volatility assumption. Assuming volatility of 10%, the OAS is 35 basis points. At 20% volatility, the OAS declines and, in this case is negative and therefore overvalued.

## EFFECTIVE DURATION AND EFFECTIVE CONVEXITY

In Chapter 4, we explained that effective duration and effective convexity are the appropriate interest rate risk measures (assuming a parallel shift in the yield curve) for a bond with an embedded option. The formulas are as follows:

$$\text{Effective duration} = \frac{V_- - V_+}{2V_0(\Delta y)}$$

$$\text{Effective convexity} = \frac{V_+ + V_- - 2V_0}{2V_0(\Delta y)^2}$$

where
- $\Delta y$ = change in rate used to calculate new values
- $V_+$ = price if yield is increased by $\Delta y$
- $V_-$ = price if yield is decreased by $\Delta y$
- $V_0$ = initial price (per $100 of par value)

# BINOMIAL METHOD

**Exhibit 17: Demonstration that the Option-Adjusted Spread is 35 Basis Points For a 6.5% Callable Bond Selling at 102.218 (Assuming 10% Volatility)**

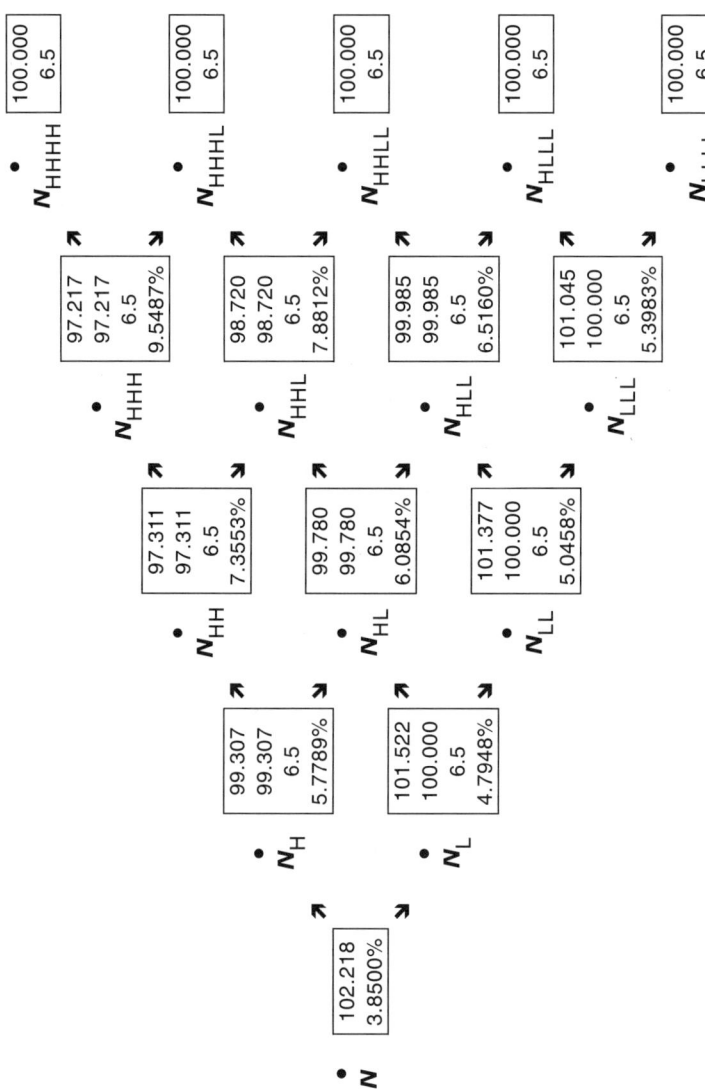

\* Each one year rate is 35 basis points greater than in Exhibit 8

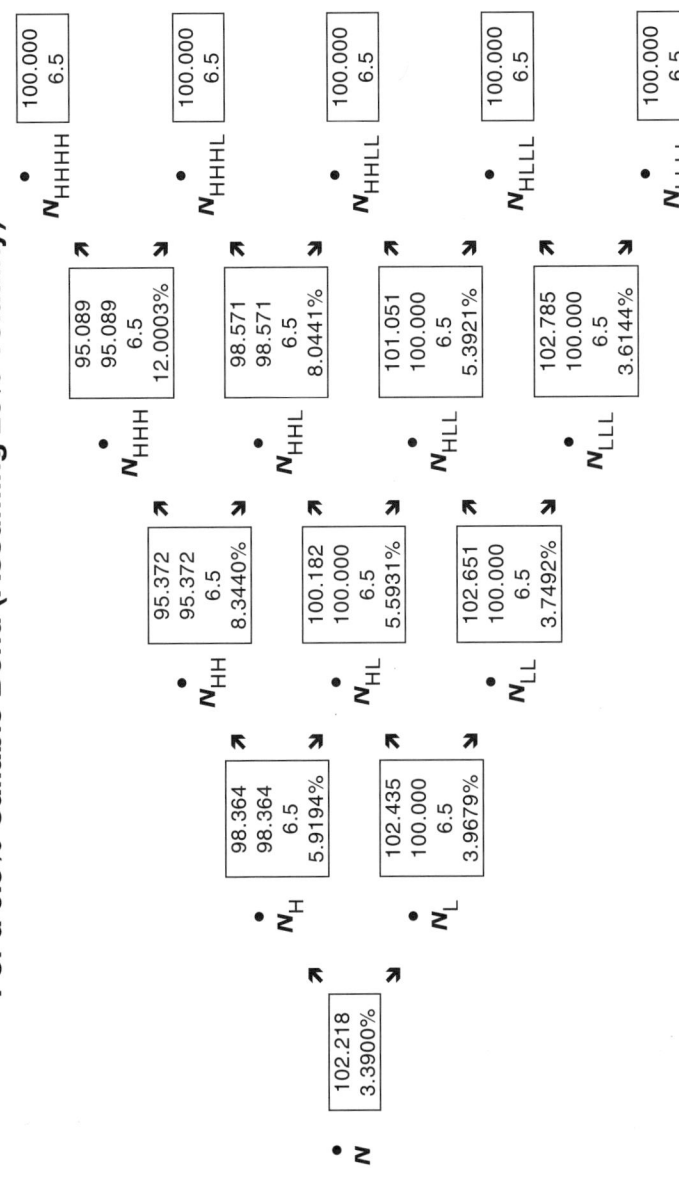

**Exhibit 18: Demonstration that the Option-Adjusted Spread is –11 Basis Points For a 6.5% Callable Bond (Assuming 20% Volatility)***

*Each one year rate is 11 basis points less than in Exhibit 13.

## 138  BINOMIAL METHOD

The procedure for calculating the value of $V_+$ to use in the formula is as follows:

***Step 1:*** Calculate the OAS for the issue.
***Step 2:*** Shift the on-the-run yield curve up by a small number of basis points ($\Delta y$).
***Step 3:*** Construct a binomial interest rate tree based on the new yield curve in Step 2.
***Step 4:*** To each of the short rates in the binomial interest rate tree, add the OAS to obtain an "adjusted tree."
***Step 5:*** Use the adjusted tree found in Step 4 to determine the value of the security, which is $V_+$.

To determine the value of $V_-$, the same five steps are followed except that in Step 2, the on-the-run yield curve is shifted down by a small number of basis points ($\Delta y$).

To illustrate how $V_+$ and $V_-$ are determined in order to calculate effective duration and effective convexity, we will use the same on-the-run yield curve that we have used in our previous illustrations assuming a volatility of 10%. The four-year callable bond with a coupon rate of 6.5% and callable at par selling at 102.218 will be used in this illustration. The OAS for this issue is 35 basis points.

Exhibit 19 shows the adjusted tree by shifting the yield curve up by an arbitrarily small number of basis points, 25 basis points, and then adding 35 basis points (the OAS) to each one-year rate. The adjusted tree is then used to value the bond. The resulting value, $V_+$, is 101.676. Exhibit 20 shows the adjusted tree by shifting the yield curve down by 25 basis points and then adding 35 basis points to each one-year rate. The resulting value, $V_-$, is 102.765.

The results are summarized below:

$\Delta y$ = 0.0025
$V_+$ = 101.676
$V_-$ = 102.765
$V_0$ = 102.218

**Exhibit 19: Determination of $V_+$ for Calculating Effective Duration and Convexity***

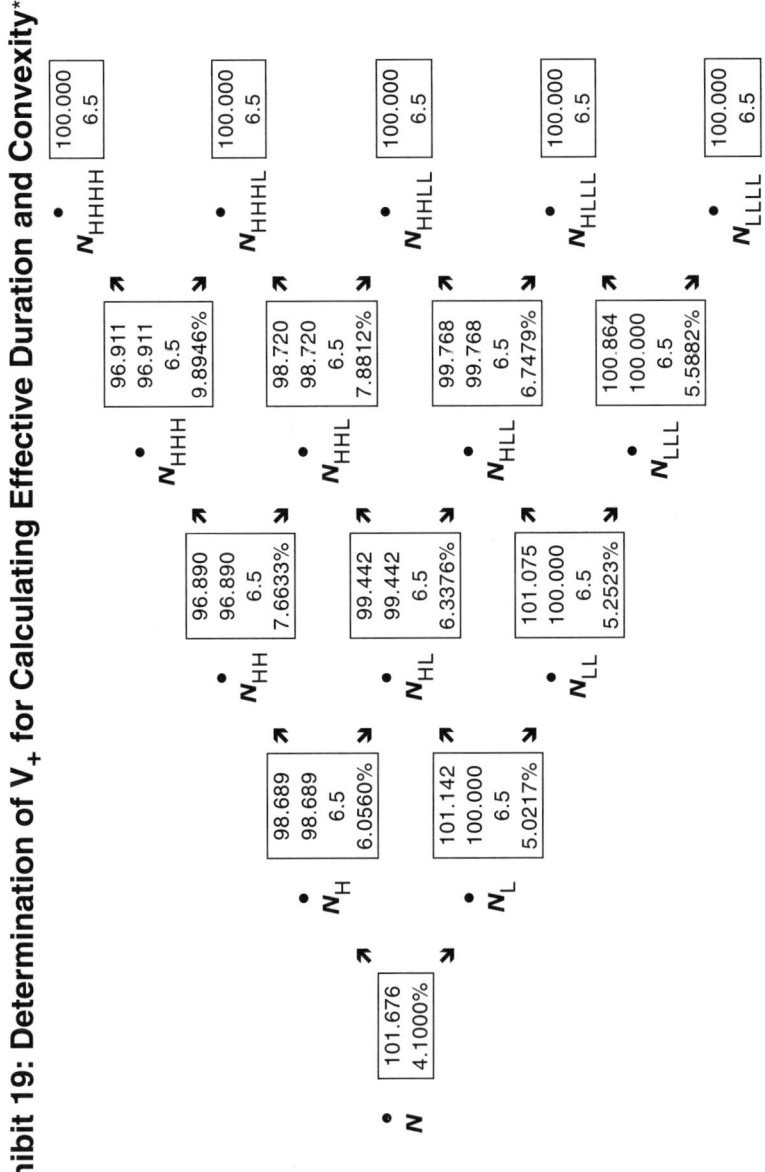

* +25 basis point shift in on-the-run yield curve.

# 140 BINOMIAL METHOD

## Exhibit 20: Determination of $V_-$ for Calculating Effective Duration and Convexity*

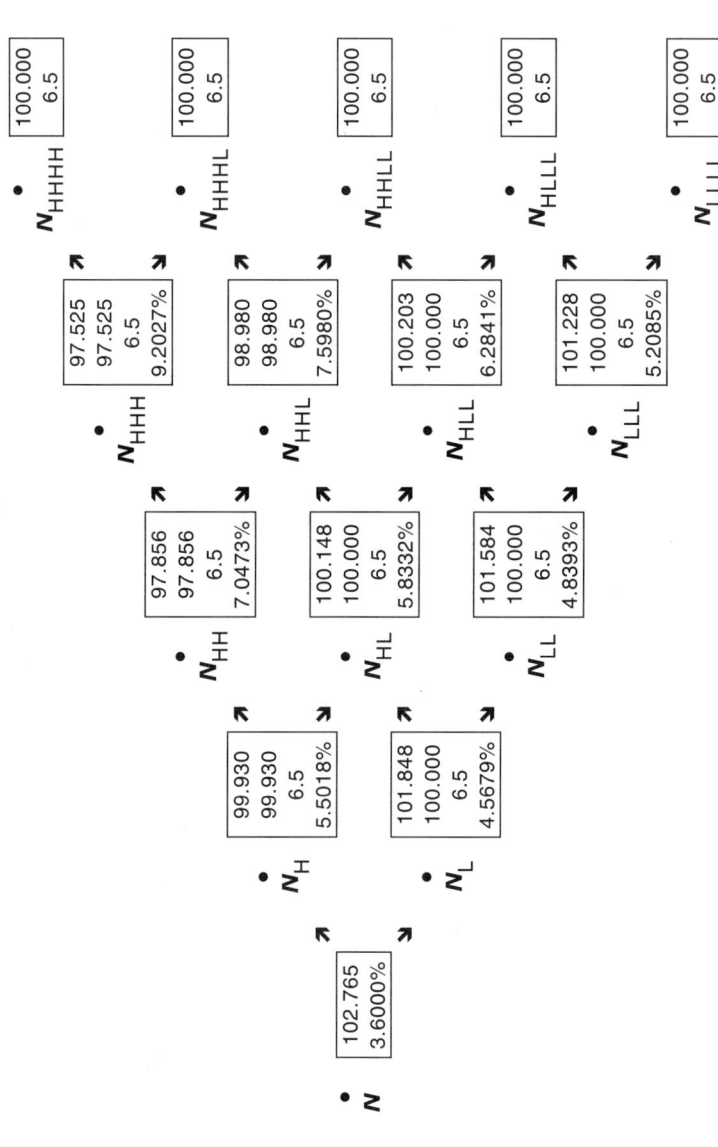

* −25 basis point shift in on-the-run yield curve.

Therefore,

$$\text{Effective duration} = \frac{102.765 - 101.676}{2(102.218)(0.0025)} = 2.1$$

$$\text{Effective convexity} = \frac{101.676 + 102.765 - 2(102.218)}{2(102.218)(0.0025)^2} = 3.9132$$

## THE CHALLENGE OF IMPLEMENTATION

To transform the basic interest rate tree into a practical tool requires several refinements. For one thing, the spacing of the node lines in the tree must be much finer. However, the fine spacing required to value short-dated securities becomes computationally inefficient if one seeks to value, say, 30-year bonds. While one can introduce time-dependent node spacing, caution is required; it is easy to distort the term structure of volatility. Other practical difficulties include the management of cash flows that fall between two node lines.

## KEY POINTS

Here are the key points of this chapter:

1. The binomial method involves generating a binomial interest rate tree based on (1) an issuer's on-the-run yield curve, (2) an assumed interest rate generation process, and (3) an assumed interest rate volatility.

2. The binomial interest rate tree is constructed by trial and error.

3. The binomial interest rate tree provides the appropriate volatility-dependent one-period rates that should be used to discount the expected cash flows of a bond.

4. The uncertainty of interest rates is introduced into the model by introducing the volatility of interest rates.

5. The standard deviation is a statistical measure of volatility.

6. The process assumes that the volatility of interest rates is measured relative to the current level of rates.

7. Using the binomial interest rate tree the value of any bond can be determined.

8. In valuing a bond using the binomial interest rate tree, the cash flows at a node are modified to take into account any embedded options.

9. The value of any embedded options is the difference between the value of an option-free bond and the value of the bond with embedded options.

10. The volatility assumption has an important impact on the theoretical value.

11. *The option-adjusted spread is the constant spread that when added to the short rates in the binomial interest rate tree will produce a valuation for the bond equal to the market price of the bond.*

12. *The required values for calculating effective duration and effective convexity are found by shifting the on-the-run yield curve, calculating a new binomial interest rate tree, and then determining the required values after adjusting the tree by adding the OAS to each short rate.*

13. *To transform the basic binomial interest rate tree into a practical tool requires several refinements.*

# 7
# MONTE CARLO METHOD

The second method for valuing bonds with embedded options is the Monte Carlo simulation, or simply Monte Carlo, method. The method involves simulating a sufficiently large number of potential interest rate paths in order to assess the value of a security along these different paths. This method is the most flexible of the two valuation methodologies for valuing interest rate sensitive instruments where the history of interest rates is important. Mortgage-backed securities (passthroughs, collateralized mortgage obligations, and stripped mortgage-backed securities) and floating-rate securities are commonly valued using this method. Some dealers use Monte Carlo simulation to value callable and putable agency and corporate bonds. Derivative instruments such as interest rate agreements (caps and floors) are also valued using Monte Carlo. We focus our attention in this chapter on the use of the Monte Carlo method to value mortgage-backed securities.

> **The objectives of this chapter are to:**
>
> 1. explain why the Monte Carlo method is used to value mortgage-backed securities;
>
> 2. show how interest rate paths are simulated in a Monte Carlo method;
>
> 3. demonstrate how the Monte Carlo method can be used to determine the theoretical value of a mortgage-backed security;

4. explain how the option-adjusted spread, effective duration, and effective convexity are computed using the Monte Carlo method;

5. explain how the option cost is calculated in the Monte Carlo method;

6. discuss the complexities of modeling collateralized mortgage obligations;

7. discuss some technical issues in the Monte Carlo method;

8. illustrate with actual deals how the OAS derived from the Monte Carlo method can be used to identify cheap and rich CMO tranches; and,

9. demonstrate modeling risk and how it can be stress tested.

## INTEREST RATE HISTORY AND PATH-DEPENDENT CASH FLOWS

For some fixed income securities and derivative instruments, the periodic cash flows are *path-dependent*. This means that the cash flow received in one period is determined not only by the current interest rate level, but also by the path that interest rates took to get to the current level.

In the case of mortgage passthrough securities (or simply, passthroughs), prepayments are path-dependent because this month's prepayment rate depends on whether there have been prior opportunities to refinance since the underlying mortgages were originated. Unlike passthroughs, the decision as to whether a corporate issuer will elect to refund an issue when the current rate is below the issue's coupon rate is not dependent on how rates evolved over time to the current level.

Moreover, in the case of adjustable-rate passthroughs (ARMs), prepayments are not only path-dependent but the periodic coupon rate depends on the history of the reference rate upon which the coupon rate is determined. This is because ARMs have periodic caps and floors as well as a lifetime cap and floor. For example, an ARM whose coupon rate resets annually could have the following restriction on the coupon rate: (1) the rate cannot change by more than 200 basis points each year and (2) the rate cannot be more than 500 basis points from the initial coupon rate.

Pools of passthroughs are used as collateral for the creation of collateralized mortgage obligations (CMOs). Consequently, for CMOs there are typically two sources of path dependency in a CMO tranche's cash flows. First, the collateral prepayments are path-dependent as discussed above. Second, the cash flow to be received in the current month by a CMO tranche depends on the outstanding balances of the other tranches in the deal. Thus, we need the history of prepayments to calculate these balances.

## THE VALUATION METHODOLOGY[1]

Conceptually, the valuation of passthroughs using the Monte Carlo method is simple. In practice, however, it is very complex. The simulation involves generating a set of cash flows based on simulated future mortgage refinancing rates, which in turn imply simulated prepayment rates.

Valuation modeling for CMOs is similar to valuation modeling for passthroughs, although, the difficulties are amplified because the issuer has sliced and diced both the prepayment risk and the interest rate risk into smaller pieces called tranches. The sensitivity of the passthroughs comprising the collateral to these two risks is not transmitted equally to every tranche. Some of the tranches wind up more sensitive to prepayment risk and interest rate risk than the collateral, while some of them are much less sensitive.

The objective of the money manager is to figure out how the

---

[1] Portions of the material in this section and the one to follow are adapted from Frank J. Fabozzi and Scott F. Richard, "Valuation of CMOs," Chapter 6 in Frank J. Fabozzi (ed.), *CMO Portfolio Management* (Summit, N.J.: Frank J. Fabozzi Associates, 1994).

OAS of the collateral, or, equivalently, the value of the collateral, gets transmitted to the CMO tranches. More specifically, the objective is to find out where the value goes and where the risk goes so that the money manager can identify the tranches with low risk and high value: the ones we want to buy. The good news is that this combination usually exists in every deal. The bad news is that in every deal there are usually tranches with low OAS, low value, and high risk.

## Using Simulation to Generate Interest Rate Paths and Cash Flows

The typical model that Wall Street firms and commercial vendors use to generate these random interest rate paths takes as input today's term structure of interest rates and a volatility assumption. The term structure of interest rates is the theoretical spot rate (or zero coupon) curve implied by today's Treasury securities. The volatility assumption determines the dispersion of future interest rates in the simulation. The simulations should be normalized so that the average simulated price of a zero-coupon Treasury bond equals today's actual price.

Each model has its own model of the evolution of future interest rates and its own volatility assumptions. Typically, there are no significant differences in the interest rate models of dealer firms and vendors, although their volatility assumptions can be significantly different.

The random paths of interest rates should be generated from an arbitrage-free model of the future term structure of interest rates. By arbitrage-free it is meant that the model replicates today's term structure of interest rates, an input of the model, and that for all future dates there is no possible arbitrage within the model. We will explain how this is done later.

The simulation works by generating many scenarios of future interest rate paths. In each month of the scenario, a monthly interest rate and a mortgage refinancing rate are generated. The monthly interest rates are used to discount the projected cash flows in the scenario. The mortgage refinancing rate is needed to determine the cash flow because it represents the opportunity cost the mortgagor is facing at that time.

If the refinancing rates are high relative to the mortgagor's original coupon rate (i.e., the rate on the mortgagor's loan), the mortgagor will have less incentive to refinance, or even a positive disincentive (i.e., the homeowner will avoid moving in order to avoid refinancing). If the refinancing rate is low relative to the mortgagor's original coupon rate, the mortgagor has an incentive to refinance.

Prepayments are projected by feeding the refinancing rate and loan characteristics, such as age, into a prepayment model. (A discussion of prepayment modeling is beyond the scope of this book.) Given the projected prepayments, the cash flow along an interest rate path can be determined.

To make this more concrete, consider a newly issued mortgage passthrough security with a maturity of 360 months. Exhibit 1 shows N simulated interest rate path scenarios. Each scenario consists of a path of 360 simulated one-month future interest rates. Just how many paths should be generated is explained later. Exhibit 2 shows the paths of simulated mortgage refinancing rates corresponding to the scenarios shown in Exhibit 1. Assuming these mortgage refinancing rates, the cash flow for each scenario path is shown in Exhibit 3.

## Calculating the Present Value for a Scenario Interest Rate Path

Given the cash flow on an interest rate path, its present value can be calculated. The discount rate for determining the present value is the simulated spot rate for each month on the interest rate path plus an appropriate spread. The spot rate on a path can be determined from the simulated future monthly rates. The relationship that holds between the simulated spot rate for month T on path n and the simulated future one-month rates is:

$$z_T(n) = \{[1+f_1(n)][1+f_2(n)]\ldots[1+f_T(n)]\}^{1/T} - 1$$

where

$z_T(n)$ = simulated spot rate for month T on path n

$f_j(n)$ = simulated future one-month rate for month j on path n

Consequently, the interest rate path for the simulated future one-month rates can be converted to the interest rate path for the simulated monthly spot rates as shown in Exhibit 4.

## Exhibit 1: Simulated Paths of One-Month Future Interest Rates

*Interest Rate Path Number*

| Month | 1 | 2 | 3 | ... | n | ... | N |
|---|---|---|---|---|---|---|---|
| 1 | $f_1(1)$ | $f_1(2)$ | $f_1(3)$ | ... | $f_1(n)$ | ... | $f_1(N)$ |
| 2 | $f_2(1)$ | $f_2(2)$ | $f_2(3)$ | ... | $f_2(n)$ | ... | $f_2(N)$ |
| 3 | $f_3(1)$ | $f_3(2)$ | $f_3(3)$ | ... | $f_3(n)$ | ... | $f_3(N)$ |
| t | $f_t(1)$ | $f_t(2)$ | $f_t(3)$ | ... | $f_t(n)$ | ... | $f_t(N)$ |
| 358 | $f_{358}(1)$ | $f_{358}(2)$ | $f_{358}(3)$ | ... | $f_{358}(n)$ | ... | $f_{358}(N)$ |
| 359 | $f_{359}(1)$ | $f_{359}(2)$ | $f_{359}(3)$ | ... | $f_{359}(n)$ | ... | $f_{359}(N)$ |
| 360 | $f_{360}(1)$ | $f_{360}(2)$ | $f_{360}(3)$ | ... | $f_{360}(n)$ | ... | $f_{360}(N)$ |

*Notation:*

$f_t(n)$ = one-month future interest rate for month t on path n

N = total number of interest rate paths

## Exhibit 2: Simulated Paths of Mortgage Refinancing Rates

*Interest Rate Path Number*

| Month | 1 | 2 | 3 | ... | n | ... | N |
|---|---|---|---|---|---|---|---|
| 1 | $r_1(1)$ | $r_1(2)$ | $r_1(3)$ | ... | $r_1(n)$ | ... | $r_1(N)$ |
| 2 | $r_2(1)$ | $r_2(2)$ | $r_2(3)$ | ... | $r_2(n)$ | ... | $r_2(N)$ |
| 3 | $r_3(1)$ | $r_3(2)$ | $r_3(3)$ | ... | $r_3(n)$ | ... | $r_3(N)$ |
| t | $r_t(1)$ | $r_t(2)$ | $r_t(3)$ | ... | $r_t(n)$ | ... | $r_t(N)$ |
| 358 | $r_{358}(1)$ | $r_{358}(2)$ | $r_{358}(3)$ | ... | $r_{358}(n)$ | ... | $r_{358}(N)$ |
| 359 | $r_{359}(1)$ | $r_{359}(2)$ | $r_{359}(3)$ | ... | $r_{359}(n)$ | ... | $r_{359}(N)$ |
| 360 | $r_{360}(1)$ | $r_{360}(2)$ | $r_{360}(3)$ | ... | $r_{360}(n)$ | ... | $r_{360}(N)$ |

*Notation:*

$r_t(n)$ = mortgage refinancing rate for month t on path n

N = total number of interest rate paths

## Exhibit 3: Simulated Cash Flow on Each of the Interest Rate Paths

| | Interest Rate Path Number | | | | | | |
|---|---|---|---|---|---|---|---|
| Month | 1 | 2 | 3 | ... | n | ... | N |
| 1 | $C_1(1)$ | $C_1(2)$ | $C_1(3)$ | ... | $C_1(n)$ | ... | $C_1(N)$ |
| 2 | $C_2(1)$ | $C_2(2)$ | $C_2(3)$ | ... | $C_2(n)$ | ... | $C_2(N)$ |
| 3 | $C_3(1)$ | $C_3(2)$ | $C_3(3)$ | ... | $C_3(n)$ | ... | $C_3(N)$ |
| t | $C_t(1)$ | $C_t(2)$ | $C_t(3)$ | ... | $C_t(n)$ | ... | $C_t(N)$ |
| 358 | $C_{358}(1)$ | $C_{358}(2)$ | $C_{358}(3)$ | ... | $C_{358}(n)$ | ... | $C_{358}(N)$ |
| 359 | $C_{359}(1)$ | $C_{359}(2)$ | $C_{359}(3)$ | ... | $C_{359}(n)$ | ... | $C_{359}(N)$ |
| 360 | $C_{360}(1)$ | $C_{360}(2)$ | $C_{360}(3)$ | ... | $C_{360}(n)$ | ... | $C_{360}(N)$ |

*Notation:*
$C_t(n)$ = cash flow for month t on path n
N = total number of interest rate paths

## Exhibit 4: Simulated Paths of Monthly Spot Rates

| | Interest Rate Path Number | | | | | | |
|---|---|---|---|---|---|---|---|
| Month | 1 | 2 | 3 | ... | n | ... | N |
| 1 | $z_1(1)$ | $z_1(2)$ | $z_1(3)$ | ... | $z_1(n)$ | ... | $z_1(N)$ |
| 2 | $z_2(1)$ | $z_2(2)$ | $z_2(3)$ | ... | $z_2(n)$ | ... | $z_2(N)$ |
| 3 | $z_3(1)$ | $z_3(2)$ | $z_3(3)$ | ... | $z_3(n)$ | ... | $z_3(N)$ |
| t | $z_t(1)$ | $z_t(2)$ | $z_t(3)$ | ... | $z_t(n)$ | ... | $z_t(N)$ |
| 358 | $z_{358}(1)$ | $z_{358}(2)$ | $z_{358}(3)$ | ... | $z_{358}(n)$ | ... | $z_{358}(N)$ |
| 359 | $z_{359}(1)$ | $z_{359}(2)$ | $z_{359}(3)$ | ... | $z_{359}(n)$ | ... | $z_{359}(N)$ |
| 360 | $z_{360}(1)$ | $z_{360}(2)$ | $z_{360}(3)$ | ... | $z_{360}(n)$ | ... | $z_{360}(N)$ |

*Notation:*
$z_t(n)$ = spot rate for month t on path n
N = total number of interest rate paths

Therefore, the present value of the cash flow for month T on interest rate path n discounted at the simulated spot rate for month T plus some spread is:

$$PV[C_T(n)] = \frac{C_T(n)}{[1+z_T(n)+K]^{1/T}}$$

where

$PV[C_T(n)]$ = present value of cash flow for month T on path n
$C_T(n)$ = cash flow for month T on path n
$z_T(n)$ = spot rate for month T on path n
$K$ = spread

The present value for path n is the sum of the present value of the cash flow for each month on path n. That is,

$$PV[Path(n)] = PV[C_1(n)] + PV[C_2(n)] + \ldots + PV[C_{360}(n)]$$

where $PV[Path(n)]$ is the present value of interest rate path n.

## Determining the Theoretical Value

The present value of a given interest rate path can be thought of as the theoretical value of a passthrough if that path was actually realized. The theoretical value of the passthrough can be determined by calculating the average of the theoretical value of all the interest rate paths. That is, the theoretical value is equal to

$$\text{Theoretical value} = \frac{PV[Path(1)] + PV[Path(2)] + \ldots + PV[Path(N)]}{N}$$

where N is the number of interest rate paths.

This procedure for valuing a passthrough is also followed for a CMO tranche. The cash flow for each month on each interest rate path is found according to the principal repayment and interest distribution rules of the deal. In order to do this, a CMO structuring model is needed. In any analysis of CMOs, one of the major stumbling blocks is getting a good CMO structuring model.

## Option-Adjusted Spread

As explained in previous chapters, the option-adjusted spread is a measure of the yield spread that can be used to convert dollar differences between value and price. It represents a spread over the issuer's spot rate curve or benchmark.

In the Monte Carlo model, the OAS is the spread K that when added to all the spot rates on all interest rate paths will make the average present value of the paths equal to the observed market price (plus accrued interest). Mathematically, OAS is the spread that will satisfy the following condition:

$$\text{Market Price} = \frac{PV[Path(1)] + PV[Path(2)] + \ldots + PV[Path(N)]}{N}$$

where N is the number of interest rate paths.

## Effective Duration and Convexity

In Chapter 4 we explained how to determine the effective duration and effective convexity for any security. These measures can be calculated using the Monte Carlo method as follows. First the bond's OAS is found using the current term structure of interest rates. Next, the initial short-term rate used to generate the interest rate paths in Exhibit 1 is increased by a small number of basis points and new paths of interest rates are generated. Given the new paths, the security is revalued holding the OAS constant. Similarly, the initial short-term rate used to generate the interest rate paths in Exhibit 1 is decreased by a small number of basis points and the security is then revalued holding the OAS constant. The two calculated values are then used in the formula for effective duration and convexity.

## Simulated Average Life

The average life of a mortgage-backed security is the weighted average time to receipt of principal payments (scheduled payments and projected prepayments). The formula for the average life is:

$$\frac{1(\text{Principal at time 1}) + 2(\text{Principal at time 2}) + \ldots + T(\text{Principal at time T})}{\text{Total principal received}}$$

where T is the number of months.

The average life reported in a Monte Carlo analysis is the average of the average lives along the interest rate paths. That is, for each interest rate path, there is an average life. The average of these average lives is the average life reported in an OAS model.

Additional information is conveyed by the distribution of the average life. The greater the range and standard deviation of the average life, the more uncertainty there is about the tranche's average life.

## Some Technical Issues

In the binomial method for valuing bonds, the interest rate tree is constructed so that it is arbitrage free. That is, if any on-the-run issue is valued, the value produced by the model is equal to the market price. This means that the tree is calibrated to the market. In contrast, in our discussion of the Monte Carlo method, there is no mechanism that we have described above that will assure the valuation model will produce a value for an on-the-run Treasury security (the benchmark in the case of agency mortgage-backed securities) equal to the market price. In practice, this is accomplished by adding a *drift term* to the short-term return generating process (Exhibit 1) so that the value produced by the Monte Carlo method for all on-the-run Treasury securities is their market price.[2] A technical explanation of this process is beyond the scope of this chapter.[3]

There is also another adjustment made to the interest rate paths. Restrictions on interest rate movements must be built into the model to prevent interest rates from reaching levels that are believed to be unreasonable (e.g., an interest rate of zero or an interest rate of 30%). This is done by incorporating *mean reversion* into the model. By this it is meant that at some point, the interest rate is forced toward some estimated average (mean) value.

Finally, the specification of the relationship between short-term rates and refinancing rates is necessary. Empirical evidence

---

[2] This is equivalent to saying that the OAS produced by the model is zero.

[3] For an explanation of how this is done, see Lakhbir S. Hayre and Kenneth Lauterbach, "Stochastic Valuation of Debt Securities," in Frank J. Fabozzi (ed.), *Managing Institutional Assets* (New York: Harper & Row, 1990), pp. 321-364.

on the relationship is necessary. More specifically, the correlation between the short-term and long-term rates must be estimated.

## Selecting the Number of Interest Rate Paths

Let's now address the question of the number of scenario paths or repetitions, N, needed to value a CMO tranche. A typical OAS run will be done for 512 to 1,024 interest rate paths. The scenarios generated using the simulation method look very realistic, and furthermore reproduce today's Treasury curve. By employing this technique, the money manager is effectively saying that Treasuries are fairly priced today and that the objective is to determine whether a specific tranche is rich or cheap relative to Treasuries.

The number of interest rate paths determines how "good" the estimate is, not relative to the truth but relative to the OAS model used. The more paths, the more average spread tends to settle down. It is a statistical sampling problem.

Most OAS models employ some form of *variance reduction* to cut down on the number of sample paths necessary to get a good statistical sample. Variance reduction techniques allow us to obtain price estimates within a tick. By this we mean that if the OAS model is used to generate more scenarios, price estimates from the model will not change by more than a tick. So, for example, if 1,024 paths are used to obtain the estimated price for a tranche, there is little more information to be had from the OAS model by generating more than that number of paths. (For some very sensitive CMO tranches, more paths may be needed to estimate prices within one tick.)

Several vendor firms have attempted to develop computational procedures that reduce the number of paths required but still provide the accuracy of a full Monte Carlo analysis. For example, BARRA has developed a procedure which it calls "modified principal component" (MPC) analysis that distills the information of a large number of interest rate paths into a considerably smaller number of paths.[4]

---

[4] For a more detailed description of the methodology, see Deepak Gulrajani, Michael Roginsky, and Ronald Kahn, "Advanced Techniques for the Valuation of CMOs," Chapter 7 in Fabozzi (ed.), *CMO Portfolio Management*.

The two panels of Exhibit 5 compare the prices of an actual CMO deal derived from full Monte Carlo analysis (Panel A) and the MPC analysis (Panel B). There are 12 tranches analyzed. A description of each tranche is given in the second column of the exhibit. For both the full Monte Carlo analysis and the MPC analysis, only 16 paths are needed for the PAC tranches A through D, the TAC tranche (G) and the accrual tranche (H). For the other tranches, a stable value is obtained with only 64 paths using the MPC analysis while a full Monte Carlo analysis requires 1,024 paths.

## ILLUSTRATIONS

In this section we use two deals to show how CMOs can be analyzed using the OAS methodology: a plain vanilla structure and a PAC/support structure.

### Plain Vanilla Structure

The plain vanilla sequential-pay CMO bond structure in our illustration is FNMA 89-97. A diagram of the principal allocation structure is given in Exhibit 6. The structure includes five tranches, A, B, C, D, and Z, and a residual class. Tranche Z is an accrual bond, and tranche D class is an IOette. The focus of our analysis is on tranches A, B, C, and Z.

The top panel of Exhibit 7 shows the OAS and the option cost for the collateral and the five classes in the CMO structure. The OAS for the collateral is 70 basis points. Since the option cost is 45 basis points, the static spread is 115 basis points (70 basis points plus 45 basis points).[5] The weighted-average OAS of all the classes (including the residual) is equal to the OAS of the collateral.

At the time this analysis was performed, April 27, 1990, the Treasury yield curve was not steep. As we noted in Chapter 2, in such a yield curve environment the static spread will not differ significantly from the traditionally computed yield spread. Thus, for the four tranches shown in Exhibit 7, the static spread is 52 for A, 87 for B, 95 for C, and 124 for D.

---

[5] Recall from Chapter 5 that the option cost is the difference between the static spread and the OAS.

## Exhibit 5: Value Derived for 12 Tranches of a Representative CMO Deal using Monte Carlo Analysis and Modified Principal Component Analysis

### Panel A: Monte Carlo Analysis

| | | Number of Paths | | | | |
|---|---|---|---|---|---|---|
| Class | Type | 16 | 64 | 256 | 1,024 | 4,096 |
| A | PAC | 103.72 | 103.71 | 103.70 | 103.71 | 103.71 |
| B | PAC | 106.50 | 106.50 | 106.48 | 106.48 | 106.48 |
| C | PAC | 106.57 | 106.57 | 106.57 | 106.57 | 106.56 |
| D | PAC | 106.08 | 106.09 | 106.09 | 106.09 | 106.09 |
| E | PAC | 90.74 | 90.47 | 90.44 | 90.40 | 90.38 |
| F | PAC IO | 9837.85 | 9882.00 | 9873.79 | 9881.06 | 9886.46 |
| G | TAC | 104.05 | 104.04 | 104.04 | 104.05 | 104.05 |
| H | Accrual | 101.75 | 101.76 | 101.76 | 101.77 | 101.77 |
| I | Support | 109.21 | 109.46 | 109.54 | 109.59 | 109.54 |
| J | PO | 62.29 | 60.51 | 59.69 | 59.44 | 59.82 |
| R | Residual | 123.39 | 124.60 | 125.08 | 125.17 | 124.97 |
| RS | Residual | 103.51 | 103.68 | 103.78 | 103.76 | 103.75 |

### Panel B: Modified Principal Component Analysis

| | | Number of Paths | | | | |
|---|---|---|---|---|---|---|
| Class | Type | 16 | 64 | 256 | 1,024 | 4,096 |
| A | PAC | 103.71 | 103.71 | 103.71 | 103.71 | 103.71 |
| B | PAC | 106.50 | 106.49 | 106.49 | 106.49 | 106.49 |
| C | PAC | 106.57 | 106.57 | 106.57 | 106.57 | 106.57 |
| D | PAC | 106.09 | 106.09 | 106.09 | 106.09 | 106.09 |
| E | PAC | 90.55 | 90.43 | 90.40 | 90.40 | 90.40 |
| F | PAC IO | 9920.20 | 9894.10 | 9892.73 | 9890.64 | 9890.80 |
| G | TAC | 104.05 | 104.05 | 104.05 | 104.05 | 104.05 |
| H | Accrual | 101.83 | 101.80 | 101.80 | 101.80 | 101.80 |
| I | Support | 109.60 | 109.53 | 109.52 | 109.52 | 109.52 |
| J | PO | 59.64 | 59.95 | 59.97 | 59.97 | 60.03 |
| R | Residual | 125.03 | 124.93 | 124.95 | 124.92 | 124.91 |
| RS | Residual | 103.76 | 103.76 | 103.77 | 103.77 | 103.77 |

Source: Deepak Gulrajani, Michael Roginsky, and Ronald Kahn, "Advanced Techniques for the Valuation of CMOs," Chapter 7 in Frank J. Fabozzi (ed.), *CMO Portfolio Management* (Summit, N.J.: Frank J. Fabozzi Associates, 1994).

## Exhibit 6: Diagram of Principal Allocation Structure for FNMA 89-97

```
                      Low    ┌─────────────────────────────────────┐
                              │                   R                 │
       Structural      ▲     ├─────────────────────────────────────┤
        Priority       │     │                   D                 │
                      High   ├────────┬────────┬─────────┬─────────┤
                              │  97A   │  97B   │  97C    │  97Z    │
                             └────────┴────────┴─────────┴─────────┘
                              ─────────────── Time ───────────────▶
```

Notice that the classes did not share the OAS equally. The same is true for the option cost. The value tended to go toward the longer bonds, something that occurs in the typical deal. Both the static spread and the option cost increase as the maturity increases. The only tranches where there appears to be a bit of a bargain are B and C. A money manager contemplating the purchase of one of these middle tranches can see that C offers a higher OAS than B and appears to bear less of the risk, as measured by the option cost. The problem a money manager may encounter is that he might not be permitted to extend out as long as the C tranche because of duration, maturity, or average life constraints.

Now let's look at modeling risk. Examination of the sensitivity of the tranches to changes in prepayments and interest rate volatility will help us to understand the interaction of the tranches in the structure and who is bearing the risk.

We begin with prepayments. Specifically, we keep the same interest rate paths as those used to get the OAS in the base case (the top panel of Exhibit 7), but reduce the prepayment rate on each interest rate path to 80% of the projected rate.

As can be seen in the second panel of Exhibit 7, slowing down prepayments does not change the OAS for the collateral and its price at all. This is because the collateral is trading close to par. Tranches created by this collateral do not behave the same way, however. The exhibit reports two results of the sensitivity analysis. First, it indicates the change in the OAS. Second, it indicates the change in the price, holding the OAS constant at the base case.

To see how a money manager can use the information in the second panel, consider tranche A. At 80% of the prepayment speed, the OAS for this class declines from 23 basis points to 8 basis points. If the OAS is held constant, the panel indicates that the buyer of tranche A would lose $0.43 per $100 par value.

## Exhibit 7: OAS Analysis of FNMA 89-97 Classes A, B, C, and Z (As of 4/27/90)

*Base Case (assumes 12% interest rate volatility)*

|  | OAS (in basis points) | Option Cost (in basis points) |
|---|---|---|
| Collateral | 70 | 45 |
| Class |  |  |
| A | 23 | 29 |
| B | 46 | 41 |
| C | 59 | 36 |
| Z | 74 | 50 |

*Prepayments at 80% and 120% of Prepayment Model (assumes 12% interest rate volatility)*

|  | New OAS (in basis points) | | Change in Price per $100 par (holding OAS constant) | |
|---|---|---|---|---|
|  | 80% | 120% | 80% | 120% |
| Collateral | 70 | 71 | $0.00 | $0.04 |
| Class |  |  |  |  |
| A | 8 | 40 | -0.43 | 0.48 |
| B | 31 | 65 | -0.86 | 1.10 |
| C | 53 | 73 | -0.41 | 0.95 |
| Z | 72 | 93 | -0.28 | 2.70 |

*Interest Rate Volatility of 8% and 16%*

|  | New OAS (in basis points) | | Change in Price per $100 par (holding OAS constant) | |
|---|---|---|---|---|
|  | 8% | 16% | 8% | 16% |
| Collateral | 92 | 46 | $1.03 | -$1.01 |
| Class |  |  |  |  |
| A | 38 | 5 | 0.42 | -0.51 |
| B | 67 | 21 | 1.22 | -1.45 |
| C | 77 | 39 | 1.22 | -1.36 |
| Z | 99 | 50 | 3.55 | -3.41 |

Source: Goldman, Sachs, & Co.

Notice that for all the tranches reported in Exhibit 7 there is a loss. How could all four tranches lose if prepayments are slowed down and the collateral does not lose value? This is because tranche D and the residual (R), which are not reported in the exhibit, got all the benefit of that slowdown. Notice that tranche Z is actually fairly well protected, so it does not lose much value as a result of the slowdown of prepayments. Tranche A by contrast is severely affected.

Also shown in the second panel of the exhibit is the second part of our experiment that tests the sensitivity of prepayments: the prepayment rate is assumed to be 120% of the base case. Once again, as the collateral is trading at close to par, its price does not move very much, about four cents per $100 of par value. In fact, because the collateral is trading slightly below par, the speeding up of prepayments will make the collateral look better while the OAS increases by only 1 basis point.

Now look at the four tranches. They all benefitted. The results reported in the exhibit indicate that a money manager who is willing to go out to the long end of the curve, such as tranche Z, would realize most of the benefits of that speedup of prepayments. Since the four tranches benefitted and the benefit to the collateral was minor, that means tranche D, the IOette, and the residual were adversely affected. In general, IO types of tranches will be adversely affected by a speedup.

Now let's look at the sensitivity to the interest rate volatility assumption, 12% in the base case. Two experiments are performed: reducing the volatility assumption to 8% and increasing it to 16%. These results are reported in the third panel of Exhibit 7.

Reducing the volatility to 8% increases the dollar price of the collateral by $1 and increases the OAS from 70 in the base case to 92. This $1 increase in the price of the collateral is not equally distributed, however, among the four tranches. Most of the increase in value is realized by the longer tranches. The OAS gain for each of the tranches follows more or less the OAS durations of those tranches. This makes sense, because the longer the duration, the greater the risk, and when volatility declines, the reward is greater for the accepted risk.

At the higher level of assumed interest rate volatility of 16%, the collateral is severely affected. The collateral's loss is distributed among the tranches in the expected manner: the longer the duration, the greater the loss. In this case tranche D and the residual are the least affected.

Using the OAS methodology, a fair conclusion can be made

about this simple plain vanilla structure: what you see is what you get. The only surprise in this structure seems to be tranches B and C. In general, however, a money manager willing to extend duration gets paid for that risk.

## PAC/Support Bond Structure

Now let's look at how to apply the OAS methodology to a more complicated CMO structure, FHLMC Series 120. The collateral for this structure is Freddie Mac 9 1/2s. A summary of the deal is provided in Exhibit 8. A diagram of the principal allocation is given in Exhibit 9.

While this deal is more complicated than the previous one, it is simple compared to the deals that have been issued in recent years. Nonetheless, it brings out all the key points about application of OAS analysis, specifically, the fact that most deals include cheap bonds, expensive bonds, and fairly priced bonds. The OAS analysis helps a money manager identify how a tranche should be classified.

There are 14 classes in this structure: nine PAC bonds (including two PAC PO bonds and a PAC IO bond), a TAC support bond, an accrual support bond, a coupon-paying support bond, and a residual bond. From Exhibit 8 it can be seen that tranches B and C are the POs because they have a coupon of 0%. From Exhibit 9 it can be seen that the underlying collateral's interest not allocated to these two PAC POs is allocated to tranche A, which is now a premium PAC with a 16% coupon. Unlike a typical mortgage-backed security backed by premium collateral, prepayments for tranche A will be slower because the underlying collateral is Freddie Mac 9 1/2s, which was not premium collateral at the time the deal was printed. Thus, with PAC A the investor realizes a high coupon rate but a much lower prepayment rate than would be experienced by a high coupon mortgage bond.

Tranches C, D, E, F, G, and H are all longer PACs. Tranche I is a PAC IO.[6] The prepayment protection for the PAC bonds is provided by the support or companion bonds. The three support bonds in this deal are tranches J, K, and Z. Tranche J is the shortest tranche (a TAC bond), and Z (an accrual bond) is the longest.

---

[6] Notice that for the PAC IO (the I bond) the coupon rate shown is 857%. Prior to 1992, all classes of a REMIC had to have some principal allocated. In this case, the original balance for the PAC IO class is $100,000.

## Exhibit 8: Summary of Federal Home Loan Mortgage Corporation — Multiclass Mortgage Participation Certificates (Guaranteed), Series 120

Total Issue: $300,000,000  
Issue Date: 12/8/89  
Structure Type: REMIC CMO  
Issuer Class: Agency  
Dated Date: 1/15/90  
Original Rating: S&P NR, Moody's NR, Fitch NR, D&P NR  
Original Settlement Date: 1/30/90  
Days Delay: 30  
Payment Frequency: Monthly; 15th day of month  

| Tranche | Original Balance ($) | Coupon (%) | Stated Maturity | Original Issue Pricing (180% PSA Assumed) | |
|---|---|---|---|---|---|
| | | | | Average Life (yr) | Expected Maturity |
| 120-A(PAC Bond) | 37,968,750 | 16.0 | 11/15/13 | 4.0 | 12/15/95 |
| 120-B(PAC Bond) | 20,500,000 | 0.0 | 2/15/11 | 3.4 | 10/15/94 |
| 120-C(PAC Bond) | 9,031,250 | 0.0 | 11/15/13 | 5.3 | 12/15/95 |
| 120-D(PAC Bond) | 12,000,000 | 9.0 | 2/15/15 | 6.3 | 9/15/96 |
| 120-E(PAC Bond) | 40,500,000 | 9.0 | 5/15/18 | 7.9 | 7/15/99 |
| 120-F(PAC Bond) | 10,000,000 | 9.0 | 1/15/19 | 10.0 | 8/15/00 |
| 120-G(PAC Bond) | 6,500,000 | 9.0 | 6/16/19 | 10.9 | 6/15/01 |
| 120-H(PAC Bond) | 33,000,000 | 9.0 | 2/15/21 | 15.5 | 4/15/18 |
| 120-I(PAC Bond) | 100,000 | 857.0 | 2/15/21 | 7.9 | 4/15/18 |
| 120-J(TAC Bond) | 99,600,000 | 9.5 | 2/15/21 | 3.2 | 10/15/99 |
| 120-K | 15,700,000 | 9.5 | 7/15/15 | 8.3 | 7/15/01 |
| 120-R | 90,000 | 9.5 | 2/15/21 | 8.1 | 4/15/19 |
| 120-S | 10,000 | 9.5 | 2/15/21 | 8.1 | 4/15/19 |
| 120-Z | 15,000,000 | 9.5 | 2/15/21 | 18.8 | 4/15/19 |

## Exhibit 8: Summary of Federal Home Loan Mortgage Corporation — Multiclass Mortgage Participation Certificates (Guaranteed), Series 120

*Structural Features*

**Prepayment Guarantee:** None

**Assumed Reinvestment Rate:** 0%

**Cash Flow Allocation:** Excess cash flow is not anticipated; in the event that there are proceeds remaining after the payments of the bonds, however, the Class 120-R Bonds will receive them. Commencing on the first principal payment date of the Class 120-A Bonds, principal equal to an amount specified in the Prospectus will be applied to the Class 120-A, 120-B, 120-C, 120-D, 120-E, 120-F, 120-G, 120-H, 120-I, and 120-J Bonds. After all other Classes have been retired, any remaining principal will be used to retire the Class 120-J, 120-A, 120-B, 120-C, 120-D, 120-E, 120-F, 120-G, 120-H, and 120-I Bonds.

**Redemption Provisions:** Nuisance provision for all Classes: Issuer may redeem the Bonds, in whole but not in part, on any Payment Date when the outstanding principal balance declines to less then 1% of the original amount.

**Other:** The PAC range is 90% to 300% PSA for the A-I bonds, and 200% PSA for the Class J Bonds.

## Exhibit 9: Principal Allocation Diagram of FHLMC Series 120

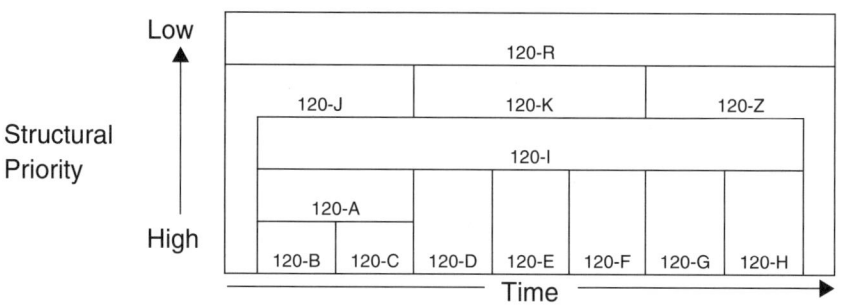

The top panel of Exhibit 10 shows the base case OAS and the option cost for the collateral and all but the residual and PAC IO classes. The collateral OAS is 72 basis points, and the option cost is 34 basis points. Thus the static spread of the collateral to the Treasury spot rate curve is 106 basis points.

The 72 basis points of OAS did not get equally distributed among the tranches — as was the case with the plain vanilla structure. Tranche J, the support TAC, did not realize a good OAS allocation, only 17 basis points, and had an extremely high option cost. Given the prepayment uncertainty associated with this support bond, its OAS would be expected to be higher. The reason for the low OAS is that this tranche was priced at issuance so that its cash flow yield was high. Using the static spread as a proxy for the spread over the Treasury yield curve, the 79-basis point spread for tranche J is high given that this appears to be a short-term tranche. Consequently, "yield buyers" probably bid aggressively for this tranche and thereby drove down its OAS, trading off "yield" for OAS. From a total return perspective, however, tranche J should have been avoided. It is an expensive bond. The two longer support bonds did not get treated as badly as tranche J: the OAS for tranches K and Z are 61 basis points and 78 basis points, respectively.

It should be apparent from the results of the base case OAS analysis reported in the top panel of Exhibit 10 where the cheap bonds are in the deal. They are the long PACs, which have a high OAS, a low option cost, and can be positively convex. These are well-protected.

## Exhibit 10 : OAS Analysis of FHLMC 120

| | Base Case (assumes 12% interest rate volatility) | |
|---|---|---|
| | OAS (in basis points) | Option Cost (in basis points) |
| Collateral | 72 | 34 |
| Class | | |
| A (PAC) | 52 | 4 |
| B (PAC PO) | 48 | -1 |
| C (PAC PO) | 64 | -7 |
| D (PAC) | 67 | 5 |
| E (PAC) | 68 | 8 |
| F (PAC) | 73 | 9 |
| G (PAC) | 75 | 9 |
| H (PAC) | 85 | 9 |
| J (Support TAC) | 17 | 62 |
| K (Support) | 61 | 58 |
| Z (Support Z) | 78 | 83 |

| | Prepayments at 80% and 120% of Prepayment Model (assumes 12% interest rate volatility) | | | | |
|---|---|---|---|---|---|
| | Base Case OAS | New OAS (in basis points) | | Change in Price per $100 par (holding OAS constant) | |
| | | 80% | 120% | 80% | 120% |
| Collateral | 72 | 69 | 77 | $0.15 | $0.22 |
| Class | | | | | |
| A (PAC) | 52 | 65 | 42 | 0.43 | -0.35 |
| B (PAC PO) | 48 | 17 | 54 | -0.71 | 0.12 |
| C (PAC PO) | 64 | 14 | 86 | -1.52 | 0.67 |
| D (PAC) | 67 | 61 | 62 | -0.24 | -0.20 |
| E (PAC) | 68 | 65 | 61 | -0.13 | -0.37 |
| F (PAC) | 73 | 76 | 63 | 0.16 | -0.59 |
| G (PAC) | 75 | 80 | 64 | 0.33 | -0.68 |
| H (PAC) | 85 | 93 | 75 | 0.56 | -0.69 |
| J (Support TAC) | 17 | 4 | 56 | -0.43 | 1.34 |
| K (Support) | 61 | 64 | 75 | 0.17 | 0.82 |
| Z (Support Z) | 78 | 85 | 114 | 0.75 | 3.77 |

## Exhibit 10(Continued): OAS Analysis of FHLMC 120

| | Interest Rate Volatility of 8% and 16% | | | | |
|---|---|---|---|---|---|
| | Base Case OAS | New OAS (in basis points) | | Change in Price per $100 par (holding OAS constant) | |
| | | 8% | 16% | 8% | 16% |
| Collateral | 72 | 91 | 51 | $0.88 | -$0.91 |
| Class | | | | | |
| A (PAC) | 52 | 57 | 43 | 0.14 | -0.31 |
| B (PAC PO) | 48 | 47 | 51 | -0.02 | 0.07 |
| C (PAC PO) | 64 | 57 | 75 | -0.15 | 0.35 |
| D (PAC) | 67 | 72 | 59 | 0.13 | -0.34 |
| E (PAC) | 68 | 74 | 56 | 0.21 | -0.59 |
| F (PAC) | 73 | 80 | 60 | 0.26 | -0.80 |
| G (PAC) | 75 | 82 | 60 | 0.26 | -0.88 |
| H (PAC) | 85 | 92 | 75 | 0.27 | -0.69 |
| J (Support TAC) | 17 | 47 | -17 | 0.54 | -0.31 |
| K (Support) | 61 | 94 | 26 | 0.95 | -1.98 |
| Z (Support Z) | 78 | 126 | 28 | 2.58 | -5.30 |

Source: Goldman, Sachs & Co.

Notice that the option costs are negative for tranches B and C, the two PAC POs. The reason is that a PO is itself an option. That is, an investor in a PO is effectively buying an option, and this explains the negative option cost. On a nonPAC PO, such as a super PO, the option cost is even more negative than it is for a PAC PO.

The next two panels in Exhibit 10 show the sensitivity of the OAS and the price (holding OAS constant at the base case) to changes in the prepayment speed (80% and 120% of the base case) and to changes in volatility (8% and 16%). This analysis shows that the change in the prepayment speed does not affect the collateral significantly, while the change in the OAS (holding price constant) and price (holding OAS constant) for each tranche is significant. For example, a slower prepayment speed, which increases the time period over which a PAC PO bondholder can recover the principal, significantly reduces the OAS and price. The opposite effect results if prepayments are faster than the base case.

Tranche A, a high-coupon short PAC bond, benefits from a slowing of prepayments, as the bondholder will receive the higher coupon for a longer time. Faster prepayments represent an adverse scenario. The PAC bonds are quite well-protected. The long PACs will actually benefit from a reduced prepayment rate because they will be earning the higher coupon interest longer. So, on an OAS basis, our earlier conclusion that the long PACs were allocated a good part of this deal's value holds up under our first stress test.

A slowdown in prepayment hurts the support tranche J and a speedup benefits this tranche. A somewhat surprising result involves the effect that the change in prepayments has on the accrual bond (the Z-bond). Notice that whether prepayment speeds are slower or faster, the OAS and the price increase. Without the use of an OAS framework, this would not intuitively be obvious.[7]

The sensitivity of the collateral and the tranches to changes in volatility are shown in the third panel of Exhibit 10. A lower volatility increases the value of the collateral, while a higher volatility reduces its value. Conversely, lower volatility reduces the value of PO instruments, and higher volatility increases the value. This can be seen for the two PAC IOs, tranches B and C, in Exhibit 10.

The long PACs continue to be fairly well-protected, whether volatility is lower or higher. In the two volatility scenarios they continue to get a good OAS, although not as much as in the base case if volatility is higher (but the OAS still looks like a reasonable value in this scenario). This reinforces our earlier conclusion concerning the investment merit of the long PACs in this deal.

## APPLICATION TO CORPORATE AND AGENCY BONDS WITH EMBEDDED OPTIONS

Some dealer firms also use the Monte Carlo method to value corporate bonds and agencies. We will illustrate this application with a simplified example of a callable corporate bond.

For a callable corporate bond, the refunding opportunities that the

---

[7] The reason for this is that at the time of this analysis there was a hump in the Treasury spot rate curve.

issuer faces will depend on how interest rates change over the life of the bond. For example, suppose that six-month interest rates are now 7%. Consider the ten possible interest rate paths for six-month interest rates for the subsequent 19 six-month periods shown in Exhibit 11 assuming that the six-month interest rates can rise or fall by 10% every six months. Exhibit 11 is the same as Exhibit 1 but with numerical values included.

The refunding opportunity for the corporation will not be based on the short-term rate but a longer-term rate that reflects how much the issuer would have to pay to refund a bond issue. Let's make the simple assumption that the refinancing rate for the corporation is 100 basis points greater than the short-term rate. Exhibit 12 shows the ten possible paths for the refunding rate, each rate in the exhibit being 100 basis points greater than in Exhibit 11. Exhibit 12 is the same as Exhibit 2 but with numerical values included. As we noted earlier in our discussion, in practice empirical evidence on the relationship between the short rate and potential refunding rate must be estimated and then incorporated into the model.

Suppose that the coupon rate on our hypothetical callable corporate bond is 8.8%, and the bond matures in 10 years but is immediately callable. Suppose further that the following rule is established for calling of the bond: If the refunding rate is below 5.8% with at least three years remaining to maturity, then the bond will be called. Given this rule for calling, the bond would not be called if five of the paths in Exhibit 12 are realized (paths 1, 2, 4, 8, and 10). Therefore, the cash flow for the bond at each six-month period is not different from that of a noncallable bond. For the other paths the bond would be called. Exhibit 13 shows the cash flow for this corporate bond given the call rule and assuming that the bond has a call price of 103 regardless of when it is called. (Exhibit 13 is the same as Exhibit 3 but with numerical values included.) In the period a bond is called, the cash flow is 107.40 (the call price of 103 plus the semiannual coupon interest of 4.40). After the call period, the cash flow is zero.

The call rule in our simplified illustration assumes that the refunding rate must be 5.8% or less and there must be at least three years remaining to maturity. In practice, the call rule will be more complex. The call rule will take into consideration the after-tax interest cost savings, the call premium (which declines over time), the legal and underwriting fees, and the time remaining to maturity.

Chapter 7  169

## Exhibit 11: Ten Possible Paths for Six-Month Rates Assuming an Initial Rate of 7% and 10% Volatility

*Path of short-term rates (%)*

| Period | 1 | 2 | 3 | 4 | 5 | 6 | 7 | 8 | 9 | 10 |
|---|---|---|---|---|---|---|---|---|---|---|
| 1 | 7.0 | 7.0 | 7.0 | 7.0 | 7.0 | 7.0 | 7.0 | 7.0 | 7.0 | 7.0 |
| 2 | 7.7 | 7.7 | 7.7 | 6.3 | 6.3 | 6.3 | 7.7 | 6.3 | 7.7 | 7.7 |
| 3 | 8.5 | 6.9 | 6.9 | 6.9 | 5.7 | 5.7 | 8.5 | 5.7 | 8.5 | 8.5 |
| 4 | 7.6 | 6.2 | 6.2 | 7.6 | 5.1 | 6.2 | 9.3 | 6.2 | 9.3 | 9.3 |
| 5 | 6.9 | 6.9 | 5.6 | 8.4 | 4.6 | 6.9 | 8.4 | 6.9 | 8.4 | 8.4 |
| 6 | 7.5 | 7.5 | 5.1 | 9.2 | 4.1 | 6.2 | 7.5 | 7.5 | 7.5 | 7.5 |
| 7 | 8.3 | 8.3 | 4.5 | 10.1 | 4.5 | 5.6 | 6.8 | 8.3 | 6.8 | 6.8 |
| 8 | 9.1 | 9.1 | 5.0 | 11.2 | 5.0 | 5.0 | 6.1 | 9.1 | 6.1 | 6.1 |
| 9 | 10.0 | 10.0 | 5.5 | 12.3 | 5.5 | 4.5 | 5.5 | 8.2 | 6.7 | 6.7 |
| 10 | 9.0 | 9.0 | 6.1 | 13.5 | 6.1 | 4.1 | 5.0 | 7.4 | 6.1 | 7.4 |
| 11 | 9.9 | 8.1 | 6.7 | 12.2 | 6.7 | 4.5 | 4.5 | 8.1 | 5.4 | 6.7 |
| 12 | 8.9 | 8.9 | 7.3 | 10.9 | 7.3 | 4.0 | 4.0 | 8.9 | 4.9 | 6.0 |
| 13 | 8.1 | 9.8 | 8.1 | 9.8 | 8.1 | 4.4 | 3.6 | 9.8 | 4.4 | 5.4 |
| 14 | 8.9 | 8.9 | 7.2 | 8.9 | 7.2 | 4.0 | 3.2 | 10.8 | 4.0 | 4.9 |
| 15 | 9.7 | 8.0 | 6.5 | 8.0 | 6.5 | 4.4 | 2.9 | 9.7 | 4.4 | 5.3 |
| 16 | 8.8 | 7.2 | 7.2 | 8.8 | 7.2 | 3.9 | 3.2 | 10.7 | 4.8 | 4.8 |
| 17 | 7.9 | 6.5 | 7.9 | 9.6 | 7.9 | 3.5 | 3.5 | 9.6 | 5.3 | 4.3 |
| 18 | 7.1 | 7.1 | 8.7 | 10.6 | 8.7 | 3.2 | 3.9 | 10.6 | 5.8 | 4.8 |
| 19 | 7.8 | 7.8 | 7.8 | 11.7 | 9.6 | 2.9 | 4.3 | 11.7 | 6.4 | 5.2 |
| 20 | 8.6 | 7.0 | 8.6 | 10.5 | 8.6 | 3.2 | 4.7 | 12.8 | 7.0 | 4.7 |

## Exhibit 12: Ten Possible Paths for the Refunding Rate Assuming It is 100 Basis Points Greater than the Short-term Rate

*Path of refunding rate (%)*

| Period | 1 | 2 | 3 | 4 | 5 | 6 | 7 | 8 | 9 | 10 |
|---|---|---|---|---|---|---|---|---|---|---|
| 1 | 8.0 | 8.0 | 8.0 | 8.0 | 8.0 | 8.0 | 8.0 | 8.0 | 8.0 | 8.0 |
| 2 | 8.7 | 8.7 | 8.7 | 7.3 | 7.3 | 7.3 | 8.7 | 7.3 | 8.7 | 8.7 |
| 3 | 9.5 | 7.9 | 7.9 | 7.9 | 6.7 | 6.7 | 9.5 | 6.7 | 9.5 | 9.5 |
| 4 | 8.6 | 7.2 | 7.2 | 8.6 | 6.1 | 7.2 | 10.3 | 7.2 | 10.3 | 10.3 |
| 5 | 7.9 | 7.9 | 6.6 | 9.4 | 5.6 | 7.9 | 9.4 | 7.9 | 9.4 | 9.4 |
| 6 | 8.5 | 8.5 | 6.1 | 10.2 | 5.1 | 7.2 | 8.5 | 8.5 | 8.5 | 8.5 |
| 7 | 9.3 | 9.3 | 5.5 | 11.1 | 5.5 | 6.6 | 7.8 | 9.3 | 7.8 | 7.8 |
| 8 | 10.1 | 10.1 | 6.0 | 12.2 | 6.0 | 6.0 | 7.1 | 10.1 | 7.1 | 7.1 |
| 9 | 11.0 | 11.0 | 6.5 | 13.3 | 6.5 | 5.5 | 6.5 | 9.2 | 7.7 | 7.7 |
| 10 | 10.0 | 10.0 | 7.1 | 14.5 | 7.1 | 5.1 | 6.0 | 8.4 | 7.1 | 8.4 |
| 11 | 10.9 | 9.1 | 7.7 | 13.2 | 7.7 | 5.5 | 5.5 | 9.1 | 6.4 | 7.7 |
| 12 | 9.9 | 9.9 | 8.3 | 11.9 | 8.3 | 5.0 | 5.0 | 9.9 | 5.9 | 7.0 |
| 13 | 9.1 | 10.8 | 9.1 | 10.8 | 9.1 | 5.4 | 4.6 | 10.8 | 5.4 | 6.4 |
| 14 | 9.9 | 9.9 | 8.2 | 9.9 | 8.2 | 5.0 | 4.2 | 11.8 | 5.0 | 5.9 |
| 15 | 10.7 | 9.0 | 7.5 | 9.0 | 7.5 | 5.4 | 3.9 | 10.7 | 5.4 | 6.3 |
| 16 | 9.8 | 8.2 | 8.2 | 9.8 | 8.2 | 4.9 | 4.2 | 11.7 | 5.8 | 5.8 |
| 17 | 8.9 | 7.5 | 8.9 | 10.6 | 8.9 | 4.5 | 4.5 | 10.6 | 6.3 | 5.3 |
| 18 | 8.1 | 8.1 | 9.7 | 11.6 | 9.7 | 4.2 | 4.9 | 11.6 | 6.8 | 5.8 |
| 19 | 8.8 | 8.8 | 8.8 | 12.7 | 10.6 | 3.9 | 5.3 | 12.7 | 7.4 | 6.2 |
| 20 | 9.6 | 8.0 | 9.6 | 11.5 | 9.6 | 4.2 | 5.7 | 13.8 | 8.0 | 5.7 |

## Exhibit 13: Cash Flow for Each Refunding Path of an 8.8%, 10-Year Corporate Bond Callable at 103

*Call Rule*: Call if refunding rate falls to 5.8% or less and has at least three years to maturity

| Period | 1 | 2 | 3 | 4 | 5 | 6 | 7 | 8 | 9 | 10 |
|---|---|---|---|---|---|---|---|---|---|---|
| 1 | 4.4 | 4.4 | 4.4 | 4.4 | 4.4 | 4.4 | 4.4 | 4.4 | 4.4 | 4.4 |
| 2 | 4.4 | 4.4 | 4.4 | 4.4 | 4.4 | 4.4 | 4.4 | 4.4 | 4.4 | 4.4 |
| 3 | 4.4 | 4.4 | 4.4 | 4.4 | 4.4 | 4.4 | 4.4 | 4.4 | 4.4 | 4.4 |
| 4 | 4.4 | 4.4 | 4.4 | 4.4 | 4.4 | 4.4 | 4.4 | 4.4 | 4.4 | 4.4 |
| 5 | 4.4 | 4.4 | 4.4 | 4.4 | 107.4 | 4.4 | 4.4 | 4.4 | 4.4 | 4.4 |
| 6 | 4.4 | 4.4 | 4.4 | 4.4 | 0.0 | 4.4 | 4.4 | 4.4 | 4.4 | 4.4 |
| 7 | 4.4 | 4.4 | 107.4 | 4.4 | 0.0 | 4.4 | 4.4 | 4.4 | 4.4 | 4.4 |
| 8 | 4.4 | 4.4 | 0.0 | 4.4 | 0.0 | 4.4 | 4.4 | 4.4 | 4.4 | 4.4 |
| 9 | 4.4 | 4.4 | 0.0 | 4.4 | 0.0 | 107.4 | 4.4 | 4.4 | 4.4 | 4.4 |
| 10 | 4.4 | 4.4 | 0.0 | 4.4 | 0.0 | 0.0 | 4.4 | 4.4 | 4.4 | 4.4 |
| 11 | 4.4 | 4.4 | 0.0 | 4.4 | 0.0 | 0.0 | 107.4 | 4.4 | 4.4 | 4.4 |
| 12 | 4.4 | 4.4 | 0.0 | 4.4 | 0.0 | 0.0 | 0.0 | 4.4 | 107.4 | 4.4 |
| 13 | 4.4 | 4.4 | 0.0 | 4.4 | 0.0 | 0.0 | 0.0 | 4.4 | 0.0 | 4.4 |
| 14 | 4.4 | 4.4 | 0.0 | 4.4 | 0.0 | 0.0 | 0.0 | 4.4 | 0.0 | 4.4 |
| 15 | 4.4 | 4.4 | 0.0 | 4.4 | 0.0 | 0.0 | 0.0 | 4.4 | 0.0 | 4.4 |
| 16 | 4.4 | 4.4 | 0.0 | 4.4 | 0.0 | 0.0 | 0.0 | 4.4 | 0.0 | 4.4 |
| 17 | 4.4 | 4.4 | 0.0 | 4.4 | 0.0 | 0.0 | 0.0 | 4.4 | 0.0 | 4.4 |
| 18 | 4.4 | 4.4 | 0.0 | 4.4 | 0.0 | 0.0 | 0.0 | 4.4 | 0.0 | 4.4 |
| 19 | 4.4 | 4.4 | 0.0 | 4.4 | 0.0 | 0.0 | 0.0 | 4.4 | 0.0 | 4.4 |
| 20 | 104.4 | 104.4 | 0.0 | 104.4 | 0.0 | 0.0 | 0.0 | 104.4 | 0.0 | 104.4 |

As explained earlier, for each path the present value of the cash flow of the bond is calculated. The discount rate used to calculate the cash flow along a path will be based on the benchmark spot rate for each six-month period. Exhibit 14 shows the benchmark spot rates for each interest rate path and is the same as Exhibit 4 with numerical values included.

Exhibit 15 shows the present value for each interest rate using the benchmark spot rates in Exhibit 14. The average of the 10 present values is the theoretical value of this callable corporate bond. In this illustration, it is 107.6

Suppose that the market price of this corporate bond is 103.3. This is less than the theoretical value of 107.6. The OAS is the spread that when added to the benchmark spot rates for each interest rate path in Exhibit 14 will produce an average price value of 103.3. This is illustrated in Exhibit 16. The first column shows the spread added to each benchmark spot rate in Exhibit 14. The next ten columns show the present value for each path based on that spread. The last column shows the average present value. Since the market price of this corporate bond is 103.3, the option-adjusted spread is 80 basis points.

Chapter 7    171

## Exhibit 14: Benchmark Spot Rate on Each Path Constructed from Six-Month Rates

| Period | 1 | 2 | 3 | 4 | 5 | 6 | 7 | 8 | 9 | 10 |
|---|---|---|---|---|---|---|---|---|---|---|
| 1 | 7.00 | 7.00 | 7.00 | 7.00 | 7.00 | 7.00 | 7.00 | 7.00 | 7.00 | 7.00 |
| 2 | 7.35 | 7.35 | 7.35 | 6.65 | 6.65 | 6.65 | 7.35 | 6.65 | 7.35 | 7.35 |
| 3 | 7.72 | 7.21 | 7.21 | 6.74 | 6.32 | 6.32 | 7.72 | 6.32 | 7.72 | 7.72 |
| 4 | 7.70 | 6.97 | 6.97 | 6.96 | 6.02 | 6.30 | 8.12 | 6.30 | 8.12 | 8.12 |
| 5 | 7.53 | 6.95 | 6.69 | 7.25 | 5.73 | 6.41 | 8.17 | 6.41 | 8.17 | 8.17 |
| 6 | 7.53 | 7.05 | 6.42 | 7.57 | 5.46 | 6.37 | 8.07 | 6.60 | 8.07 | 8.07 |
| 7 | 7.64 | 7.22 | 6.15 | 7.94 | 5.33 | 6.26 | 7.89 | 6.84 | 7.89 | 7.89 |
| 8 | 7.83 | 7.46 | 6.01 | 8.34 | 5.29 | 6.10 | 7.66 | 7.13 | 7.66 | 7.66 |
| 9 | 8.07 | 7.75 | 5.95 | 8.77 | 5.31 | 5.92 | 7.42 | 7.25 | 7.56 | 7.56 |
| 10 | 8.17 | 7.88 | 5.96 | 9.24 | 5.39 | 5.73 | 7.17 | 7.26 | 7.41 | 7.54 |
| 11 | 8.33 | 7.90 | 6.02 | 9.51 | 5.50 | 5.62 | 6.93 | 7.34 | 7.23 | 7.46 |
| 12 | 8.38 | 7.99 | 6.13 | 9.62 | 5.65 | 5.48 | 6.68 | 7.48 | 7.03 | 7.34 |
| 13 | 8.36 | 8.13 | 6.28 | 9.64 | 5.84 | 5.40 | 6.44 | 7.66 | 6.83 | 7.19 |
| 14 | 8.39 | 8.18 | 6.35 | 9.59 | 5.94 | 5.30 | 6.21 | 7.88 | 6.63 | 7.02 |
| 15 | 8.48 | 8.17 | 6.36 | 9.48 | 5.98 | 5.24 | 5.99 | 8.01 | 6.47 | 6.91 |
| 16 | 8.50 | 8.11 | 6.41 | 9.43 | 6.05 | 5.15 | 5.82 | 8.17 | 6.37 | 6.78 |
| 17 | 8.46 | 8.01 | 6.50 | 9.45 | 6.16 | 5.06 | 5.68 | 8.26 | 6.31 | 6.63 |
| 18 | 8.39 | 7.96 | 6.62 | 9.51 | 6.30 | 4.95 | 5.58 | 8.39 | 6.28 | 6.53 |
| 19 | 8.36 | 7.95 | 6.68 | 9.62 | 6.47 | 4.84 | 5.51 | 8.56 | 6.28 | 6.46 |
| 20 | 8.37 | 7.90 | 6.78 | 9.67 | 6.58 | 4.76 | 5.47 | 8.77 | 6.32 | 6.37 |

## Exhibit 15: Calculation of Theoretical Value of Callable Corporate Bond: Present Value of Each Interest Rate Path

| Period | 1 | 2 | 3 | 4 | 5 | 6 | 7 | 8 | 9 | 10 |
|---|---|---|---|---|---|---|---|---|---|---|
| 1 | 4.25 | 4.25 | 4.25 | 4.25 | 4.25 | 4.25 | 4.25 | 4.25 | 4.25 | 4.25 |
| 2 | 4.09 | 4.09 | 4.09 | 4.12 | 4.12 | 4.12 | 4.09 | 4.12 | 4.09 | 4.09 |
| 3 | 3.93 | 3.96 | 3.96 | 3.98 | 4.01 | 4.01 | 3.93 | 4.01 | 3.93 | 3.93 |
| 4 | 3.78 | 3.84 | 3.84 | 3.84 | 3.91 | 3.89 | 3.75 | 3.89 | 3.75 | 3.75 |
| 5 | 3.66 | 3.71 | 3.73 | 3.68 | 93.25 | 3.76 | 3.60 | 3.76 | 3.60 | 3.60 |
| 6 | 3.52 | 3.57 | 88.85 | 3.52 | 0.00 | 3.65 | 3.47 | 3.62 | 3.47 | 3.47 |
| 7 | 3.38 | 3.43 | 0.00 | 3.35 | 0.00 | 3.55 | 3.36 | 3.48 | 3.36 | 3.36 |
| 8 | 3.24 | 3.28 | 0.00 | 3.17 | 0.00 | 3.46 | 3.26 | 3.32 | 3.26 | 3.26 |
| 9 | 3.08 | 3.13 | 0.00 | 2.99 | 0.00 | 82.60 | 3.17 | 3.19 | 3.15 | 3.15 |
| 10 | 2.95 | 2.99 | 0.00 | 2.80 | 0.00 | 0.00 | 3.09 | 3.08 | 3.06 | 3.04 |
| 11 | 2.81 | 2.87 | 0.00 | 2.64 | 0.00 | 0.00 | 73.86 | 2.96 | 2.98 | 2.94 |
| 12 | 2.69 | 2.75 | 0.00 | 2.50 | 0.00 | 0.00 | 0.00 | 2.83 | 70.94 | 2.86 |
| 13 | 2.58 | 2.62 | 0.00 | 2.39 | 0.00 | 0.00 | 0.00 | 2.70 | 0.0 | 2.78 |
| 14 | 2.47 | 2.51 | 0.00 | 2.28 | 0.00 | 0.00 | 0.00 | 2.56 | 0.00 | 2.71 |
| 15 | 2.36 | 2.41 | 0.00 | 2.20 | 0.00 | 0.00 | 0.00 | 2.44 | 0.00 | 2.64 |
| 16 | 2.26 | 2.33 | 0.00 | 2.10 | 0.00 | 0.00 | 0.00 | 2.32 | 0.00 | 2.58 |
| 17 | 2.17 | 2.26 | 0.00 | 2.01 | 0.00 | 0.00 | 0.00 | 2.21 | 0.00 | 2.53 |
| 18 | 2.10 | 2.18 | 0.00 | 1.91 | 0.00 | 0.00 | 0.00 | 2.10 | 0.00 | 2.47 |
| 19 | 2.02 | 2.10 | 0.00 | 1.80 | 0.00 | 0.00 | 0.00 | 1.98 | 0.00 | 2.41 |
| 20 | 45.98 | 48.09 | 0.00 | 40.61 | 0.00 | 0.00 | 0.00 | 44.23 | 0.00 | 55.76 |
| Total | 103.3 | 106.4 | 108.7 | 96.15 | 109.5 | 113.3 | 109.8 | 103.1 | 109.8 | 115.6 |

Average present value = Theoretical value = 107.6

## Exhibit 16: Determination of the OAS: Present Value of Each Path and Average Present Value Using Various Spreads

| Spread (bp) | Present Value of Path | | | | | | | | | | Average Present value |
|---|---|---|---|---|---|---|---|---|---|---|---|
| | 1 | 2 | 3 | 4 | 5 | 6 | 7 | 8 | 9 | 10 | |
| 40 | 100.6 | 103.5 | 107.5 | 93.73 | 108.5 | 111.5 | 107.9 | 100.4 | 107.7 | 112.4 | 105.4 |
| 50 | 100.0 | 102.9 | 107.3 | 93.14 | 108.3 | 111.1 | 107.4 | 99.77 | 107.2 | 111.6 | 104.9 |
| 60 | 99.35 | 102.2 | 107.0 | 92.55 | 108.0 | 110.7 | 106.9 | 99.13 | 106.7 | 110.8 | 104.3 |
| 70 | 98.70 | 101.5 | 106.7 | 91.97 | 107.8 | 110.3 | 106.5 | 98.49 | 106.2 | 110.1 | 103.8 |
| 80 | 98.06 | 100.8 | 106.4 | 91.40 | 107.5 | 109.9 | 106.0 | 97.86 | 105.7 | 109.3 | 103.3 |
| 90 | 97.43 | 100.2 | 106.1 | 90.83 | 107.3 | 109.5 | 105.5 | 97.24 | 105.3 | 108.6 | 102.8 |
| 100 | 96.80 | 99.58 | 105.9 | 90.26 | 107.1 | 109.1 | 105.1 | 96.62 | 104.8 | 107.9 | 102.3 |
| 110 | 96.18 | 98.93 | 105.6 | 89.70 | 106.8 | 108.7 | 104.6 | 96.00 | 104.3 | 107.1 | 101.8 |
| 120 | 95.56 | 98.29 | 105.3 | 89.14 | 106.6 | 108.3 | 104.2 | 95.39 | 103.8 | 106.4 | 101.3 |

Chapter 7  173

## KEY POINTS OF CHAPTER

Here are the key points of this chapter:

1. The Monte Carlo method is the most flexible of the two valuation methodologies for valuing fixed-income securities whose periodic cash flows are path-dependent.

2. A path-dependent cash flow is one in which the cash flow received in one period is determined not only by the current interest rate level, but also by the path that interest rates took to get to the current level.

3. The cash flow of mortgage-backed securities is path dependent and consequently the Monte Carlo is commonly used to value these securities.

4. The Monte Carlo method is also used to value floating-rate securities and derivative instruments such as caps and floors.

5. The Monte Carlo method involves randomly generating many scenarios of future interest rate paths.

6. The interest rate paths are generated based on some volatility assumption for interest rates.

7. The random paths of interest rates should be generated from an arbitrage-free model of the future term structure of interest rates.

8. The Monte Carlo method applied to mortgage-backed securities involves randomly generating a set of cash flows based on simulated future mortgage refinancing rates.

9. The theoretical value of a security on any interest rate path is the present value of the cash flow on that path where the spot rates are those on the corresponding interest rate path.

10. The theoretical value of a security is the average of the theoretical values over all the interest rate paths.

11. In the Monte Carlo method, the option-adjusted spread is the spread that when added to all the spot rates on all interest rate paths will make the average present value of the paths equal to the observed market price (plus accrued interest).

12. The model is calibrated to the market by adding a drift term.

13. Mean reversion is included in the model to prevent interest rates from reaching unrealistic rates.

14. The effective duration and effective convexity are calculated using the Monte Carlo method by holding the OAS constant and shifting the term structure up and down.

15. The average life reported in the Monte Carlo method is the average of the average lives from all the interest rate paths and information about the distribution of the average life is useful.

16. The number of interest paths analyzed is determined by a variance reduction rule.

17. Vendors have developed procedures to reduce the number of paths needed to value a security.

18. When the Monte Carlo method is used to value a mortgage-backed security, a prepayment model is needed to obtain the cash flow on each interest rate path.

19. When the Monte Calro method is used to value a callablle bond, a call rule is needed to obtain the cash flow on each interest rate path.

# 8
# VALUATION OF INVERSE FLOATERS

Floating-rate securities are securities whose coupon rate is reset at specified dates at some spread to a reference rate. In recent years, inverse floating-rate securities have been introduced to the fixed-income market. The coupon rate on an inverse floating-rate security, or simply, *inverse floater*, changes in the direction opposite to that of some reference rate or market rate.

**The objectives of this chapter are to:**

1. explain how an inverse floater is created;

2. set forth a methodology for valuing an inverse floater;

3. explain how a change in the shape of the yield curve affects the value of an inverse floater;

4. show the price volatility characteristics of an inverse floater when interest rates change;

5. explain the relationship between an inverse floater and an interest rate swap; and,

6. explain the different types of inverse floaters created in the collateralized mortgage obligation and municipal bond markets.

### Exhibit 1: Creation of an Inverse Floater

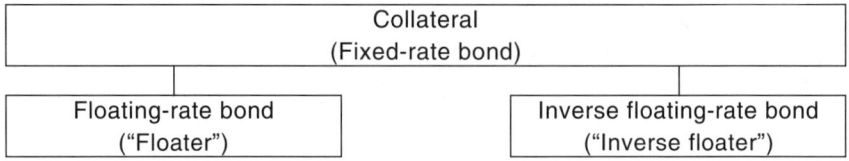

## CREATION OF INVERSE FLOATERS

Inverse floaters exist in the corporate bond market, the municipal bond market, and the mortgage-backed securities market. In general, an inverse floater is created from a fixed-rate security. The security from which the inverse floater is created is called the *collateral*. From the collateral two bonds, or *tranches*, are created: a floater and an inverse floater. This is depicted in Exhibit 1.

### Conditions that Must Be Satisfied

The two tranches are created such that (1) the total coupon interest paid to the two tranches in each period is less than or equal to the collateral's coupon interest in each period, and (2) the total principal paid in any period to the two tranches is less than or equal to the collateral's total principal in each period. Equivalently, the floater and inverse floaters are structured so that the cash flow from the collateral in each period will be sufficient to satisfy the obligation of the two tranches.

For example, consider a 10-year 7.5% coupon semiannual-pay bond. Suppose $100 million of the bond is used as collateral to create a floater with a principal of $50 million and an inverse floater with a principal of $50 million. Suppose that the reference rate is LIBOR and that the coupon rate for the floater and the inverse floater are reset every six months based on the following formula:

> Floater coupon: LIBOR + 1%
> Inverse floater coupon: 14% − LIBOR

Notice that the total principal of the floater and inverse floater equals the principal of the collateral, $100 million. The weighted average of the coupon rate of the combination of the two tranches is:

> 0.5 (LIBOR + 1%) + 0.5 (14% − LIBOR) = 7.5%

Thus, regardless of the level of LIBOR, the combined coupon rate for the two tranches is the coupon rate of the collateral, 7.5%.

There is one problem with the coupon formulas given above. Suppose that LIBOR exceeds 14%. Then the formula for the inverse floater will be negative. To prevent this from happening a restriction, or *floor*, is placed on the coupon rate for the inverse floater. Typically, the floor is set at zero. Because of the floor, the coupon rate on the floater must be restricted so that the coupon interest paid to the two tranches does not exceed the collateral's coupon interest. In our hypothetical structure, the maximum coupon rate that must be imposed on the floater is 15%. Thus, when a floater and an inverse floater are created from the collateral, a floor is imposed on the inverse and a cap is imposed on the floater.

In our simple structure, we assumed an equal allocation of the par value between the two tranches. This need not happen, and, as explained later in this chapter, in the mortgage-backed securities market typically less than half of the collateral's principal is allocated to the inverse floater.

## General Formula for Inverse Floater Coupon

In general, a wide range of allocations of the collateral's principal are possible, permitting an infinite number of possibilities for the formula for the inverse floater. The general formula for the inverse floater is: $K - L \times R$ where R is the reference rate, and K and L are values that can be selected by the creator of the floater and the inverse floater.

Let's interpret the two parameters. K is the maximum coupon rate that the inverse floater can realize; that is, it is the *inverse cap*. This occurs when the reference rate is zero. L is the *coupon leverage*, or simply, *leverage*. It indicates the multiple by which the coupon rate will change for a 100 basis point change in the reference rate. For example, if L is 4, this means that the coupon rate on the inverse floater will change 400 basis points for each 100 basis point change in the reference rate (subject to any restrictions imposed on the coupon rate). Thus, the general formula for the coupon rate of an inverse floater can be expressed as follows:

$$\text{Inverse Cap} - \text{Leverage} \times \text{Reference Rate}$$

Any cap or floor imposed on the coupon rate for the floater and the inverse floater must be selected so as to maintain the integrity of the combined coupon rate. That is, the combined coupon rate must be less than or equal to the collateral's coupon rate. The relationships among the parameters for the collateral, floater, and inverse floater are shown in Exhibit 2.

The amount of leverage is not determined arbitrarily by the creator of the inverse floater. Rather, it is dictated by client inquiries and/or market demand for other issues that have been recently created.

## VALUING AN INVERSE FLOATER

As emphasized throughout this book, the value of any financial asset is the present value of its expected cash flow. It is difficult to value an inverse floater in these terms because of uncertainty about future values for the reference rate. Fortunately, the valuation of an inverse floater is not complex, as we shall see.

### Fundamental Principle

We can express the relationships among the collateral, the floater, and the inverse floater as follows:

Collateral = Floater + Inverse floater

This relationship applies to cash flows as well as valuation. That is, the sum of the value of the floater and the value of the inverse floater must be equal to the value of the collateral from which they are created. If this relationship is violated, arbitrage profits are possible.

An alternative way to express the relationship is:

Value of inverse floater = Value of collateral − Value of floater

This expression states that the value of an inverse floater can be found by valuing the collateral and valuing the floater, then calculating the difference between these two values. In this case, the value of an inverse floater is not found directly, but is instead inferred from the value of the collateral and the value of the floater.

## Exhibit 2: Relationships for Principal and Coupon for Creation of Floater and Inverse Floater Tranches[*]

*Parameters for collateral:*
Collateral principal
Collateral coupon rate

*Parameters for floater tranche:*
Floater spread
Floater cap
Floater floor
Current value of reference rate

*Parameters for inverse floater tranche:*
Coupon leverage
Inverse floater cap
Inverse floater floor

*Relationships:*

Floater coupon = Current value of reference rate + Floater spread

$$\text{Floater principal} = \frac{\text{Coupon leverage} \times \text{Collateral principal}}{(1 + \text{Coupon leverage})}$$

Inverse principal = Collateral principal − Floater principal

Inverse interest = (Collateral principal × Collateral coupon rate) − (Floater principal × Floater coupon rate)

$$\text{Floater cap} = \frac{\text{Collateral coupon}}{\text{Floater principal}}$$

$$\text{Inverse floor} = \frac{\text{Inverse interest when floater coupon at cap}}{\text{Inverse principal}}$$

$$\text{Inverse cap} = \frac{\text{Inverse interest when floater coupon at floor}}{\text{Inverse principal}}$$

---

[*] Assumes that all of the collateral principal and interest will be distributed to the floater and inverse floater.

# 180  VALUATION OF INVERSE FLOATERS

The value of the collateral is obtained using the valuation methodologies described in previous chapters. The expected cash flows of the collateral must be discounted at appropriate rates that reflect the inherent risk associated with the collateral. The appropriate discount rate depends on (1) the spot rate curve, and (2) the option-adjusted spread of the collateral to the appropriate benchmark spot rate curve.

## Valuing the Floater

The value of a floater depends on two factors: (1) the spread over the reference rate, and (2) the cap on the floater. A floater with a cap can be viewed as a package with an uncapped floater (a floater without a cap) and a cap. That is:

Capped floater = Uncapped floater − Floater cap

The reason for subtracting the value of the cap from the value of an uncapped floater is that the holder of a capped floater has effectively sold a cap.

Assuming that the spread over the reference rate required by the market has not changed since issuance, the uncapped floater should sell at its par value. The value of a capped floater thus can be expressed as follows:

Value of capped floater = Par value − Value of floater cap

If the reference rate plus the spread is far below the floater cap rate, the value of the cap will be close to zero, and the capped floater will trade at par value. However, if the reference rate plus the spread is close to the cap rate or above it, the value of the floater cap will be positive, and the value of a capped floater will be less than its par value.

The question therefore is how to determine the value of the cap embedded in the floater. The Monte Carlo methodology described in Chapter 7 can be used. What is important to understand here is that there are two key factors that affect the value of a cap: (1) the relationship between the current reference rate plus the spread and the cap rate on the floater, and (2) the expected volatility of the reference rate. The farther the reference rate plus the spread is below the floater cap rate, the less the value of the cap. As the reference rate plus the spread approaches the cap rate, the value of the cap increases. With respect to expected volatility of the reference rate, a cap increases in value the greater the expected volatility.

Given that the floater created from the collateral is a capped floater, the value of an inverse floater can be expressed as:

Value of inverse floater = Value of collateral − Value of capped floater

The factors that affect the value of inverse floaters are the factors that affect the value of the collateral and the value of a capped floater.

## Leverage and Valuation

It is informative to recast the valuation of inverse floaters by looking at the importance of the leverage that is selected. Suppose that the creator of the floaters and inverse floaters divides the collateral into 100 bonds, 20 inverse floater bonds and 80 floater bonds.[1] This means that the leverage in this structure is 4:1 of floater bonds to inverse floater bonds. Then, the following relationship must hold:

100 (Collateral price) = 20 (Inverse price) + 80 (Floater price)

This can also be expressed as:

20 (1 + 4) (Collateral price) = 20 (Inverse price) + 20 (4) (Floater price)

Dividing both sides by 20, we get:

(1 + 4) (Collateral price) = (Inverse price) + 4 (Floater price)

This can be generalized for any leverage L as follows:

---

[1] William R. Leach, "A Portfolio Manager's Perspective of Inverses and Inverse IOs," Chapter 10 in Frank J. Fabozzi (ed.), CMO Portfolio Management (Summit, NJ: Frank J. Fabozzi Associates, 1994).

$$(1+L)(\text{Collateral price}) = (\text{Inverse price}) + L(\text{Floater price})$$

Solving for the inverse price we have:

$$\text{Inverse price} = (1+L)(\text{Collateral price}) - L(\text{Floater price})$$

There are two important implications of this price relationship. First, typically it is not difficult to price the floater. The greater difficulty is often in determining the collateral's price. Notice the implication of mispricing the collateral. *The greater the leverage, the greater the impact of mispricing of the inverse floater resulting from mispricing the collateral.* Specifically, every one point mispricing of the collateral results in a $1+L$ point mispricing of the inverse floater. So with a leverage of 3, a 4 point mispricing of the inverse results for each one point mispricing of the collateral.

The second implication is that the price of the inverse floater is not related to the level of the reference rate as long as the floater cap is not affected. What in fact affects the price performance of an inverse floater is explored next.

## PERFORMANCE OF AN INVERSE FLOATER

A common misconception is that the value of an inverse floater should change in a direction opposite from the change in the reference rate. Thus, if the reference rate falls, the value of an inverse floater should rise. This view is incorrect because, as we just explained, the value of an inverse floater is not solely dependent on the reference rate. The reference rate affects the value of the inverse floater only through its effect on the value of the cap of the capped floater, and does not take into consideration the other factors that we have noted will affect the value of an inverse floater.

To see the importance of these relationships for the value of an inverse floater and to make the analysis simple, let's assume that an inverse floater and floater are created from the on-the-run 10-year Treasury issue. While the creation of such securities is not being done at the time of this writing, the basic principles are illustrated and can be extended to more complicated collateral such as corporate bonds, municipal bonds, and collateralized mortgage obligations. The assumptions for the illustration are:

- The reference rate for the floater and inverse floater is the six-month Treasury bill rate which is currently 6%. (Thus, the reference rate is a short-term rate.)
- The coupon rate for the floater is the six-month Treasury bill rate flat. That is, there is no spread.
- The cap for the floater is 5%.
- The yield on the 10-year Treasury is 9.5% and the yield on a 9-year Treasury is 9.3%.

Now consider three scenarios one-year from now. For each scenario we make an assumption about

(1) the reference rate one year from now,
(2) the expected volatility of the reference rate one year from now, and
(3) the yield on a nine-year Treasury.

We will look at the effect one year from now on the value of the collateral (the original 10-year Treasury) and the value of the capped floater. The difference between these two values is the value of the inverse floater.

***Scenario 1:*** In this scenario, it is assumed that six months from now:

(1) the reference rate declines to 4%,
(2) expected volatility of the six-month Treasury bill rate declines, and
(3) the yield on a 9-year Treasury increases from its current rate of 9.3% to 11%.

Thus, in Scenario 1, one year from now it is assumed that short-term Treasury rates have declined and intermediate-term rates have increased. This means that the Treasury yield curve has steepened in the short to intermediate term range.

## 184 VALUATION OF INVERSE FLOATERS

Given this scenario, the value of the capped floater will increase for two reasons. First, today the coupon rate on the floater would be 6% in the absence of the floater cap. Because of the floater cap, the coupon rate is 6%. One year from now, the capped floater's value increases because the coupon rate falls below the cap (the new coupon rate is 5%), thereby reducing the value of the cap. Second, expected volatility for the reference rate decreases. The value of the collateral declines because the yield on the 9-year Treasury rises.

Since the value of an inverse floater is the difference between the value of the collateral (which has decreased) and the value of the capped floater (which has increased), the value of the inverse floater has declined. *Notice that this occurs despite the fact that the reference rate is assumed to decline in this scenario.*

**Scenario 2:** In this scenario, it is assumed that one year from now:

(1) the reference rate rises to 7%,
(2) expected volatility of the six-month Treasury bill rate increases, and
(3) the yield on a 9-year Treasury declines from its current rate of 9.3% to 7.6%.

In this scenario it is assumed that short-term rates rise and intermediate-term rates fall. This means that the Treasury yield curve has flattened in the short to intermediate term range.

Two factors cause the value of the floater to decrease because the value of the cap increases. First, the reference rate has risen above the cap rate so one year from now the coupon rate is even further below the market rate. Second, the expected volatility has increased.

Now consider the collateral. Its value will increase. Consequently, the value of the inverse floater will increase. *Notice that this occurs even though the reference rate for the inverse floater has increased.*

**Scenario 3:** In this last scenario, the following is assumed one year from now:

(1) the reference rate declines to 4% (as in Scenario 1),
(2) expected volatility of the reference rate decreases (as in Scenario 1), and

(3) the yield on a 9-year Treasury declines from its current rate of 9.3% to 7.6% (as in Scenario 2).

Under this scenario, the value of the collateral will rise. The value of the inverse floater can either rise or fall, as the collateral has risen in value and the capped floater has risen in value. The net effect depends on the relative increases of the collateral and the capped floater.

These illustrations make it clear that the change in the shape of the yield curve is the key factor that affects the performance of an inverse floater. There are two factors that have not been introduced into the analysis yet since we have dealt with a hypothetical inverse floater created from a Treasury issue. The following will affect how non-Treasury collateral and the floater created will affect the value of the inverse floater: (1) how the spread of the floater changes and (2) the option-adjusted spread at which the collateral trades relative to its benchmark spot rate curve.

Typically, dealers analyze inverse floaters for a potential buyer by modeling the performance under various scenarios. Usually, performance assumptions cover a rise or decline in interest rates of up to 300 basis points. Such analysis can be misleading for several reasons. First, there is no such thing as an "interest rate." Rather there is a structure of interest rates as depicted by the yield curve, and we demonstrated above that changes in the shape of the yield curve can affect the value of an inverse floater. Simply assuming that "interest rates" rise or fall by a particular number of basis points means that all interest rates along the Treasury yield curve change by the same amount (that is, that there is a parallel shift in the Treasury yield curve). Our discussion should make it clear that the value of an inverse floater requires more in-depth analysis than one simple assumption of parallel shifts in the yield curve.

## Duration of an Inverse Floater

The duration of an asset is a measure of its price sensitivity to a change in interest rates. Because valuations are additive (that is, the sum of the floater and the inverse floater equals the value of the collateral), durations (properly weighted) are additive as well. Thus, the duration of the inverse floater is related to the duration of the collateral and the duration of the floater.

Assuming that the duration of the floater is close to zero, it can be shown that the duration of an inverse floater is:[2]

$$\text{Duration of inverse floater} = (1 + L)(\text{Duration of collateral}) \times \frac{\text{Collateral price}}{\text{Inverse price}}$$

Thus, the duration of an inverse floater will be a multiple of the duration of the collateral. In the case where the principal from the collateral is split equally between the floater and the inverse floater, L is equal to one and the duration of the inverse floater is two times the duration of the collateral.

## INTERPRETATION OF AN INVERSE FLOATER POSITION

Since the capped floater and inverse floater are created from fixed-rate collateral, the following relationship is true:

Long a fixed-rate collateral = Long a capped floater + Long an inverse floater

Recasting this relationship in terms of an inverse floater, we can write

Long an inverse floater = Long a fixed-rate collateral − Long a capped floater

Or, equivalently,

Long an inverse floater = Long a fixed-rate collateral + Short a capped floater

Thus, the owner of an inverse floater has effectively purchased fixed-rate collateral and shorted a capped floater. But shorting a floater is equivalent to borrowing funds, where the interest cost of the funds is a floating rate where the interest rate is the reference rate plus the spread. Consequently, the owner of an inverse floater has effectively purchased a fixed-rate asset with borrowed funds.

There is another capital market instrument that shares a similar characteristic with an inverse floater, an interest rate swap. One party to an interest rate swap receives a fixed rate and pays a floating rate. With the exception of the cap on the floater, the owner of an inverse floater receives fixed and pays floating. Thus, it should not be surprising that the swap market has also been used to value inverse floaters.

---

[2] Leach, "A Portfolio Manager's Perspective of Inverses and Inverse IOs," p. 159.

## Exhibit 3: Creation of a CMO Inverse Floater Class

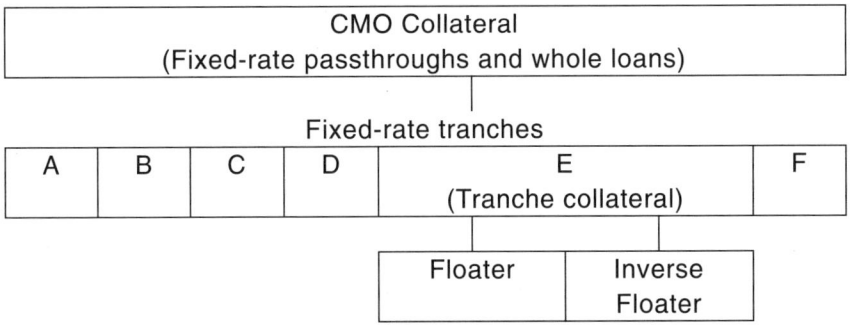

## CMO INVERSE FLOATER TRANCHES

The largest issuance of inverse floaters has been in the CMO market. In 1990, 1991, and 1992, issuance of agency CMOs was $97.0 billion, $185 billion, and $317 billion, respectively. Inverse issuance as a percentage of CMO issuance for these three years was 1.7%, 2.9%, and 2.4%, respectively.[3]

In describing CMO inverse floaters we must modify our terminology. In our earlier discussion, we referred to the fixed-rate bond from which the floater and inverse floater were created as the collateral. We referred to the floater and inverse floater as tranches. The term collateral to participants in the CMO market refers to the passthroughs or whole loans from which the CMO was created. The collateral is then carved up to create various tranches. From any fixed-rate tranche, a floater and an inverse floater can be created.

The term "collateral" for the floater and the inverse floater can be misleading in the CMO market. It could mean the collateral for the CMO deal or it could mean the fixed-rate tranche. To avoid confusion, we will refer to the collateral for the entire CMO deal as the *CMO collateral* and the fixed-rate tranche from which the floater and inverse floater are created as the *tranche collateral*.

This is depicted in Exhibit 3. The CMO collateral is shown at the top of the exhibit. From the CMO collateral, six fixed-rate tranches are created, denoted A, B, C, D, E, and F. From fixed-rate tranche E, a floater and an inverse floater are created.

---

[3] Leach, "A Portfolio Manager's Perspective of Inverses and Inverse IOs," p. 155.

## Exhibit 4: Inverse Classification Composition

| Passthrough (%) | | CMO Structure (%) | | Coupon Index (%) | |
|---|---|---|---|---|---|
| 30 Year FN/FH | | 60 Companion | 51 | LIBOR | 60 |
| 15 Year FN/FH | | 20 Sequential | 14 | COFI | 24 |
| Balloon FN/FH | | 10 PAC | 10 | CMT | 15 |
| GNMA | | 8 TAC | 9 | Other | 1 |
| Whole Loan | | 2 Other | 16 | | |
| | 100 | | 100 | | 100 |

Source: *Source*: William R. Leach, "A Portfolio Manager's Perspective of Inverses and Inverse IOs," Chapter 10 in Frank J. Fabozzi (ed.), *CMO Portfolio Management* (Summit, NJ: Frank J. Fabozzi Associates, 1994), p. 155.

Any type of bond class can be divided into a floater and an inverse floater. That is, a floater and inverse combination can be created from companion (or support) tranches, sequential-pay tranches, PAC tranches, and TAC tranches. The reference rate has been primarily LIBOR, the Eleventh District Cost of Funds Index (COFI), or the Constant Maturity Treasury. Exhibit 4 shows the composition of the inverse floater market as of 1992 by type of collateral, by underlying fixed-rate CMO structure, and by coupon index.

Inverse floaters with a wide variety of leverages are available in the market. Market participants refer to *low leverage* inverse floaters as those with a leverage between 0.5 and 2.1; *medium leverage* as those with a leverage greater than 2.1 but not exceeding 4.5, and; *high leverage* as those with a leverage greater than 4.5.

## Valuing CMO Inverse Floaters

The basic principles that we described earlier about valuing inverse floaters apply to CMO inverse floaters. The added dimension that increases the complexity of the valuation process is the impact of prepayments. Prepayments affect the value of the CMO collateral; in turn, the value of the CMO collateral affects the value of the collateral tranche. Because the collateral tranche's value changes, the value of the inverse floater changes.

## Average Life and Duration

The average life of an inverse floater is the same as the average life of the tranche collateral. The average life for the tranche collateral depends on the expected prepayment speed. As we explained earlier, the duration of the floater is a multiple of the duration of the collateral from which it was created.

## Variants in CMO Inverse Structuring[4]

In the CMO market, there are several variants of the inverse floater that have been created. The first is the inverse interest-only (IO) floater. In this structure the inverse floater tranche is further divided into two tranches: a principal only tranche and a tranche that receives only coupon interest. The coupon interest varies inversely with the reference rate.

The second variant is what is called a *strike bond* or a *two-tiered index bond* (TTIB). In this structure, the inverse floater has a coupon that varies as follows: (1) when the reference rate is above a designated rate, the coupon rate is capped at the designated rate, (2) when the reference rate is below a designated rate, a floor is set for the coupon rate at the designated rate, and (3) when the reference rate is between the cap and floor, the coupon rate has the standard formula for an inverse floater. The reason the bond is called a strike bond is that the designated rates for the cap and the floor are referred to as strike rates.

## MUNICIPAL INVERSE FLOATERS

Inverse floaters have been created in the municipal bond market by one of the following transactions:

(1) a municipal dealer buys in the secondary market a fixed-rate municipal bond, places it in a trust, and the trust then issues a floating-rate security and an inverse floating-rate bond; or,
(2) a new fixed-rate municipal issue is underwritten by an investment banking firm, places it in a trust, and the trust then issues a floating-rate security and an inverse floating-rate bond.

---

[4] For a more detailed discussion of municipal inverse floaters, see Chapters 4 and 15 in Frank J. Fabozzi, T. Dessa Fabozzi, and Sylvan G. Feldstein, *Municipal Bond Portfolio Management* (Burr Ridge, IL: Business One Irwin, 1994).

(3) an investment banking firm underwrites a long-term fixed-rate municipal bond and simultaneously enters into an interest rate swap for a time that is generally less than the term to maturity of the bond. The investor owns an inverse floater for the term of the swap which then converts to a fixed-rate bond (the underlying) at the end of the swap term.

Note that in the first two transactions, both a floating-rate security and an inverse floating-rate bond are created. In the third transaction, only an inverse floating-rate bond is created.

When a floater is created, the coupon rate on it is reset based on the results of a Dutch auction. The auction can take place anywhere between 7 days and 35 days. The coupon rate on the floater changes in the same direction as market rates. The resulting inverse floater receives the residual interest; that is, the coupon interest is the difference between the coupon interest on the collateral and the coupon rate that has been reset on the floater as a result of the auction. Thus, the coupon rate on the inverse floater changes in the opposite direction of market rates.

The use of the swap market to create an inverse floater eliminates the need for selling the floaters through a Dutch auction. The issuer locks in the cost of the bond at issuance, which is the interest cost of the underlying bond to maturity plus the difference between the fixed payments made and the floating rates received on the underlying swap for the term of the swap. These products are generically called *indexed inverse floaters*. The investor has the option of converting the indexed inverse floater to a fixed-rate bond before the end of the swap term by unwinding the swap. The cost of the conversion is satisfied either up-front or is satisfied by adjusting the fixed rate the investor was to begin receiving at the end of the initial swap term.

Most of the floaters and inverse floaters that have been created in the municipal bond market at the time of this writing have been created by dividing the principal equally between the two classes. That is, if the collateral has a par value of $100 million, the par value for both the floater and inverse floater is $50 million. As explained earlier, this means that the duration of an inverse floater will have roughly twice the duration of the collateral.

Several investment banking firms active in the municipal bond market have developed proprietary products. Merrill Lynch's institutional products are called FLOATS and RITES (Residual Interest Tax Exempt Securities). These products are created using the first two transactions discussed above. Merrill Lynch has an inverse floating-rate bond that it markets to retail investors which it calls TEEMS (Tax Exempt Enhanced Municipal Securities) that is created by means of the third type of transaction. Goldman Sachs' proprietary products are called PARS (Periodic Auction Reset Securities), which are floaters, and INFLOS, which are inverse floaters. Lehman Brothers' proprietary products are called RIBS (Residual Interest Bonds) and SAVRS (Select Auction Variable Rate Securities).

# KEY POINTS OF CHAPTER

Here are the key points of this chapter:

1. Inverse floaters are created from fixed-rate debt instruments.

2. To prevent the coupon interest on a reset date from becoming negative for an inverse floater, there is an interest rate floor.

3. Typically the inverse floater's floor is set at zero.

4. Because of the floor on the inverse floater, a cap is set on the accompanying floater.

5. The leverage of an inverse floater indicates the number of basis points that the coupon rate changes for a given change in the reference rate.

6. The value of an inverse floater is determined by the value of the collateral and the corresponding floater.

7. The factors that affect the value and performance of an inverse floater are those that affect the value of the collateral from which it is created and the value of the floater.

8. In the case of a CMO inverse floater, an important factor is the prepayment rate that affects the CMO collateral.

9. The valuation of the collateral becomes critical because mispricing the collateral results in a mispricing of the inverse floater by 1 plus the leverage.

10. The performance of an inverse floater is determined by the change in the shape of the yield curve.

11. A decline in the reference rate will not necessarily increase the value of the inverse floater despite the fact that the coupon rate is increased.

12. The duration of an inverse floater is a multiple of the duration of the collateral.

13. The owner of an inverse floater has effectively purchased a fixed-rate asset and borrowed on a floating-rate basis.

14. An inverse floater position is similar in characteristic to a interest rate swap position.

# 9
# VALUATION OF CONVERTIBLE SECURITIES

A convertible security is a security that can be converted into common stock at the option of the securityholder. These securities include convertible bonds and convertible preferred stock.

> **The objectives of this chapter are to:**
>
> 1. describe the basic features of a convertible and exchangeable security;
>
> 2. explain the traditional valuation methodology that has been used to value convertible securities;
>
> 3. explain the factors that complicate the valuation of convertible securities;
>
> 4. describe and illustrate the state-of-the-art option-based valuation methodology for valuing a convertible security; and,
>
> 5. demonstrate the risk/return characteristics of a convertible security versus the ownership of the underlying common stock.

## BASIC FEATURES OF CONVERTIBLE SECURITIES

The conversion provision of a convertible security grants the securityholder the right to convert the security into a predetermined number of shares of common stock of the issuer. A convertible security is therefore a security with an embedded call option to buy the common stock of the issuer. An *exchangeable security* grants the securityholder the right to exchange the security for the common stock of a firm *other* than the issuer of the security. For example, some Ford Motor Credit convertible bonds are exchangeable for the common stock of the parent company, Ford Motor Company. Throughout this chapter we use the term convertible security to refer to both convertible and exchangeable securities.

In illustrating the calculation of the various concepts described below, we will use the General Signal Corporation (ticker symbol "GSX") 5 3/4% convertible issue due June 1, 2002. Information about the issue and the stock of this issuer is provided in Exhibit 1.

### Conversion Ratio

The number of shares of common stock that the securityholder will receive from exercising the call option of a convertible security is called the *conversion ratio*. The conversion privilege may extend for all or only some portion of the security's life, and the stated conversion ratio may change over time. It is always adjusted proportionately for stock splits and stock dividends. For the GSX convertible issue the conversion ratio is 25.32 shares. This means that for each $1,000 of par value of this issue the securityholder exchanges for GSX common stock, he will receive 25.32 shares.

At the time of issuance of a convertible security, the issuer effectively grants the securityholder the right to purchase the common stock at a price equal to:

$$\frac{\text{Par value of convertible security}}{\text{Conversion ratio}}$$

This price is referred to in the prospectus as the *stated conversion price*. Sometimes the issue price of a convertible security may not be equal to par. In such cases, the stated conversion price at issuance is usually determined by the issue price.

## Exhibit 1: Information About General Signal Corporation Convertible Bond 5 3/4% Due June 1, 2002 and Common Stock

*Convertible bond*
Market price (as of 10/7/93): $106.50
Issue proceeds: $100 million
Issue date: 6/1/92
Maturity date: 6/1/02
Non-call until 6/1/95

Call price schedule
| | |
|---|---|
| 6/1/95 | 103.59 |
| 6/1/96 | 102.88 |
| 6/1/97 | 102.16 |
| 6/1/98 | 101.44 |
| 6/1/99 | 100.72 |
| 6/1/00 | 100.00 |
| 6/1/01 | 100.00 |

Coupon rate: 5 3/4%
Conversion ratio: 25.320 shares of GSX shares per $1,000 par value
Rating: A3/A-

*GSX common stock*
Expected volatility: 17%
Dividend per share: $0.90 per year
Dividend yield (as of 10/7/93): 2.727%
Stock price: $33

The conversion price for the GSX convertible issue is:

$$\text{Conversion price} = \frac{\$1,000}{25.32} = \$39.49$$

## Call Provisions

Almost all convertible issues are callable by the issuer. This is a valuable feature for issuers who deem the current market price of their stock undervalued enough so that selling stock directly would dilute the equity of current stockholders. The firm would prefer to raise common stock over incurring debt, so it issues a convertible setting the conversion ratio on the basis of a stock price it regards as acceptable. Once the market price reaches the conversion price, the firm will want to see the conversion happen in view of the risk that the stock price may drop in the future. This gives the firm an interest in forcing conversion, even though this is not in the interest of the owners of the security whose price is likely to be adversely affected by the call.

Typically there is a non-call period (i.e., a time period from the time of issuance that the convertible security may not be called). The GSX convertible issue had a non-call period at issuance of three years. There are some issues that have a provisional call feature that allows the issuer to call the issue during the non-call period if the price of the stock reaches a certain price. For example, Whirlpool Corporation zero-coupon convertible bond due 5/14/11 could not be called before 5/14/93 unless the stock price reached $52.35, at which time the issuer had the right to call the issue. In the case of Eastman Kodak zero-coupon convertible bond due 10/15/11, the issuer can not call the issue before 10/15/93 unless the common stock traded at a price of at least $70.73 for at least 20/30 trading days.

The call price schedule of a convertible security is specified at the time of issuance. Typically, the call price declines over time. The call price schedule for the GSX convertible issue is shown in Exhibit 1. In the case of a zero-coupon convertible bond, the call price is based on an accreted value. For example, for the Whirlpool Corporation zero-coupon convertible, the call price on 5/14/93 is $28.983 and thereafter accretes daily at 7% per annum compounded semiannually. So, if the issue is called on 5/14/94, the call price would be $31.047 ($28.983 times $1.035^2$).

## Putable Provision

A put option grants the bondholder the right to require the issuer to redeem the issue at designated dates for a predetermined price. Some convertible bonds are putable. For example, Eastman Kodak zero-coupon convertible bond due 10/15/11 is putable. The put schedule is as follows: 32.35 if put on 10/15/94; 34.57 if put on 10/15/95; 36.943 if put on 10/15/96; 51.486 if put on 10/15/01; and, 71.753 if put on 10/15/06. The GSX convertible issue is not putable.

Put options can be classified as "hard" puts and "soft" puts. A hard put is one in which the convertible security must be redeemed by the issuer only for cash. In the case of a soft put, the issuer has the option to redeem the convertible security for cash, common stock, subordinated notes, or a combination of the three.

## TRADITIONAL ANALYSIS OF CONVERTIBLE SECURITIES

### Minimum Value of a Convertible Security

The *conversion value* or *parity value* of a convertible security is the value of the security if it is converted immediately.[1] That is,

Conversion value = Market price of common stock × Conversion ratio

The minimum price of a convertible security is the greater of

1. Its conversion value, or
2. Its value as a security without the conversion option — that is, based on the convertible security's cash flows if not converted (i.e., a plain vanilla security). This value is called its *straight value* or *investment value*. The valuation principles set forth in the previous chapters should be used to determine the straight value.

If the convertible security does not sell for the greater of these two values, arbitrage profits could be realized. For example, suppose the conversion value is greater than the straight value, and the security trades at its straight value. An investor can buy the convertible security at the straight value and convert it. By doing so, the investor realizes a gain equal to the difference between the conversion value and the straight value. Suppose, instead, the straight value is greater than the conversion value, and the security trades at its conversion value. By buying the con-

---

[1] Technically, the standard textbook definition of conversion value given here is theoretically incorrect because as bondholders convert, the price of the stock will decline. The theoretically correct definition for the conversion value is that it is the product of the conversion ratio and the stock price *after* conversion.

vertible at the conversion value, the investor will realize a higher yield than a comparable straight security.

For the GSX convertible issue, the conversion value on 10/7/93 per $1,000 of par value was equal to:

$$\text{Conversion value} = \$33 \times 25.32 = \$835.56$$

Therefore, the conversion value per $100 of par value was 83.556.

To simplify the analysis of the straight value of the bond, we will discount the cash flows to maturity by the yield on the 10-year on-the-run Treasury at the time, 5.32%, plus a credit spread of 70 basis points that appeared to be appropriate at that time. The straight value using a discount rate of 6.02% and assuming same day settlement for theoretical purposes only is 98.19. Actually, the straight value would be less than this because no recognition was given to the call feature. Since the minimum value of the GSX convertible issue is the greater of the conversion value and the straight value, the minimum value is 98.19.

## Market Conversion Price

The price that an investor effectively pays for the common stock if the convertible security is purchased and then converted into the common stock is called the *market conversion price* or *conversion parity price*. It is found as follows:

$$\text{Market conversion price} = \frac{\text{Market price of convertible security}}{\text{Conversion ratio}}$$

The market conversion price is a useful benchmark because once the actual market price of the stock rises above the market conversion price, any further stock price increase is certain to increase the value of the convertible security by at least the same percentage. Therefore, the market conversion price can be viewed as a break-even point.

An investor who purchases a convertible security rather than the underlying stock, pays a premium over the current market price of the stock. This premium per share is equal to the difference between the market conversion price and the current market price of the common stock. That is,

Market conversion premium per share =
Market conversion price − Current market price

The market conversion premium per share is usually expressed as a percentage of the current market price as follows:

Market conversion premium ratio =
$$\frac{\text{Market conversion premium per share}}{\text{Market price of common stock}}$$

Why would someone be willing to pay a premium to buy the stock? Recall that the minimum price of a convertible security is the greater of its conversion value or its straight value. Thus, as the common stock price declines, the price of the convertible security will not fall below its straight value. The straight value therefore acts as a floor for the convertible security's price.

Viewed in this context, the market conversion premium per share can be seen as the price of a call option. As explained in Chapter 5, the buyer of a call option limits the downside risk to the option price. In the case of a convertible security, for a premium, the securityholder limits the downside risk to the straight value of the security. The difference between the buyer of a call option and the buyer of a convertible security is that the former knows precisely the dollar amount of the downside risk, while the latter knows only that the most that can be lost is the difference between the convertible security's price and the straight value. The straight value at some future date, however, is unknown; the value will change as interest rates in the economy change.

The calculation of the market conversion price, market conversion premium per share, and market conversion premium ratio for the GSX convertible issue based on market data as of 10/7/93 is shown below:

$$\text{Market conversion price} = \frac{\$1{,}065}{25.32} = \$42.06$$

Market conversion premium per share = $42.06 − $33 = $9.06

$$\text{Market conversion premium ratio} = \frac{\$9.06}{\$33} = 0.275 = 27.5\%$$

## Current Income of Convertible Security Versus Common Stock

As an offset to the market conversion premium per share, investing in the convertible security rather than buying the stock directly, generally means that the investor realizes higher current income from the coupon interest paid in the case of a convertible bond and dividends in the case of a convertible preferred than would be received as common stock dividends paid on the number of shares equal to the conversion ratio. Analysts evaluating a convertible security, typically compute the time it takes to recover the premium per share by computing the *premium payback period* (which is also known as the *break-even time*). This is computed as follows:

$$\frac{\text{Market conversion premium per share}}{\text{Favorable income differential per share}}$$

where the favorable income differential per share is equal to the following for a convertible bond:

$$\frac{\text{Coupon interest} - (\text{Conversion ratio} \times \text{Common stock dividend per share})}{\text{Conversion ratio}}$$

And, for convertible preferred stock:

$$\frac{\text{Preferred dividends} - (\text{Conversion ratio} \times \text{Common stock dividend per share})}{\text{Conversion ratio}}$$

Notice that the premium payback period does *not* take into account the time value of money.

For the GSX convertible issue, the market conversion premium per share is $9.06. The favorable income differential per share is found as follows:

$$\text{Coupon interest from bond} = 0.0575 \times \$1{,}000 = \$57.50$$
$$\text{Conversion ratio} \times \text{Dividend per share} = 25.32 \times \$0.90 = \$22.79$$

Therefore,

$$\text{Favorable income differential per share} = \frac{\$57.50 - \$22.79}{25.32} = \$1.37$$

and

$$\text{Premium payback period} = \frac{\$9.06}{\$1.37} = 6.6 \text{ years}$$

Without considering the time value of money, the investor would recover the market conversion premium per share in about 6.6 years.

## Downside Risk with a Convertible Security

Investors usually use the straight value as a measure of the downside risk of a convertible security, because the price of the convertible security cannot fall below this value. Thus, the straight value acts as the *current* floor for the price of the convertible bond. The downside risk is measured as a percentage of the straight value and computed as follows:

$$\text{Premium over straight value} = \frac{\text{Market price of convertible security}}{\text{Straight value}} - 1$$

The higher the premium over straight value, all other factors constant, the less attractive the convertible security.

Despite its use in practice, this measure of downside risk is flawed because the straight value (the floor) changes as interest rates change. If interest rates rise (fall), the straight value falls (rises) making the floor fall (rise). Therefore, the downside risk changes as interest rates change.

For the GSX convertible issue, since the market price of the convertible security is 106.5 and the straight value is 98.19, the premium over straight value is

$$\text{Premium over straight value} = \frac{\$106.50}{\$98.19} - 1 = 0.085 = 8.5\%$$

## The Upside Potential of a Convertible Security

The evaluation of the upside potential of a convertible security depends on the prospects for the underlying common stock. Thus, the techniques for analyzing common stocks discussed in books on equity analysis should be employed.

## INVESTMENT CHARACTERISTICS OF A CONVERTIBLE SECURITY

The investment characteristics of a convertible security depend on the common stock price. If the price is low, so that the straight value is considerably higher than the conversion value, the security will trade much like a straight security. The convertible security in such instances is referred to as a *fixed-income equivalent* or a *busted convertible*.

When the price of the stock is such that the conversion value is considerably higher than the straight value, then the convertible security will trade as if it were an equity instrument; in this case it is said to be a *common stock equivalent*. In such cases, the market conversion premium per share will be small.

Between these two cases, fixed-income equivalent and common stock equivalent, the convertible security trades as a *hybrid security*, having the characteristics of both a fixed-income security and a common stock instrument.

## AN OPTION-BASED VALUATION APPROACH

In our discussion of convertible securities, we did not address the following questions:

1. What is a fair value for the conversion premium per share?
2. How do we handle convertible securities with call and/or put options?
3. How does a change in interest rates affect the stock price?

Consider first a noncallable/nonputable convertible security. The investor who purchases this security would be entering into two separate transactions: (1) buying a noncallable/nonputable straight security and (2) buying a call option (or warrant) on the stock, where the number of shares that can be purchased with the call option is equal to the conversion ratio.

The question is: What is the fair value for the call option? The fair value depends on the factors discussed in Chapter 5 that affect the price of a call option. While the discussion in that chapter focused on options where the underlying is a fixed-income instrument, the principles apply also to options on common stock. One key factor is the expected price volatility of the stock: the more the expected price volatility, the greater the value of the call option. The theoretical value of a call option can be valued using the Black-Scholes option pricing model. As a first approximation to the value of a convertible security, the formula would be:

Convertible security value =
Straight value + Value of the call option on the stock

The value of the call option is added to the straight value because the investor has purchased a call option on the stock.

Now let's add in a common feature of a convertible security: the issuer's right to call the security. The issuer can force conversion by calling the security. For example, suppose that the call price is 103 and the conversion value is 107. If the issuer calls the security, the optimal strategy for the investor is to convert the security and receive shares worth $107.[2] The investor, however, loses any premium over the conversion value that is reflected in the market price. Therefore, the analysis of convertible securities must take into account the value of the issuer's right to call. This depends, in turn, on (1) future interest rate volatility, and (2) economic factors that determine whether it is optimal for the issuer to call the security. The Black-Scholes option pricing model cannot handle this situation.

To link interest rates and stock prices together (the third question we raise above), statistical analysis of historical movements of these two variables must be estimated and incorporated into the model.

Valuation models based on an option pricing approach have been suggested by several researchers.[3] These models can generally be classified as one-factor or multi-factor models. As we explained in Chapter 3, by factor we mean the stochastic variables that are assumed to drive the value of a convertible security. The obvious candidates for factors are the price movement of the underlying common stock and the movement of interest rates. According to Mihir Bhattacharya and Yu Zhu of Merrill

---

[2] Actually, the conversion value would be less than $107 because the per share value after conversion would decline.

Lynch Equity Capital Markets, the most widely used convertible valuation model has been the one-factor model and the factor is the price movement of the underlying common stock.[4]

Specifically, the valuation model is based on the solution to a partial differential equation. The no arbitrage conditions that the convertible bond price must satisfy is:[5]

$$\frac{\delta V}{\delta t} + \frac{1}{2}\sigma^2 S^2 \frac{\delta^2 V}{\delta r^2} + rs\frac{\delta V}{\delta S} = rV$$

where

$V$ = Value of convertible bond = $V(S,t)$
$S$ = Price of the underlying stock
$t$ = time
$r$ = short rate
$\delta^2$ = instantaneous variance of the stock price return

The characteristics of the issue such as the maturity, coupon rate, conversion ratio, call and put provisions, and changing conversion ratios and provisional call features are incorporated into the boundary conditions to solve the partial differential equation.

For the GSX convertible issue, the solution to the partial differential equation as of 10/7/93, assuming that the standard deviation of the stock price return is 17%, is 106.53. This value is equal to the actual market price at the time of 106.5 which suggests that the issue is fairly priced.

---

[3] See, for example: Michael Brennan and Eduardo Schwartz, "Convertible Bonds: Valuation and Optimal Strategies for Call and Conversion," *Journal of Finance* (December 1977), pp. 1699-1715; Jonathan Ingersoll, "A Contingent-Claims Valuation of Convertible Securities," *Journal of Financial Economics* (May 1977), pp. 289-322; Michael Brennan and Eduardo Schwartz, "Analyzing Convertible Bonds," *Journal of Financial and Quantitative Analysis* (November 1980), pp. 907-929; and, George Constantinides, "Warrant Exercise and Bond Conversion in Competitive Markets," *Journal of Financial Economics* (September 1984), pp. 371-398.

[4] Mihir Bhattacharya and Yu Zhu, "Valuation and Analysis of Convertible Securities," Chapter 36 in Frank J. Fabozzi and T. Dessa Fabozzi (eds.), *The Handbook of Fixed Income Securities* (Burr Ridge, IL: Business One-Irwin, 1994).

[5] Bhattacharya and Zhu.

The difference between the value of the convertible bond as determined from the valuation model and the straight value (properly adjusted for the call option granted to the issuer and any put option) is the value of the embedded call option for the stock. That is,

Value of the embedded call option for underlying stock =
Theoretical value of convertible bond − Straight value

For the GSX convertible issue, since the theoretical value for the issue is 106.53 and the straight value is 98.19 (recall that this was not adjusted for the issuer's call option), the approximate value of the embedded call option for the underlying stock is 8.34.

The valuation model as applied to the GSX issue indicated that the issue was fairly priced. Exhibit 2 compares the theoretical value of Motorola's Liquid Yield Option Notes (LYONs)[6] to the actual market price of the convertible issue from the issue date (9/7/89) to 3/26/93. During this period, the price of Motorola's stock increased from $28 1/16 to $65 1/4. In January 1991, the market conversion premium ratio reached a high of 44%. The exhibit indicates that the valuation appears to track the market price well.

Because the inputs into the valuation model are not known with certainty, it is important to test the sensitivity of the model. As an example, the Merrill Lynch theoretical valuation model was used to value as of November 20, 1992 the Whirlpool Corporation zero-coupon bond due 5/14/11 (a LYON) assuming the following as a base case: a common stock price of 43 5/8, volatility for the stock price at 25.21%, a constant dividend yield, a yield to maturity of 8.10%, and a yield to put of 6.98%. The theoretical value for the Whirlpool issue for this base case was $33.16.[7] The market price for this issue at the time was $33, so the issue appeared to be cheap relative to its theoretical value.

---

[6] LYON is a Merrill Lynch trademark name for zero-coupon convertible bonds that are both callable and putable.

[7] Preston M. Harrington II, Bernie Moriarty, and Hareesh Paranjape, *LYONs Review*, November/December 1992 Quarterly Update, Merrill Lynch, Pierce, Fenner & Smith, Inc., p. 104.

# 208 VALUATION OF CONVERTIBLE SECURITIES

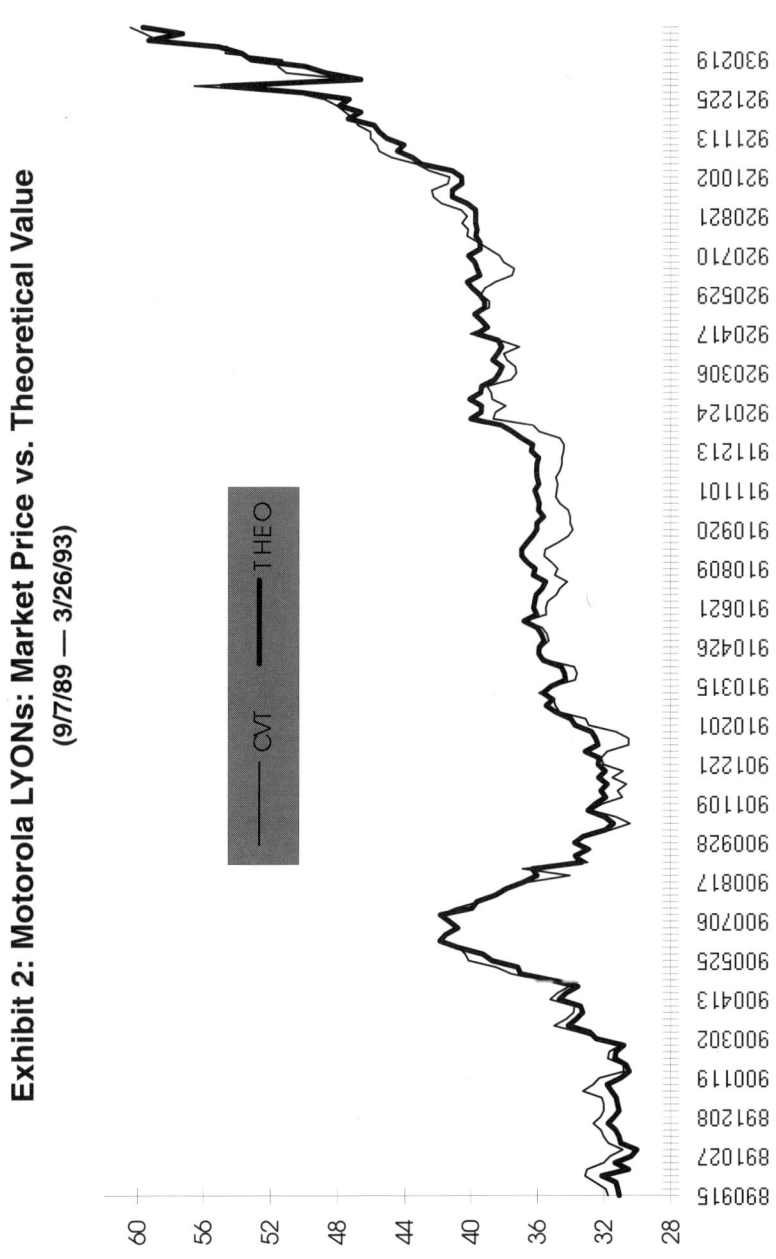

**Exhibit 2: Motorola LYONs: Market Price vs. Theoretical Value (9/7/89 — 3/26/93)**

Source: Mihir Bhattacharya and Yu Zhu of Merrill Lynch Equity Capital Markets.

Tests of the sensitivity of the model to the base case inputs indicated the following for the theoretical value as of November 20, 1992 and also one year later by changing each input:

|  | Theoretical value (% change) | | | |
|---|---|---|---|---|
|  | 11/20/92 | | 11/20/93 | |
| Base case | $33.16 | | $33.33 | |
| Stock volatility = 20% | 32.67 | (-1.0%) | 33.07 | (0.2%) |
| Stock price up 25% | 39.52 | (19.8%) | 39.46 | (19.6%) |
| Stock price down 25% | 29.59 | (-10.3%) | 30.93 | (-6.3%) |
| Interest rate down 100 bp | 33.47 | (1.44%) | 33.66 | (1.9%) |
| Interest rate up 100 bp | 32.89 | (-0.3%) | 33.05 | (0.15%) |

The results for the stock volatility analysis indicate that if stock price volatility is 20% rather than the 25.21% assumed in the base case, the theoretical value as of November 20, 1992 would be less. This is expected since the value of a call option on a stock is lower the lower the expected stock price volatility. Thus, while the Whirlpool issue would be cheap relative to its market price of $33 if stock price volatility is 25.21%, it is expensive if stock price volatility is 20%.

## THE RISK/RETURN PROFILE OF A CONVERTIBLE SECURITY

Let's use the GSX convertible issue and the valuation model to look at the risk/return profile by investing in a convertible issue or the underlying common stock.

Suppose on 10/7/93 an investor is considering the purchase of either the common stock of GSX or the 5 3/4% convertible issue due 6/1/02. The stock can be purchased in the market for $33. By buying the convertible bond, the investor is effectively purchasing the stock for $42.06 (the market conversion price per share). Exhibit 3 shows the total return for both alternatives one year later assuming (1) the stock price does not change, (2) it changes by ±10%, and (3) it changes by ±25%. The convertible's theoretical value is based on the Merrill Lynch valuation model.

## Exhibit 3: Comparison of One-Year Return for GSX Stock and Convertible Issue for Assumed Changes in Stock Price

Beginning of horizon: 10/7/93
End of horizon: 10/07/94
Price of GSX stock on 10/7/93: $33.00
Assumed volatility of GSX stock return: 17%

| Stock price change (%) | GSX stock return (%) | Convertible's theoretical value | Convertible's return (%) |
|---|---|---|---|
| -25 | -22.24 | 100.47 | -0.16 |
| -10 | -7.24 | 102.96 | 2.14 |
| 0 | 2.76 | 105.27 | 4.27 |
| 10 | 12.76 | 108.12 | 6.90 |
| 25 | 27.76 | 113.74 | 12.08 |

If the GSX's stock price is unchanged, the stock position will underperform the convertible position despite the fact that a premium was paid to purchase the stock by acquiring the convertible issue. The reason is that even though the convertible's theoretical value decreased, the income from coupon more than compensates for the capital loss. In the two scenarios where the price of GSX declines, the convertible position outperforms the stock position because the straight value provides a floor for the convertible. In contrast, the stock position outperforms the convertible position in the two cases where the stock rises in price because of the premium paid to acquire the stock via the convertible's acquisition.

One of the critical assumptions in this analysis is that the straight value does not change except for the passage of time. If interest rates rise, the straight value will decline. Even if interest rates do not rise, the perceived creditworthiness of the issuer may deteriorate, causing investors to demand a higher yield. The illustration clearly demonstrates that there are benefits and drawbacks of investing in convertible securities. The disadvantage is the upside potential give-up because a premium per share must be paid. An advantage is the reduction in downside risk (as determined by the straight value).

## KEY POINTS

Here are the key points of this chapter:

1. Convertible and exchangeable securities can be converted into shares of common stock.

2. The conversion ratio is the number of common stock shares for which a convertible security may be converted.

3. All convertible securities are callable and some are putable.

4. The conversion value is the value of the convertible bond if it is immediately converted into the common stock.

5. The market conversion price is the price that an investor effectively pays for the common stock if the convertible security is purchased and then converted into the common stock.

6. The premium paid for the common stock is measured by the market conversion premium per share and market conversion premium ratio.

7. The straight value or investment value of a convertible security is its value if there was no conversion feature.

8. The minimum value of a convertible security is the greater of the conversion value and the straight value.

9. A fixed-income equivalent (or a busted convertible) refers to the situation where the straight value is considerably higher than the conversion value so that the security will trade much like a straight security.

10. A common stock equivalent refers to the situation where the conversion value is considerably higher than the straight value so that the convertible security trades as if it were an equity instrument.

11. A hybrid equivalent refers to the situation where the convert-

ible security trades with characteristics of both a fixed-income security and a common stock instrument.

12. While the downside risk of a convertible security usually is estimated by calculating the premium over straight value, the limitation of this measure is that the straight value (the floor) changes as interest rates change.

13. An advantage of buying the convertible rather than the common stock is the reduction in downside risk.

14. The disadvantage of a convertible relative to the straight purchase of the common stock is the upside potential give-up because a premium per share must be paid.

15. An option-based valuation model is a more appropriate approach to value convertible securities because of the multiple embedded options.

16. There are various option-based valuation models: one-factor and multiple-factor models.

17. The most common convertible bond valuation model is the one-factor model in which the one factor is the stock price return.

18. Incorporated into the boundary conditions to solve the partial differential equation to determine the theoretical value of a convertible bond are the characteristics of the issue such as the maturity, coupon rate, conversion ratio, call and put provisions, and changing conversion ratios and provisional call features.

19. Because the inputs into the valuation model are not known with certainty, it is important to test the sensitivity of the model to changes in these inputs.

20. A critical input of the valuation model is the volatility of the stock's return.

# INDEX

## A

Accelerating sinking fund provisions, 13
  see Bond
Accrual
  bond, 156, 161, 167
  support bond, 161
  tranche, 156
Adjustable-rate
  mortgages (ARMs), 146, 147
  passthroughs, 146
After-tax basis, 127
Agency bonds
  see Callable, Putable
  embedded options, application, 167-172
Agency CMOs, 187
Agency mortgage-backed securities, 154
Amortization class, see Planned, Targeted
Arbitrage, 148
  arguments, 45-46, 65, 66
  profit, 28, 29, 33, 103, 178
Arbitrage-free model, 148, 173
ARM, see Adjustable-rate
Asset, see Financial
Asset/liability management, 64
At the money, 99
Average life, 174, 188-189
  see Simulated
  constraints, 158

## B

Balloon maturity, 4
Basis points, 11,

Benchmark
  rates, 17
  spot rate, 170
  curve, 38, 39
  zero-coupon rate curve, 38
BEY, see Bond-equivalent
Biased expectations theory, 56, 63-64
Binomial
  interest rate, 131
  interest rate tree, 109, 111-117, 119, 123, 127, 129, 135, 138, 142, 143
  construction, 117-123
  lattice method, 103
  method, 12, 109-144, 154
Black-Scholes option pricing model, 205
Bond(s), 1
  see Accrual, Agency, Bullet, Callable, Convertible, Corporate, Default-free, Fixed-rate, Floater, Floating-rate, Index, Industrial, Interest-only, Inverse, Mortgage, Municipal, Non-callable, Nonputable, Non-Treasury, Option-free, Planned, Principal-only, Putable, Residual, Short-term, Strike, Support, Two-tiered, Zero-coupon
  accelerating sinking fund provisions, 4
  characteristics, 78-79
  embedded options
    components, 97-103
    valuation, 93-108
  indentures, call/refunding provisions, 3
  price quotations, 25
  price sensitivity, 84, 91
  price volatility, 78, 79, 85
  put provision, 4
  valuation, 93, 96, 145, 154
  value, 116, 118, 120, 121, 129

213

214    INDEX

Bond-equivalent yield (BEY), 23, 25, 47-49, 55
Bootstrapping, 21, 40, 110
Break-even
  point, 200
  time, 202
Bullet
  bonds, 42
  maturity, 85
Busted convertible security, 204, 211

# C

Call
  date, 96, 97
  feature, 93
  option, 4, 94, 97-99, 102, 129, 196, 204, 207
  see Embedded
  limits, 201
  price, 98
  value, determination, 127
  premium, 168
  price, 124, 127, 205
  protection, 3
  provisions, 13, 197-198, 206
  see Bond
Callable
  agency bond, 145
  bond, 7, 30, 42, 82, 89, 93-98, 105, 108, 109, 127, 129, 131,138
  see Noncallable
  disadvantages, 94-96
  corporate bond, 83, 94, 145, 167, 170
  valuation, 124-127
  security, 94
Cap(s), 6, 127, 145, 147, 178, 189
  see Capped, Floater, Inverse, Uncapped
  value, 182
Cap rate, 180, 181, 184
  see Floater
Capital gain, 78
Capital loss, 78

Capped floater, 180, 182, 184, 186
Cash flow, 1, 6
  see Default-free, Path-dependent, Periodic
  discounting, 7-10, 17
  estimation, 2-7, 17
  generation, simulation, 148-149
CATs, 19
Ceiling, 6
CIR, see Cox-Ingersoll-Ross
CMO, see Collateralized
COFI, see Eleventh
Collateral, 158, 161, 167, 176, 177, 180-182, 184
  see Collateralized, Fixed-rate, Non-Treasury, Tranche
  coupon rate, 178
  option-adjusted spread, 148
  premium, 161
  principal, 177, 186
  tranche, 188
Collateralized mortgage obligations (CMO), 12, 83, 145, 147, 156, 183
  see Agency, Fixed-rate
  analysis, illustrations, 156-167
  collateral, 187, 188
  inverse floater
    tranches, 187-189
    valuation, 188
  inverse structuring, 189
  structuring model, 152
  tranche, 148, 155
Common stock, 1, 6, 195, 197, 198, 200, 205, 206, 209, 211
  see Convertible security
  dividends, 202
Companion tranches, 188
Constant
  maturity Treasury, 188
  spread, 135
Continuous variable, 69
Continuous-time stochastic process
  discrete-time stochastic process comparison, 70
Contractual due date, 2, 13
Conversion

option, 199
parity price, 200
premium, 204
  *see* Market
price, *see* Market
provision, 6
ratio, 196-197, 206
value, 200
Convertible bonds, 195, 202
  *see* Zero-coupon
Convertible preferred stock, 195
Convertible security/securities, 6, 12, 14
  *see* Busted, Fixed-income
  current income, common stock comparison, 202-203
  downside risk, 203
  features, 196-199
  investment characteristics, 204
  minimum value, 199-200
  risk/return profile, 209-210
  traditional analysis, 199-203
  upside potential, 203
  valuation, 195-213
Convex, 76
  curve, 94
Convexity, 85-89, 91
  *see* Effective, Modified, Negative, Option-adjusted, Positive
  measurement, 87
  percentage price change, 87-88
Corporate(s), 40
  *see* Zero-coupon
  bonds, 12, 33, 34, 36, 124, 127, 170, 182
    *see* Callable, Option-free
    embedded options, application, 167-172
  issuer, 37
  security, 36
  trustee, 4
  zero, 36
  zero-coupon securities, 35
Coupon, 78
  *see* Inverse, Treasury, Zero-coupon
  bond, 8, 40, 87
  index, 188

interest, 18, 177, 190, 192
interest payment, 2, 3
  *see* Option
leverage, 177
payment, 2, 29, 116, 121
  *see* Option
reset formula, 5
reset rate, 6
security, *see* Treasury
stripping, 29
Treasury, 22
  security, 23, 24
Coupon-paying support bond, 161
Cox-Ingersoll-Ross specification (CIR), 73-74
Credit
  rating, 37
    *see* Investment
  risk, 10, 39
  spread, 34, 35, 37, 110
    *see* Zero-coupon
  term structure, 38, 43
Creditors, 64
Current
  floor, 203
  price, *see* Security

# D

Debt instruments, *see* Fixed-rate
Debt obligations, 3
Default
  forward probability, 37
  probability, 36, 37
  risk, 10, 36
Default-free
  bonds, 33
  cash flow, 26
  securities, 17, 33
    *see* Zero-coupon
  spot rate, 25
    curve, 38
  zero-coupon instrument, 41
Depreciation, 2

Derivative instruments, 145
Discount
  function, 25-26
  rate, 8, 11, 14, 34, 119, 149, 170, 180
  securities, 18
Discounting process, 123
Discrete variable, 69
Discrete-time stochastic process, *see* Continuous-time
Dividend(s)
  *see* Common stock
  yield, 207
Dothan specification, 73
Drift rate, 71
  dynamics, 72
Duration, 11, 15, 75, 81, 82, 88, 89, 91, 158, 188-189, 193
  *see* Effective, Inverse, Macaulay, Modified, Option-adjusted

# E

11th District Cost of Funds, *see* Eleventh
Effective convexity, 88-89, 109, 135-141, 143, 153
Effective duration, 12, 91, 109, 135-141, 143, 153
  modified duration comparison, 82-84
Eleventh District Cost of Funds, 5
  Index (COFI), 188
Embedded call option, 98, 196, 207
Embedded options, 3, 4, 6, 12, 13, 33, 75, 83-85, 93, 99, 103, 107, 108, 111, 135, 142
  *see* Agency, Bonds, Corporate
  extension, 127-129
Equity, 197
  issue, 2
Exchange provision, 6
Exchangeable security, 6, 196
Expectations, *see* Local, Return-to-maturity
Expectations theory, 55, 66, 67
  *see* Biased, Pure
Expiration date, 102, 103

# F

Face value, 4
Fair value, 204
Financial asset, 1, 2, 9, 13
Fixed-income
  equivalent convertible security, 204, 211
  instrument, 205
  market, 39, 175
  security, 2, 7-14, 75, 83, 91, 146, 173
Fixed-rate
  bond, 187, 190
  CMO, 188
  collateral, 186
  debt instruments, 192
  municipal bond, 189, 190
  security, 176
  tranche, 187
Flat yield curve, 66
Floater(s), 178, 180, 181, 183, 187
  *see* Capped, Interest-only, Inverse, Uncapped
  bonds, 181
  *see* Inverse
  cap, 184, 186
  cap rate, 181
  valuation, 180-181
Floating-rate
  bond, 189
  *see* Inverse
  instruments, 4
  note, 127
  securities, 5-6, 14, 145, 173, 175, 189, 190
  *see* Inverse
FLOATS, 191
Floor(s), 6, 129, 145, 147, 177, 178, 189
  *see* Current
Forward
  probability, *see* Default
  rate(s), 11, 45-55, 63, 66-68, 110, 123
  *see* Implied, Short-term, Spot rates
  derivation, 46-51

rate curve, 50
  see Treasury

## H

Humped yield curve, 55, 64, 66
Hybrid security, 204

## I

Implied forward rates, 66
In the money, 99
Income
  see Convertible, Net
  differential, 202
Indentures, see Bond
Index bond, see Two-tiered
Indexed inverse floaters, 190
Industrial bond, 38
Interest
  see Coupon, Residual
  distribution rules, 152
  payment, see Coupon
  volatility, see Option
Interest rate, 3, 5, 7-9, 14, 41, 62-64, 79, 85, 91, 94, 107, 153, 168, 185, 204
  see Binomial, Option, Short-term, Static
  agreements, 145
  behavior models, 65
  changes, 12, 15, 75
    price sensitivity measurement, 11, 75-92
  environment, 94
    see Static
  generation process, 142
  history, 146-147
  level, 146
  models, 148
  path, 103, 149, 152-155, 158, 168, 170, 173, 174
    see Scenario
  generation, simulation, 148-149

number selection, 155-156
risk, 67, 80-85, 135, 147
sensitive instruments, 145
swap, 175, 186, 190, 193
term structure, 45
  theories, 55-65
tree, 103, 141, 154
  see Binomial
uncertainty, 6-7
volatility, 30, 96, 97, 100, 102, 104, 129, 135, 142, 158, 205
  introduction, 111
Interest-only
  floater, see Inverse
  strip (IO/IOette), 156, 160
  bond, see Planned
Intrinsic value, 99-100, 107
Inverse cap, 177
Inverse floater(s), 5
  see Indexed
  bonds, 181
  coupon, formula, 177-178
  creation, 176-178
  duration, 185-186
  interest-only floater, 189
  performance, 182-186
  position, interpretation, 186-187
  tranches, 189
    see Collateralized
  valuation, 175-193
Inverse floating-rate
  bond, 190, 191
  security/securities, 5, 175
Inverted yield curve, 66
Investment
  grade corporate rating, 37
  horizon, 46, 53, 58, 60, 62, 63, 67
  value, 199, 211
IO/IOette, see Interest-only
Issue(s), 146
  see On-the-run, Treasury
Issue date, 4
Issuer, 2, 3, 6, 7, 13, 36, 94, 96-98, 110, 124, 127, 190, 196, 197, 205, 207
  see Corporate
Ito process, 71-72

## L

Leverage, 178, 181-182
  see Coupon
Liability, 64
  see Asset/liability
LIBOR, see London
Liquidity, 19
  premium, 63, 68
  theory, 56, 63
Local expectations, 60
Lognormal random walk, 112
London Interbank Offered Rate (LIBOR),
  5, 176, 177, 188

## M

Macaulay duration, 12, 84
Market
  conversion premium, 201, 202, 211
  conversion price, 200-202
  participants, 12
  sector, 40
  segmentation theory, 55, 64-65, 66
  value, 29, 30, 119
Maturity/maturities, 18
  see Balloon, Bullet, Return-to-maturity,
    Term to maturity
  date, 2, 3, 6, 9, 96
  levels, 11
  range, 64, 68
  sectors, 64
  strategy, 67
  Treasury, see Constant
  value, 18, 26, 118, 121
Mean reversion, 154
Mean-reversion process, 72
Mean-Reverting Square Root Diffusion
  model, 74
Model, see Arbitrage-free, Black-
  Scholes, Collateralized, Interest rate,
  Multiple-factor, One-factor, Option-
  adjusted, Option-based, Prepayment,
  Structuring

Modeling
  see Prepayment, Valuation
  risk, 93, 106, 108, 158
Modified convexity, 88-89
Modified duration, 12, 91
  see Effective
Modified principal component (MPC),
  155, 156
Monte Carlo
  method, 12, 145-174
  methodology, 180
  simulation, 145
    method, 103, 108
Mortgage(s)
  see Adjustable-rate
  bond, 161
  loan, 1
    balance, 94
    prepayment provision, 4-5, 13
  obligations, see Collateralized
  passthrough securities, 105, 146, 149
  rate, 7
  refinancing rate, 147, 148, 173
Mortgage-backed security/securities, 12,
  82, 89, 94, 106, 145, 153, 161, 173
  see Agency, Collateralized, Stripped
  market, 176
Mortgagor, 148-149
Multiple-factor models, 212
Municipal
  bond(s), 182-183
    see Fixed-rate
  market, 175, 189, 190
  term structure, 39-40
  inverse floaters, 189-191
  security, see Tax

## N

Negative convexity, 95, 96
Net income, 2
Node, 111, 121, 122, 129
  line, 141
  spacing, see Time-dependent

value determination, 115-116
Nominal
  spread, 30
  spread measure, 42
  yield spread, 32, 97
    see Static
Non-call period, 198
Noncallable
  bond, 94, 95, 97, 98, 168
  straight security, 204
  Treasury securities, 2
Noncash outlay, 2
Non-parallel yield curve shifts, 85, 91
  price sensitivity, 84-85
Nonputable
  bond, 94
  straight security, 204
Non-Treasury
  bond, 30, 31
  collateral, 185
  issue, 31, 32
  securities, 2, 13

# O

OAS, see Option-adjusted
Obligations, see Debt
One-factor model(s), 65, 68, 206, 212
  see Term structure
On-the-run
  issue, 121
  Treasury issue, 110
  Treasury security, 154
  yield, 117
  yield curve, 97, 110, 123, 129, 138, 143
Opportunity cost, 148
Option(s)
  see Bonds, Call, Conversion, Embedded, Put
  buyer, 100
  cost, 104-106, 158, 164, 166
  coupon
    interest payment, 100, 103, 108
    payments, 103

expected interest volatility, 102
price, 100, 102
  see Call
pricing model, see Black-Scholes
short-term risk-free interest rate, 102-103, 108
time to expiration, 102
value, affecting factors, 99-100
value, influencing factors, 101-103
Option-adjusted
  convexity, 89
  duration, 83, 91
  spread (OAS), 12, 93, 104, 108, 109, 131-135, 143, 153, 158, 160, 164, 166, 170, 173, 180
    see Collateral, Weighted-average, Zero
  methodology, illustrations, 156-167
  model, 155
Option-based valuation, 195, 204-209
  model, 212
Option-free bond, 75, 89, 90, 94, 95, 109, 124, 129, 142
  price volatility characteristics, 76-79
  properties, 76-78
  tree, valuation, 123-124
  valuation, 110-111
Option-free corporate bond, 123
Out of the money, 99

# P

PAC, see Planned
Par value, 4, 28, 180, 190
Parallel
  shift, 82, 83, 85, 91
  yield curve shift assumption, 80
PARS, see Periodic
Passthroughs, 145, 146, 152
  see Adjustable-rate, Mortgage
Path-dependent cash flows, 146-147
Payment, see Coupon, Interest, Option, Prepayment, Principal, Repayment
Percentage price change, 90

*see* Convexity
Periodic
  Auction Reset Securities (PARS), 191
  cash flow, 173
  coupon rate, 147
Plain vanilla
  security, 199
  structure, 156-161, 164
Planned amortization class
  IO bond, 161, 164, 167
  PO bond, 161, 166
  support bond structure, 161-167
  tranche, 156, 188
PO, *see* Principal-only
Positive convexity, 95
Preferred
  habitat theory, 64, 65, 68
  stock, 1
Premium, 3, 19, 100, 210, 211
  *see* Call, Conversion, Liquidity, Market, Risk, Yield
  collateral, 161
  payback period, 202, 203
Prepayment(s), 147, 158
  model, 174
  modeling, 149
  provisions, *see* Mortgage
  rate, 158
  risk, 147
  speed, 158, 166, 189
Present value, 1
  *see* Scenario
Price
  *see* Call, Call option, Conversion, Current, Market, Security, Stock, Strike
  appreciation, 78
    potential, 94, 96
  change, *see* Convexity, Percentage
  compression, 95
  risk, 59
  sensitivity, *see* Bond, Interest rate, Non-parallel, Security
Price volatility, 75, 76, 175, 205
  *see* Bond, Option-free, Security
Price/yield relationship, 76, 78, 86, 90, 94, 95

Principal
  *see* Collateral
  payments, 153
  repayment, 6, 13, 152
    alteration provisions, 2-5
    date, 5
Principal-only strip (PO), 161
  bond, *see* Planned
Probability of default, *see* Default
Probability distribution, 70
Probability of solvency, *see* Solvency
Probability theory, 69
Pure expectations theory, 56, 58-63, 67
  drawbacks, 58-59
  interpretations, 59-63
Put option, 99, 100, 102, 103, 127, 129, 198
Put provisions, 13, 206
  *see* Bond
Putable
  agency bond, 145
  bond, 7, 30, 42, 82, 98, 105, 106, 109, 127, 129, 131
  *see* Nonputable
  bondholder, 98
  corporate bond, 145
  provision, 198-199

# R

Random
  variable, 69
  walk, *see* Lognormal
Real estate, 1
Reconstituting, 29
Reference rate, 5, 14
Refinancing
  costs, 7
  rate, 149, 154
  *see* Mortgage
Refunding, 3
  opportunity, 167, 168
  protection, 3
  provisions, 13

INDEX 221

*see* Bond
rate, 168
Reinvestment risk, 62, 94, 96
Repayment, *see* Principal
Reset formula, *see* Coupon
Residual
  bond, 161
  interest, 190
  Interest Tax Exempt Securities (RITES), 191
Return-to-maturity expectations, 62, 63
Risk
  *see* Convertible security, Credit, Default, Interest-rate, Modeling, Prepayment, Price, Reinvestment, Sector
  measures, 10-11, 14
  premium, 33, 63, 64, 68
Risk-return characteristics, 195
Risk/return profile, *see* Convertible security
RITES, *see* Residual

## S

SAVRS, *see* Select
Scenario interest rate path, present value calculation, 149-152
Sector risks, 39
Security/securities
  *see* Callable, Convertible, Corporate, Coupon, Default-free, Discount, Exchangeable, Fixed-income, Fixed-rate, Floating-rate, Hybrid, Inverse, Municipal, Noncallable, Nonputable, Non-Treasury, Treasury, Zero-coupon
  holder, 2
  current price, 102
  price sensitivity, 15, 80, 83
  price volatility, 80
Select Auction Variable Rate Securities (SAVRS), 191
Sensitivity, 166

*see* Bond, Interest rate, Non-parallel, Price, Security
analysis, 158
Separate Trading of Registered Interest and Principal Securities STRIPS, 19
Sequential-pay tranches, 188
Short rates, volatility, 65
Short-term
  bonds, 62
  forward rates, *see* Spot rates
  risk-free interest rate, *see* Option
Simulated average life, 153-154
Sinking fund, 127
  *see* Accelerating, Bond
  requirement, 4
Solvency, 36
  probability, 37
Spot rate(s), 11, 32, 34, 50, 52, 60, 66, 110, 123, 149, 153
  *see* Benchmark, Default-free, Theoretical, Treasury
  curve, 25, 26, 30, 32, 41, 96, 104, 108, 153
  *see* Benchmark, Default-free, Treasury
  short-term forward rates, relationship, 51-52
  valuation role, 17-44
Spread, 5, 180
  *see* Constant, Credit, Nominal, Option-adjusted, Static, Yield
  curve, *see* Zero-coupon
  measure, *see* Nominal, Yield
Standard deviation, 114-115
Standard & Poor's 500, 5
Standard Weiner process, 70-71
Static interest rate, 97
  environment, 105
Static spread, 30-33, 38-39, 96, 97, 104, 105, 156, 164
  determination, 30-32
  nominal yield spread, divergence comparison, 32
Static valuation methodology, 96-97
Static yield spread, 97

Stochastic
  process, 12, 70
    see Continuous-time, Discrete-time
  variable, 70-72
Stock
  see Common, Preferred
  price, 198
  volatility analysis, 209
Straight value, 199, 203, 204, 207, 210, 211
Strike
  bond, 189
  price, 99, 100, 102
  rate, 189
Strip, see Interest-only, Principal-only
Stripped
  mortgage-backed securities, 145
  Treasury securities, 19
    see Zero-coupon
Stripping, 27
  see Coupon
STRIPS, see Separate
Structuring
  see Collateralized
  model, see Collateralized
Support bond, 161
  see Accrual, Coupon-paying, Targeted
  structure, see Planned
Support tranche, 188
  J, 167
Swap
  see Interest-rate
  market, 190

# T

TAC, see Targeted
Targeted amortization class (TAC)
  support bond, 161
  tranche, 156, 188
Tax Exempt Enhanced Municipal Securities (TEEMS), 191
Taxable entities, 19
TEEMS, see Tax

Term to maturity, 78, 79
Term structure, 25, 30, 103, 107, 131, 141, 153
  see Credit, Interest, Municipal
  one-factor model, 69-74
    alternative specifications, 72-74
  relationship, 19
  theories, 45, 55-74
Theoretical spot rate, 14, 17, 23, 24, 25, 49, 54-55
  curve, 97
  construction, 21-25
Theoretical value, 131, 135
  see Volatility
  determination, 152
TIGRs, 19
Time to expiration, see Option
Time value, 100, 107, 203
Time-dependent node spacing, 141
TR, see Trust
Tranche, 147, 148, 156, 158, 164, 176, 177
  see Accrual, Collateral, Collateralized, Companion, Fixed-rate, Inverse, Planned, Sequential-pay, Support, Targeted
Treasury/Treasuries, 155, 183-185
  see Constant, Coupon, Maturity, Non-Treasury
  bill, 22, 41, 46, 47, 49
  rate, 183
  bond, see Zero-coupon
  coupon security, 2, 19, 22, 27, 29, 41
    pricing/spot rate application, 26
  forward rate curve, 66
  issue, 185
    see On-the-run
  security/securities, 7, 9, 17, 21, 26, 27, 33, 35, 42, 49
    see Noncallable, On-the-run, Stripped, Zero-coupon
  spot rate, 11, 31, 32
    basis, 26-30
    curve, 30, 35, 37, 42, 53, 66, 164
  yield curve, 9, 18-20, 21, 30, 31, 66, 164, 183-185

zero, 37
Tree, see Binomial, Interest rate, Option-free
Trust receipts (TRs), 19
Two-factor models, 65
Two-tiered index bond, 189

## U

Uncapped floater, 180
Underwriting fees, 168
U.S. Department of the Treasury, 82
U.S. Treasury, 27
   see Treasury

## V

Valuation, 181-182
   see Bonds, Convertible, Corporate, Floater, Inverse, Option-based, Option-free, Spot, Static
   contemporary approach, 9-10
   definition, 1
   methodology/ methodologies, 103-106, 147-156
      drawbacks, 96-97
      illustrations, 156-167
      model, 11, 12, 15, 75, 80, 83, 85, 104, 154, 207, 212, 213
   modeling, 147
   principles, 1-16
   traditional approach, 8
Value, see Bond, Call, Cap, Conversion, Convertible, Fair, Intrinsic, Investment, Market, Maturity, Node, Option, Straight, Theoretical, Time, Volatility
Variable, see Continuous, Discrete, Random, Stochastic
Variance
   reduction techniques, 155
   term, dynamics, 72-74
Vasicek specifications, 73
Volatility, 73, 114-115, 117, 129, 131, 138, 166, 167, 180, 181, 183, 184
   see Interest, Interest rate, Option, Price, Short rates, Zero
   analysis, see Stock
   assumption, 118, 119, 121, 135, 148
   parameter, 114
   statistical measure, 142
   theoretical value, 129-135

## W

Wasting asset, 102
Weighted average, 176
Weighted-average OAS, 156
Weiner process, see Standard

## Y

Yield, 19, 23, 25, 28, 55, 90, 94-96, 164
   see Bond-equivalent, Dividend, On-the-run, Price/yield
Yield curve, 18, 32, 39, 40, 42, 46, 63, 64, 66, 75, 82, 85, 88, 91, 96, 97, 175, 185, 192
   see Flat, Humped, Inverted, On-the-run, Parallel, Treasury
   shift, see Non-parallel
Yield premium, 30, 64
Yield spread, 104, 131, 153, 156
   see Nominal, Static
   measure, drawbacks, 30
Yield to maturity, 22, 26, 29, 30, 207
   effects, 79

## Z

Zero, see Corporate, Treasury
Zero volatility OAS, 104, 108
Zero-coupon
   bond, 8, 9, 62, 63, 67
   convertible bond, 198
   corporates, 37

credit spread, 43
default-free security, 25
instrument, 9, 14, 22, 27, 28, 41
  see Default-free
rate, 11
  curve, see Benchmark
securities, 18, 36, 37
  see Corporate
spread, 38
  curve, 35
stripped Treasury securities, 29
Treasury bond, 148
Treasury securities, 18, 19, 22, 23, 29, 53, 54

# IT'S EASIER TO HIT THE NAIL ON THE HEAD IF YOU'VE GOT A HANDLE ON WHAT YOU'RE DOING

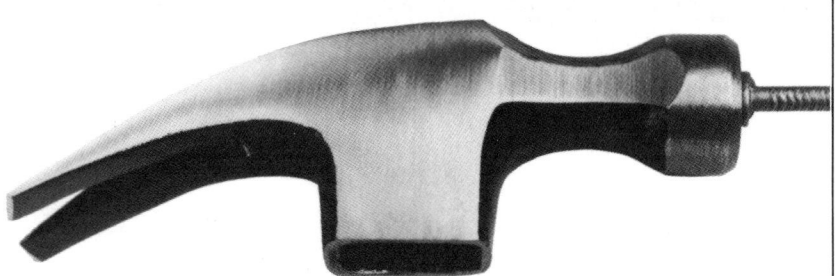

The right tools can make any task easier and the results more professional. And when it comes to constructing, analyzing and evaluating your fixed income portfolio, the right tools come from BARRA.

We all know that the fixed income marketplace is complex and constantly evolving. As an investment architect, it's your job to keep on top of it all. At BARRA, it's our job to help you understand the risks associated with these ever-changing instruments, and how they interact to affect your portfolio. Simply stated, we help you drive the nail straighter to build a stronger foundation.

BARRA tools are the most complete and sophisticated available. We cover just about any asset type you can think of, including complex CMOs, exchange-traded futures, and options on futures. And since our tools reduce each of these asset types to a common framework, you can analyze, compare, and then integrate them into a single portfolio.

BARRA tools actually help you become a master portfolio builder. We tell you which of your investment strategies paid off and which didn't. By measuring your exposure to important factors, we help you better understand how to tailor your portfolio's aggregate risk. We even let you create what-if scenarios to forecast returns influenced by changing interest rates, sector spreads, and other economic variables.

As a BARRA user, you'll have all the information needed to build portfolios that best reflect your investment objectives and your own expertise. In fact, we'll not only give you a handle on what you're doing, we'll make sure your grasp on it is very firm.

**BARRA**
**TOOLS OF THE TRADE**

Berkeley • Tokyo • New York • London • Paris • Frankfurt • Hong Kong • Sydney • Montreal

# ANDREW KALOTAY
## ASSOCIATES, INC.

## *Making Debt Pay*

Andrew Kalotay Associates, a leading authority on the valuation of fixed income securities, offers corporate and sovereign borrowers tailored advice that brings dramatic improvement in portfolio performance. Whether restructuring existing debt, assessing new financial products, or honing a trading strategy, selective clients depend on our proven analytics to safeguard their balance sheets. Under our direct guidance, borrowers carried out more than seven billion dollars in primary market transactions in 1992 alone.

## *Precision You Can Trade On*

- *BondVal:* Option-adjusted arbitrage-free bond valuation

- *SwapVal:* Valuation for interest-rate swaps, forward swaps, and options on swaps

- *DerivVal:* Interest rate cap, floor, and collar valuation

- *FloatVal:* Arbitrage-free valuation for ARMs, CMT floaters, and other complex variable-rate instruments

- *PortVal:* Fair value and OAS analysis for fixed income portfolios

- *PortSim:* Scenario-dependent cashflows and optimization

- *BondRef:* Refunding efficiency for calls, tenders, and open-market purchases

- *NewBond:* New issue structuring and comparative analysis

25 East 9th Street □ New York, New York 10003
(212) 979-7177 □ Fax: (212) 475-6438

# BondCalc®

BondCalc is a pricing and analytical system that constructs the cash flows for ALL types of fixed income securities with **after tax, leveraging** and **multicurrency** capabilities. It specializes in private placements, bank loans, high yield securities, municipals, emerging market debt, convertibles and other corporate securities.

- Portfolios have all cash flows for projections and precise calculations.
- Total return and performance attribution can be calculated.
- BondCalc performs swap analysis, matrix pricing, zero spot curve pricing and other valuation techniques.
- Uses implied forward yield curve or 2-dimensional interest rate forecasts to value make-whole calls, swaps and horizon analysis work-outs.
- Equity portion of convertibles valued using artificial intelligence techniques for range of stock growth rates.

Output consists of:
(1) Results returned to the screen,
(2) Over 50 preset analytical graphs and reports, and
(3) A report and graph writer with over 170 columns to choose from.

All output is publication quality and can be imported into spreadsheets.

## BondCalc Corporation

295 Greenwich St. #3B
New York NY 10007-1050
Phone 212.587.0097 / Fax 212.587.9142

# FOR THE BEST FINANCIAL RESULTS

# HIRE THE BEST FINANCIAL EXPERTISE

**MYERS-KOHL CORPORATION
SEARCH & PLACEMENT
DIVISION**

**The Best Expertise in
Locating and Placing Highly
Qualified Professionals in**

- Asset/Liability Management
- Interest Rate Risk
- Funds Transfer Pricing
- Treasury Systems
- Investment Management
- Asset Securitization
- Structured Finance

"We have used Myers-Kohl's search and placement services to recruit top-notch candidates for our asset/liability department since 1989. Their professionalism and comprehension of our personnel needs have assisted us in developing a strong team."

H. Walter Young
Vice President, A/L Manager
Banc One Corporation

"Working with Myers-Kohl was a big help in our recent employment search. Their evaluation procedure and interest rate risk questionnaire were especially useful because they knew the right questions to ask."

James H. Walters
Senior Vice President
Old Kent Corporation

# MYERS-KOHL
CORPORATION

*Leaders In Interest Rate Risk and Capital Adequacy Analysis Since the '70s.*

**For Information On How We Work Contact:**
Deedee Myers, Senior Vice President
Corporate Headquarters
4350 E. Camelback Rd, Suite 250B  Phoenix, AZ  85018
602/840-7837      602/840-7909 fax

*Phoenix*            *Boston*            *New York*

# FOR ALL ASSET-BACKED SECURITIES

ONLY ONE SOURCE PROVIDES A FULL RANGE OF INDEPENDENT EXPERTISE, ANALYTICAL SOFTWARE AND COMPREHENSIVE DATABASES

## THE TREPP GROUP

A LEADING INDEPENDENT SOURCE OF STRUCTURED FINANCE FOR MAJOR FINANCIAL FIRMS SINCE 1979, WITH THE ASSET BACKED SECURITIES GROUP, A THOMSON FINANCIAL SERVICES COMPANY.

## STRUCTURING REVERSE ENGINEERING ANALYTICS

### SOLID EXPERTISE
- Structuring specialists work closely with underwriters, issuers, rating agencies, and trustees
- Reverse engineering specialists provide the best coverage in existing securities

### ADVANCED ANALYTICAL SOFTWARE
- Structure and issue new securities
- Reverse engineer any asset-backed security before or after closing
- Analyze tranche characteristics

### BEST COVERAGE IN NON-PARTISAN DATABASES
- Security Master for Whole Loan and Agency CMOs, Private Labels, MBSs, ARMs, and other ABSs
- Detailed collateral and paydown structures
- Cashflows and daily pricing

**ANY ASSET**
MBSs
Mortgages
Second Mortgages
Title I
Credit Card Receivables
Auto Loan Receivables
ARMs
Graduated Payment MBSs
Tiered Payment MBSs
Leases
Other Financial Assets

**ANY ISSUE**
Whole Loan
Double-A Pass Through
Agency
RTC
Commercial Mortgage
Multi-family
Private

**ANY STRUCTURE**
Senior/Subordinate
LOC Backed
Bond Insured
IOs
IOettes
Floaters
Inverse Floaters
IO Floaters
POs
PACs
TACs
Partial PACs
Sticky Jump Zs
Non-Sticky Jump Zs

CONTACT
BETH GRANT

477 MADISON AVE.
NEW YORK, NY 10022
(212) 754-1010
(212) 832-6738 FAX

THE TREPP GROUP

**Portfolio Management. Trading. Analytics. Accounting.** If you manage fixed income securities, you need an array of sophisticated investment software. And if you thought you couldn't find it all from one vendor, think again. Thomson Investment Software is the premier source for fixed-income software, from front office systems to high-end analytics.

# The Fixed Income Software Resource

**PORTIA®** - As the market's leading portfolio management software system, PORTIA offers comprehensive support for even the most complex security types, from CMOs to asset-backeds. PORTIA captures front-office trade information and allows you to integrate it with sophisticated analytics and accounting. And a flexible, easy to use report writer lets you examine data any way you like.

**Gifford Fong** - Thomson Investment Software is an authorized marketing agent for GFA software systems, a name synonymous with the most advanced fixed-income analytics available today. PORTIA data can easily be transferred into a variety of GFA systems for option-adjusted analysis, horizon analysis, performance attribution, and more.

**Almont Portfolio Manager** - Thomson Investment Software also offers Almont Portfolio Manager, a powerful system for fixed income securities accounting and reporting. With complete support for mortgage-backeds, CMOs, and asset-backed securities, APM is one of the few systems available to provide full FASB 91 accounting.

*For more information on Thomson Investment Software's fixed-income software solutions, call 617.345.2700.*

**Thomson Investment Software**
22 Pittsburgh Street
Boston, MA 02210

# Staggering!

## Muller Data climbs by 20% – again.

No other pricing service boasts a *52% market share* among mutual fund groups with muni assets in excess of $1 billion\*. And no other pricing service covers the breadth of the industry that we do *every single day*.

Over the past four years, Muller Data has grown faster than any other pricing service in North America. So fast that we're now the leader in securities evaluations, providing accurate, consistent price movements time after time.

We're continually upgrading our technology to provide the most efficient and cost effective services available – whether you're an individual fund manager, or a large firm responsible for billions of dollars of portfolio money. Call us, and you'll see that it's not just our growth that's staggering.

\* *Based on Lipper Analytical Services, 9/30/93*

**Muller Data Corporation**

*A Thomson Financial Services Company*

1-800-US-MULLER

## For PCs and Workstations

# Build Your Own CMO Analysis System.

Intex Solutions provides complete and accurate tools to help you easily build your own CMO analysis system. Of course, Intex's portfolio analytics and timely deal models match all industry benchmarks; only Intex, though, gives you the independence and flexibilty to perform more advanced CMO analysis yourself and to integrate your results with other systems.

For calculations, cashflows, vector analysis and more, call Intex today.

*At Last Count...*

**Intex CMO Database**
Over 30,000 bonds, modeled and updated every month

### FOR DEVELOPERS:
Intex's flexible C-Callable Subroutines save you time and effort, so you can move on to other projects sooner.

### FOR END USERS:
Harness the power and convenience of Microsoft Excel with CMO Analyst™, the first and only spreadsheet add-in of its kind.

*Ask about Intex's popular Bond and MBS analytics, too!*

(617) 449-6222   Fax (617) 444-2318
35 Highland Circle, Needham, MA 02194

# Ernst & Young
## Consultants for:

- *Public and Corporate Finance*

  Advance Refundings
  Collateralized Mortgage Obligations
  Mortgage Revenue Bonds
  Rebate Computations
  Cash Flow Models and Yield

---

**Birmingham**     1900 AmSouth Harbert Plaza
                   Birmingham, AL 35203
                   (205) 251-2000  Telecopy:(205)226-7469

**Jacksonville**   One Independent Drive, Suite 1800
                   Jacksonville, FL 32202
                   (904) 358-2000 Telecopy(904) 358-4597

**Memphis**        1400 One Commerce Square
                   Memphis, TN 38103
                   (901) 526-0500 Telecopy(901)577-6340

**Tucson**         One South Church Avenue, Suite 1100
                   Tucson, AZ 85701
                   (602) 622-5801 Telecopy (602)624-1361

PORTFOLIO MANAGEMENT FOR THE 90's:

# GLOBAL INVESTMENT MANAGER II™

Seasoned in the 80's in the architecture of the 90's. Our clients in banking, brokerage, money management, mutual funds are convinced: with all the automation, analytics, interfaces, flexibility and cost effectiveness, **Global Investment Manager II is the system of the decade. Ask them! Call for references.**

Los Angeles (310) 478-4015
New York (212) 575-7518

## We'll help you put it all together.

- Multiuser, multitasking.
- Standard reports so flexible that each system can be unique.
- Relational database access to all data for analysis and reports.
- Mature in Unix/Relational Database Technology
- True Multi-Currency Processing
- Exact AIMR Performance
- Wrap Fee Automation
- Complete Audit Trail

- DTC and Custodian Auto-Matching/Reconciliations
- Multiple Daily AutoPricing Interfaces
- Automated, Integrated Asset Allocation/Block Trading System
- Pooled Asset Automation
- Complete Manager, Client and Tax Reporting
- Report Writer
- Unexcelled Accounting Accuracy
- Full Technical Support

### *Integrated* Decision Systems, Inc.

*The fitting solution in portfolio management.*

1950 Sawtelle Blvd., Suite 255, Los Angeles, CA 90025

Is this your programmer on fixed income analytics?

*N*ow your programmers can build sophisticated in-house fixed income analysis systems without fear. The TIPS Fixed Income Calculations Library contains over 500 functions which enable programmers to reproduce exactly industry standard numbers. Results which until now have been available only on outside analytic services.

*E*xtensive coverage of US and foreign government securities, US agency securities, corporate securities, municipal securities, and US and foreign CDs.

*U*sed by a wide range of firms, large and small, in the US and abroad, including:

- Pension Funds
- Insurance companies
- Brokerage firms
- Banks
- Money managers
- Software developers

## Subroutine Libraries available for:

- IBM Mainframe
- Digital Vax
- Tandem
- Sun Sparc
- IBM RS/6000
- HP 700, 800
- DOS
- OS/2
- Macintosh
- and others

*F*ree *no risk* trial version of the library is available configured for use with your development environment.

(908) 522-8950